Dr. Edward Maynard

"Letters from the Land of the Tsar 1845-1846"
America's Pioneering Dental Surgeon
Turned Civil War Gun Inventor

Edward Maynard by George Willoughby Maynard, 1881
National Portrait Gallery, Smithsonian Institution; Gift of the Artist

By Rodney S. Hatch III

Published By:

IRON HORSE PUBLISHING

AS STRONG AS THE NAME IMPLIES

First Edition

Printed in the United States of America

Library of Congress Control Number: 2010931713

ISBN 978-0-615-37617-2

Cover Design by Wendy Hammond of FancyPantsStudio.com

Illustrated by Fran Mergerdichian of FranMergerdichian.com

Copies of this book may be ordered directly from the author by mailing $60.00 plus $5.00 for shipping $65.00 total to:

Rodney Hatch
PO Box 433
North Salem, NY 10560
IronHorsePublishing@yahoo.com

Dedicated to:

My Parents Rodney Sage Hatch Jr. and Madeline Staniford Hatch

And to:

Dr. Edward Maynard and his wife Ellen Sophia Doty Maynard, George Willoughby Maynard, James Lemuel Hatch and his wife Nellie Maynard Hatch, George Edward Hatch and his wife Anna Sage Hatch, Marjorie Hatch, Rodney Sage Hatch Sr. and his wife Greeta Gray Hatch

Each successive generation held on to these letters, which after one hundred and sixty years and five generations could have so easily been thrown out.

Acknowledgement

The research and writing of this book has consumed a fair amount of my time over the past year and a number of people have been instrumental in allowing me access to information that has made this book more complete. Many thanks to Thomas Bower, Judy Chelnick, James Hughes and David Miller of the National Museum of American History at the Smithsonian Institution for their assistance in allowing me access to Dr. Maynard's various collections. Thank you to the National Portrait Gallery, Smithsonian Institution, for the use of the fabulous portrait of Dr. Maynard by George Willoughby Maynard and the Alexander Gardner photograph of Dr. Maynard from 1864. Thanks to Scott Swank, the Curator of the Dr. Samuel D. Harris National Museum of Dentistry in Baltimore, Maryland for a picture of Dr. Maynard in later life. Thanks to Sara Mascia, the Curator of The Historical Society, serving Sleepy Hollow and Tarrytown for pictures of Dr. Maynard's home in Tarrytown. Special thanks to Fran Megerdichian, a neighbor, friend and especially gifted artist who helped in recreating Dr. Maynard's sketches from his letters. Thanks also to Douglas Cox and last but not least thanks to my wife, Lydia, who put up with me using her computer at times when she had wanted to use it. I have since bought my own.

"Who are all these people?
What could they mean to me?
Born in different times and places
Their importance you may not see

Early settlers of this land
Struggles I'll never know
Each one played an important part
Helping both Country and Family grow

Who are all these people?
What do they mean to me?
If not for their lives and struggles
I clearly wouldn't be!"

By Rodney S. Hatch III

Foreword

This book is the direct result of my passionate interests in my genealogy, my interest in American history and my interest in the history of the development of firearms from the early flintlocks to more modern cartridge guns. Without my interest in each area, this book and these letters would have been lost to time.

In the spring of 1997, I was in the beginning stages of researching my family's genealogy when I came upon a musty brown paper shopping bag in an old metal filing cabinet which my Father had stored in his garage in upstate New York since 1969. The filing cabinet had belonged to my Grandfather and it had sat, for the most part unnoticed, in the back of our garage ever since my Grandfather had passed away in 1969. In the bag was my great-great grandfather's, James L. Hatch, Civil War enlistment and discharge documents from his service as a Hospital Steward in the Civil War, documents pertaining to his having worked for the U.S. Treasury after the Civil War and other old miscellaneous documents and letters. At the bottom of the pile was a stack of transcribed letters about an inch thick, nineteen letters totaling one hundred and thirty four pages. Each transcribed letter was held together by a rusted paper clip and the top page read:

Copied from a letter written by Mr. George Maynard to his sister Nellie (Mrs. James L. Hatch)

Dear Sister Nellie

Herewith I send you the "Ring letter" and a typed copy of the 1st letter written from St. Petersburg. You will see that father has written of some very <u>intimate</u> matters – and some of the letters go farther on intimate subjects so it would be perhaps as well that you should look them over privately.

The letter of which I send you a copy has faded so much that I had difficulty in reading it – most of the others are all in much the same state. The "Ring letter" is the most legible of all.

With love, George.

The next page read:

Copied from an outside wrapper around old letters.

"Letters from Edward Maynard to his wife
While in Europe in 1845-1846 –
To be read by his children in their old age"

The above is on the old wrapper around the letters
inside this one. I have read the letters and
am strongly of the opinion the request should
be strictly followed.

George W. Maynard
March 14, 1894

The third page read:

Copied from inside wrapper around old letters.

Edward Maynard
Tarrytown
N.Y.

Letters from Edward Maynard to
His wife: written while in Europe in
1845-1846. To be preserved for his children
To read in their old age.

I remember thinking to myself, what had I stumbled upon? What did "The Ring Letter" mean? Why were these letters kept? I proceeded to spend the better part of a night reading through this stack of nineteen letters. As I read through these letters, the writer started talking about guns and patents and dental procedures. Who was this Edward Maynard, obviously a relative, I read through the letters probably half a dozen times, which was both time consuming and somewhat laborious as the style of writing is clearly that of the mid 19th century and flows in a manner that I am not used to. With a little research, I came to realize that Dr. Edward Maynard, the writer of these letters was my great-great-great grandfather. His eldest daughter Marcia Ellen "Nellie" Maynard Hatch was my great-great grandmother; she had married James L. Hatch, my great-great grandfather.

Dr. Edward Maynard was a very well known 19th century firearms inventor, I had heard of the Maynard Carbine of Civil War fame. He was also a prominent dentist who had lived the better part of his life in Washington D.C. He was considered to have had one of the finest scientific minds of his day. Of his many gun inventions, he is best known for the Maynard Tape Primer Lock, the development of the first metallic cartridge and the design and development of the first breech loading rifle known as the Maynard rifle or carbine, which saw use in the Civil War.

These letters that I had discovered were the letters Dr. Maynard wrote home in 1845 and 1846 to his wife as he had travelled to St. Petersburg, Russia and through Europe to try and sell the patent to his tape primer lock system to various heads of state. In the spring of 1845 he had sold his patented tape primer lock to the U.S. Government. After this sale to the U.S., he believed that he could make a sizeable fortune selling this invention in Russia and Europe, so he organized an overseas business trip and set sail in early July 1845.

At the time, I thought these letters were interesting and should probably be shared with interested American historians and Maynard gun enthusiasts. Several people who knew I had found them and to whom I had described them expressed an interest in the 'gun sections' of the letters but in my mind, the 'gun sections' of these letters are but a small part of the letters. The letters in their entirety tell a much greater story of a 19th century inventor and entrepreneur seeking his fortune overseas, when to do so was no small undertaking. Dr. Maynard left his wife, Ellen, with three small children at home in Washington D.C. on a journey that would take fifteen months. He also left his thriving Washington dental practice, in an attempt to make a fortune by selling his Patented Tape Primer Lock System to the Governments of Russia, Prussia, France, Belgium, England, Scotland and Ireland.

Dr. Maynard left Springfield Massachusetts on July 3, 1845 for St. Petersburg, Russia where he arrived on September 21, 1845. He anticipated being home by Christmas of that year. Instead, he met many unexpected obstacles and delays, the least of which were the Russian ways of doing business, which made his trip go from the anticipated six months to close to fifteen months. He eventually returned safely to his wife and children in September 1846.

The letters to his wife, Ellen were written in a time when there were no modern conveniences, no running water, or electricity, no modern form of transport, so I imagine Dr. Maynard sitting by a the glow of wax candle in his boarding room at night, at times when the temperatures outside in St. Petersburg were 40 degrees below zero, describing to Ellen, his wife, his days events as they unfolded, his meetings with the heads of foreign governments regarding his invention, his performing dental operations, his descriptions of the people he met and got to know, the places he visited, and the things he did to occupy his time. These letters when sent to his wife Ellen in either Washington D.C. or Cooperstown, New York, where they summered, took anywhere from three to eight weeks to be delivered home.

As Dr. Maynard's funds started to dwindle because of unexpected delays, he started performing dental operations in order to raise funds. He is credited as being the first dental surgeon to use gold fillings in cavities in America. As a result of his deteriorating financial circumstances in St. Petersburg, which caused him to perform dental operations in order to raise funds; he is also credited as being the first dentist to introduce this procedure to Europe. As the word spread of his prowess as a dental surgeon, his reputation would lead to his performing dental procedures for the Imperial Family of Tsar Nicholas I of Russia, which in turn would lead Tsar Nicholas I to offer him the position of "Dentist to the Imperial Family" with the additional rank of Major.

Much to my chagrin, the original letters in Dr. Maynard's own hand writing have been lost to time. In reading his letters home he mentions many sketches that he drew to better describe that about which he wrote. Dr. Maynard was apparently a gifted draftsman, adept at making drawings and sketches. To have lost these to time is a tragedy. In instances where these sketches could be re-created based on his written description, I have taken the liberty of doing so.

In the fall of 2008, I called a first cousin of my Father's who I have never met. I was looking for family pictures or any other Family information for my genealogical research. He mentioned these Maynard letters which he had a copy of and he kindly shared with me a picture of the ring in "the Ring Letter". He owns this magnificent ring given to Dr. Maynard in 1846 by Her Imperial Highness the Grand Duchess Helen which is mentioned and described in these letters. This ring is such an integral part of Dr. Maynard's story, his trip and his time spent as Dentist to the Imperial Family of Russia. The existence of 'The Magnificent Ring" brought all of these Maynard letters back to my attention and in many ways completed the story told by these letters.

When my great Grandfather who was Edward Maynard's only grandson to live to maturity died, his daughter, my great Aunt Marjorie, had these Maynard letters re-typed so that both she and her brother, my Grandfather, would have a copy of them. What I found and forms the basis of this book is my Grandfather's copy of these letters.

These letters tell a fascinating story of a year in the life of a nineteenth century entrepreneur, dental surgeon and gun inventor. They tell a story that involves a bit of American history, a bit of American gun and business history, a bit of dental history, and a bit of history of St. Petersburg, Russia. It also contains many other observations by Dr. Maynard of his travels and experiences throughout the rest of Europe. Some of his observations about people and customs have changed little since his time spent there. These letters also mention numerous people that Dr. Maynard came to know during his time abroad; Major George Whistler, Colonel Charles Todd, Mr. Henry Wheaton, Grand Duke Michael of Russia, Her Royal Highness Grand Duchess Helen of Russia and her children, Dr. Brewster a fellow dentist and Mr. and Mrs. Clemson; all notable historical figures of the time in their own right.

For me, they contain a bit of my own families genealogy, as not only is Dr. Maynard my direct ancestor but his wife to whom he wrote these letters, Ellen Sophia Doty Maynard was a direct descendent of Edward Doty, who was one of the original passengers on the Mayflower which landed in Plymouth, Massachusetts in 1620.

I can only presume that Dr. Edward Maynard kept these letters that he had written to his wife as a sort of journal and documentation of his historic trip to St. Petersburg and Europe in 1845 and 1846. By his own estimation, while he was in St. Petersburg, there were "only about half a dozen or perhaps ten, including women, Americans in Petersburg all counted. Children not counted." I suspect he had the foresight to know that his travels were so unique, that they should be documented, as he did in these letters. Very few Americans would have made this sort of trip in that time, fewer still would have had such an invention that would have necessitated meeting with the heads of state or Kings of these foreign governments. Dr. Maynard's revolutionary Tape Primer Lock System had the potential to appeal to the armies of these countries and it would have required proper diplomatic introductions at the highest level of governments in order for him to even get a meeting with the Tsar of Russia, the King of Prussia or the King of Belgium.

I have acquired and read numerous articles and pamphlets about Dr, Edward Maynard since I learned of my relationship to him. They generally describe his guns, their role in the Civil War and his gum related inventions. This book tells a different story about him; it is a story about his experiences surrounding his trying to sell his Patented Tape Primer Lock in Russia and Europe in 1845. It also tells the personal side of his life from 1846 until his death in 1891. His letters to his wife in this book remain unedited. I think he would be happy to know that what he wrote in 1845 and 1846 has been saved by his descendents and has been made available to a larger interested audience in the 21st Century. I think Dr. Maynard would be very pleased with this book and were he able to communicate with me I think he would say "Thank you".

Rodney S. Hatch III

American College of Dentists

Journal of the American College of Dentists

1940 - 1941

COMMITTEE ON DENTAL HISTORY

W. N. HODGKIN, *Chairman*, Warrenton, Va.

W. H. ARCHER, 804 Professional Bldg., Pittsburgh, Pa.; H. L. BANZHAF, 1217 W. Wisconsin Ave., Milwaukee, Wis.; E. E. HAVERSTICK, 346 N. Boyle Ave., St. Louis, Mo.; J. BEN ROBINSON, 42 S. Greene St., Baltimore, Md.

January 25, 1941

Mr. R. S. Hatch
Rochester, New York

Dear Mr. Hatch;

I am anxious to contact some relative of Dr. Edward Maynard, inventor of the Maynard rifle and a dentist of Washington in the period 1835-1890. For purposes of dental history I wish to supplement the information gleaned from available records with that which could be gained only from a member of the family.

From obituary notice I have learned that one of his daughters was a Mrs. Hatch residing in Rochester at the time of his death, and so hope I can find one by that name who is a descendant.

May I hear from you, presuming I have addressed a proper party, and will you advise of anyone in the family most likely to be of aid if you have little information of Dr. Maynard?

With thanks for your cooperative interest, I am,

Sincerely yours,

W. N. Hodgkin
Warrenton, Va.

Letter found April 2009 written by Mr. W. N. Hodgkin, Chairman of the Committee on Dental History, Journal of the American College of Dentists, in January 1941 to Mr. R. S. Hatch, great-grandson of Dr. Maynard and grandfather of the author, requesting family information about Dr. Maynard.

Table of Contents

Front cover of Maynard letter from 1845-1846, found among original stack of letters.

Chapter 1

Beginnings

Edward Maynard was born on a farm in upstate New York in the town of Madison on April 26, 1813. The town of Madison is located between Syracuse and Schenectady, New York, and in the early 1800's it would have been a rural wilderness. Edward was the son of Moses Maynard and Chloe Butler Maynard. He was descended of early New England Puritan stock, his earliest American ancestor, John Maynard came from England and arrived and settled in America in 1630 eventually settling in Sudbury Massachusetts. Edward's Father, Moses was both a farmer and a sheriff in Madison. He was a Major in the New York State Militia and he served as the Sheriff of Madison. He was a member of the New York State legislature from 1816 to 1817 and he also owned a tavern. His grandfather, Lemuel Maynard served in the American Revolution as a corporal in Captain James Hosley's Company, Colonel William Prescott's Regiment Massachusetts Militia, "Lexington Alarm", April 19, 1775.

As a young boy, Edward attended the village school and Hamilton Academy from which he received an appointment to the Military Academy at West Point in 1831. His appointment as a cadet to West Point was from De Witt Clinton, the Governor of New York State. Unfortunately due to ill health and a fragile disposition, he resigned from West Point during his first year and took to studying civil engineering, law, drawing, architecture and anatomy. In 1835 he decided to pursue a career in dentistry, working first as an associate with a dentist in Utica, New York. He displayed an early knack for making his own dental instruments and was adept at forging iron and working with gold. He moved to Washington D.C. in 1836 and set up his own practice which he was involved with for the better part of the rest of his life.

From his earliest days in dentistry, Maynard showed an unusual inquisitiveness for the profession, designing and inventing numerous instruments for his own use which became well known to the profession and later widely used by other dentists. His most notable dental invention was a hand held drill stock. In 1838, he was the first dentist to successfully use gold foil to fill the nerve cavity, including nerve canals in molar and bicuspid teeth. This is an operation that he introduced in Europe in 1845 and is mentioned in his letters. From 1843 to 1846, Dr. Maynard was a co-editor of the "American Journal of Dental Science." He discovered the great diversity of situation, form and capacity of the maxillary antra which was made known to the Faculty of the Baltimore College of Dental Surgery in 1846 where it was officially acknowledged. From 1846 on, this discovery by Maynard was regarded as being of utmost importance in the treatment of diseased superior maxillaries.

His announcement of the existence of dental fibrils, based upon his discovery that sensitive dentine could be cut with less pain in particular directions than in opposite ones, was discussed, and was reported in the Transactions of the American Society of Dental Surgeons before such discovery was confirmed with the use of a microscope.

In short, at a time when most people had lost all of the teeth in their mouth due to decay by their mid thirties; at a time when there was no such thing as dental hygiene, and at a time when to solve a dental problem meant a visit to a local barber or local blacksmith where one's tooth would be pulled with pliers and a shot of whiskey; Dr. Maynard was a cutting edge innovator to the dental profession, developing dental tools, techniques and practices that would revolutionize the world of dentistry, dental care and oral surgery. His inventive genius allowed him to design and build numerous instruments and tools that would facilitate the practice of dentistry, and allow people to both keep the teeth in their mouths while reducing the effects of tooth decay.

On September 3, 1838 Edward Maynard married Ellen Sophia Doty in Sherburne, New York. She was born October 15, 1817 and was the daughter of Moses Doty and Elizabeth Pike Dorrance. Moses Doty, her father, was born in Hardwick Massachusetts July 2, 1758 and was a soldier in the Revolution serving as a Fifer in Captain Billing's Company, Colonel Learned's Regiment Massachusetts Militia October 7, 1775 and as a Fifer in Captain Morse's Company, Massachusetts Continental Infantry under Colonel Putnam, March 1, 1777. Muster Rolls from 1777 show his rank as a Fife Major. He lived in Wardsburg, N.Y., Wilmington, VT and Williamstown, Massachusetts before moving to Troy, New York about 1800 where he kept a famous tavern 'At the Sign of The Red Lion'. Ellen was a direct descendent of Edward Doty, who was one of the original passengers on the Mayflower that landed at Plymouth Massachusetts in 1620. By 1845, Dr. Edward Maynard and his wife Ellen had three boys, Edward born 1840, George Willoughby born March 5, 1843 and John Doty born 1843.

Edward Maynard's interest in guns from an early age and his inventive scientific mind, combined with his early ambitions to attend West Point and serve in the Army must have planted an interest in his head for tinkering with firearms. Most young men in early American farming life would have been interested in guns and would have certainly been adept at shooting a gun for hunting, protection, and survival. Surely Maynard liked guns from his earliest days. These confluences of interests most certainly lead to Dr. Maynard's first firearms invention, of which over the course of his lifetime there would be many.

Chapter 2
Revolutionary Invention

In the early 1800's there were many developments in gun design that would bring an end to the flintlock method of gun ignition which had been in use since the 1630's. Flintlock guns relied upon the spark created when the hammer and its attached flint hit the guns frizzen. A frizzen is a piece of steel on the priming pan lid which when opened, exposes the priming powder. This system required a flash pan to be primed with a small amount of very finely ground gun powder. Prior to cocking the hammer, the flash pan lid or frizzen is closed. After the trigger is pulled and the hammer has made contact between the flint and the frizzen, a spark is created which is directed into the flash pan causing the gun powder to ignite. The resulting flame passes through a small vent hole in the barrel that leads to the combustion chamber, igniting the main powder charge which in turn makes the gun to fire.

Above: British Long Land Pattern flintlock musket marked Vernon 1762, note the piece of flint held in the hammer and the metal frizzen that it hits to create a spark above the pan. This method of gun ignition remained in use for almost 200 years. (Author's collection)

The flintlock system was found to be awkward and time consuming and was officially replaced by the US army in 1842 by the adaptation of its first percussion musket. The percussion system required the gun operator to place a small brass cap filled with gunpowder on to a nipple which would cause ignition when hit by the hammer. While more efficient than the flintlock method it still had its drawbacks. These developments would prompt a number of firearms inventors to attempt to come up with gun ignition systems that were easy to use, reliable and which would increase the shooters ability to reload and fire his gun more quickly.

3

In March of 1845 Dr. Maynard patented a system of priming for firearms, to take the place of the recently adapted percussion cap. Maynard's invention involved connecting a series of individually self contained percussion primers in a waterproof paper tape and a means of applying these tape primers to every kind of gun. The Maynard Tape Primer System, as seen below, was an attempt to increase reliability and speed the loading process of a rifle, musket or pistol. The tape primer consisted of thin wafers of percussion compound cemented between two narrow strips of paper, equally spaced and varnished for waterproofing. Each premier was equidistant from each other so as to insure that other primers on the strip would not explode in conjunction with any other primer being exploded. The Maynard Tape Primer Lock System consisted of a hammer and a self contained magazine compartment, which held a roll of tape primers. Additionally this system incorporated an internal ratchet that would advance the roll of primers as the hammer was cocked. The compartment or magazine and tape primer advancing mechanism was sealed by a cover which was either hinged or sliding which could be closed shut with a latch or lever. As the hammer was cocked, a primer was pushed over the nipple by an arm and lever which was synchronized with the hammer mechanism. The fulminated mercury cap would detonate when the trigger was pulled and the hammer fell, striking the cap and simultaneously a sharp edge on the rear of the hammer face would cut off that segment of the paper strip. This system eliminated the need to place a percussion cap on the nipple by hand. It was also designed so that it could be affixed to any type of firearm be it a cannon, musket, rifle or pistol.

Below: Maynard Tape Primer Lock with magazine door open and a roll of Tape Primers installed in the magazine compartment on a Harpers Ferry Model 1855 U.S. Percussion Rifle.

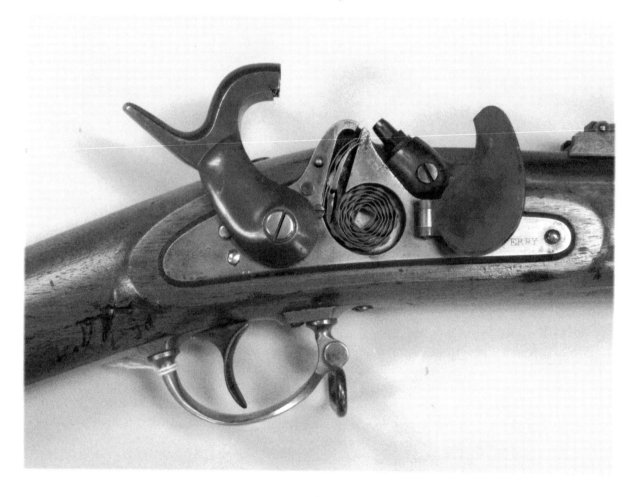

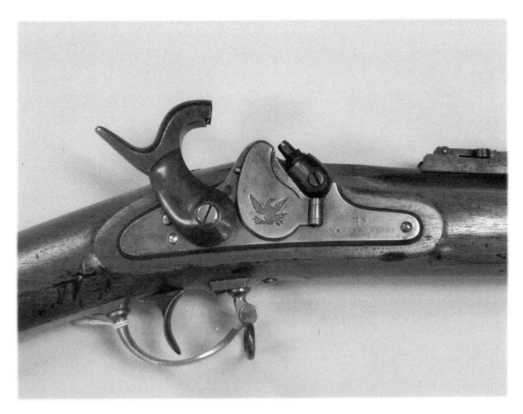

Above: Maynard Tape Primer Lock with magazine door in closed position stamped with Federal Eagle.

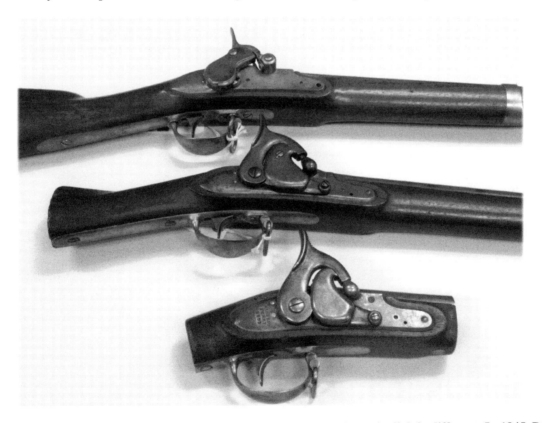

Above: Three of Dr. Maynard's Tape Primer Lock Models; each one is slightly different. In 1845, Dr Maynard travelled to St. Petersburg, Russia and through Europe with these three models which have cut stocks and barrels. The shortened length would have facilitated his travelling with them.

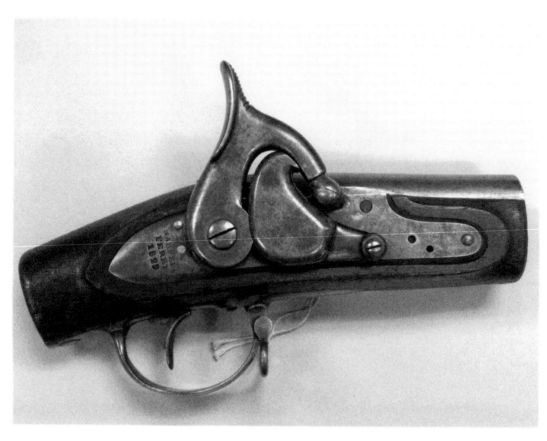

Above: Dr. Maynard's Patented Tape Primer Lock model marked Harpers Ferry 1829. Below: Tape Primer Lock with Tape Primer Roll in place with magazine door cover that swings up and down.

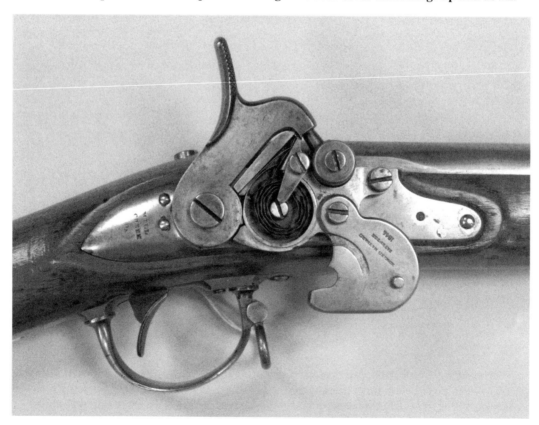

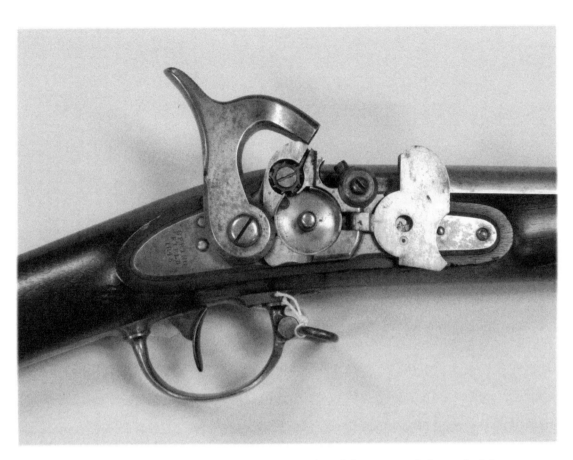

Variations on Maynard Tape Primer Lock; Above hinged door cover; below swivel door cover.

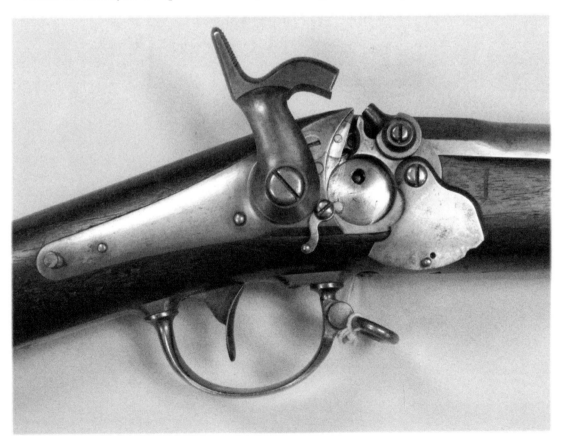

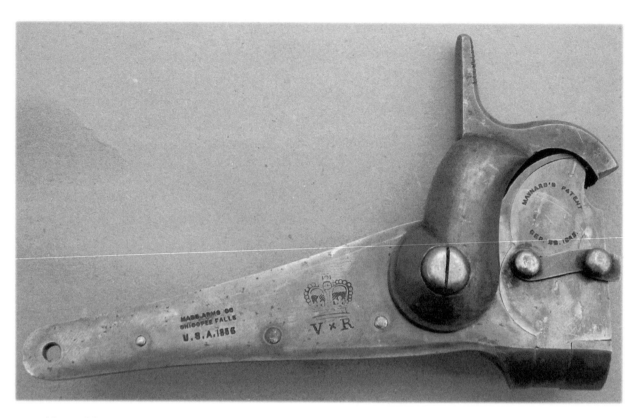

Above: Maynard Tape Primer Lock stamped Maynard's Patent Sep 22, 1845 on door of magazine, Manufactured and stamped by Mass. Arms Co. Chicopee Falls. This particular lock is from an 1856 British Greene carbine. Below: Same lock as above with magazine door open.

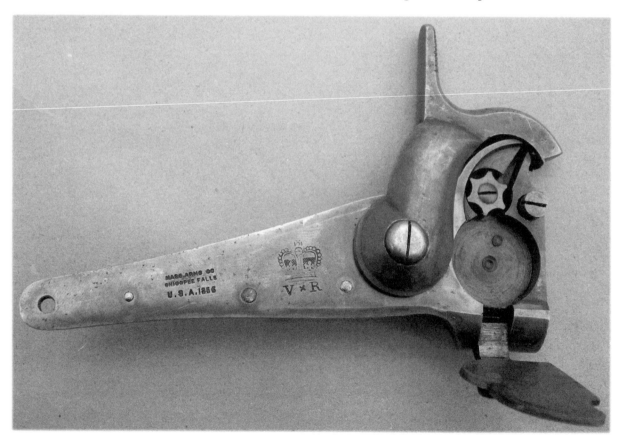

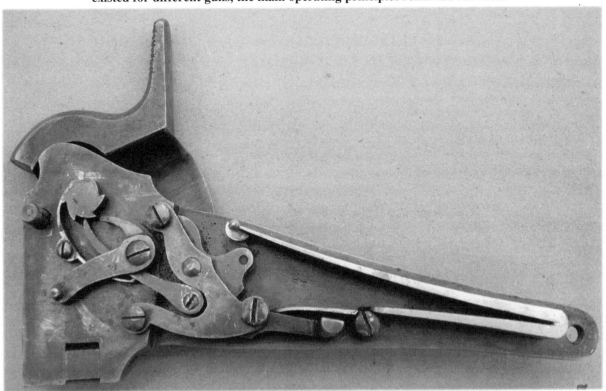

Maynard's tape primers were made up of two layers of paper on which small caplets of a fulminating compound were sandwiched at intervals and then glued together and covered in varnish. This roll of tape primers was placed in a round compartment fitted into the weapon's lock. When the hammer was cocked a linkage to a ratchet arm or finger advanced the tape placing a cap over the nipple. The arm would place the primed caplet over the nipple and the weapon was ready to fire.

Above: Two unopened tape primers in original wrapping and a section of tape primer showing round lozenges of fulminate in varnished paper.

Chapter 3

U.S. Government Tests and Purchase

In 1842 the United States Government adopted the first percussion rifle and musket for military use. The US Army was continuously looking for ways to advance firearms reliability and ease of use. On January 15, 1845 Dr. Maynard wrote to the U.S. Governments Secretary of War William Wilkins:

"The new percussion gun-lock and priming, for the purpose of trying which your department granted me the use of a number of muskets some months since, have, it is believed, been brought to such a degree of perfection as to justify me in asking for an official trail and report of the fitness for the purpose intended. Not having funds to enable me to do so, I have not secured my patents abroad, as it is necessary, in other countries than ours, that the patentee should be either the inventor or his legal representative, I trust you, sir, will see and admit the propriety, as an act of simple justice to me, of having the proposed trail made in the presence of those only who shall be appointed to make it (except the inventor or his friends), and that they be directed to give no information of the invention, excepting such shall be embraced in their official report; of having the trail and report made as early as practicable, consistent with a series of thorough experiments; and having the trail made at some military post within this District, at the nearest point where the government has troops."

"Every principle upon which my invention rests is so simple, demonstrable and self evident that the whole range of experiments can be made within a short time and with the military means near at hand, without resorting to protracted trails at points distant and detached. Without this precaution as regards secrecy, time and distance in making the trail and report, I should hazard the invasion of my invention, with the loss of every benefit that I might expect from abroad."

"You can, sir, readily appreciate the importance to me of an early decision. In the first place, it grows out of my desire to make the result available; and secondly as foreign governments having large armies and navies have signified, through their ministers here, their anxiety to have the earliest possible use of the invention, it is but fair also to presume that the report should be favorable, the United States Government would be as anxious to have the benefits of its adoption at the earliest practicable moment, I ask your favorable consideration of my suggestions."

On January 21, 1845, Special Order No. 3 was issued by Assistant Adjutant General L. Thomas, Adjutant General's Office, Washington, D.C., which directed, by order of the Secretary of War, that Brevet Brigadier Generals G.M. Brooke and George Gibson, and Captain Alfred Mordecai, of the Ordnance, be detailed as a board (in conjunction with such officers of the Navy as would be designated by the head of that department) to meet at Washington Arsenal as soon as practicable, for the purpose of examining the invention of Dr. Maynard, and reporting upon its adaptation to the service. Commodore Charles Stewart and Commodore Levin M. Powell of the U.S. Navy were appointed to serve on the Board by the Secretary of the Navy S.Y. Mason.

On January 29, 1845 the Board met in pursuance of the above orders, and proceeded to examine the percussion lock offered by Dr. Maynard. The lock was taken to pieces by Dr. Maynard, and its construction and operation, together with the arrangement of the primers, were explained by him to the board. In the musket which was presented for this purpose, the priming apparatus was adapted to a common flint-lock, in which the following alterations were made:

1) The pan, the battery, and the battery spring were removed, and the cock was replaced by a percussion hammer of a peculiar form.

2) The new magazine for percussion primers was placed on the outer face of the lock-plate, just in front of the hammer, where it was held by two screws; one in the old hole for the battery screws; the other principal one, in the center of the magazine, passing through a new hole in the lock-plate and serving as a pivot for the magazine, which by means of small set screws could be adjusted in its position so as to present the primers in the requisite manner to the action of the hammer.

3) The cone was screwed into a seat which itself was screwed into the side of the barrel in the place occupied by the former vent; the outer end of this seat was supported also by the lock-plate, for which purpose a suitable support was inserted in the notch of the pan.

The orange brown colored tape primer submitted were formed as previously described, of little lozenges of percussion powder spaced equally apart at small intervals between two slips of paper, which were cemented together and varnished in order to secure the powder from the action of moisture. The primers were formed into a coil by Dr. Maynard and placed in the magazine with one end just protruding through the small slit in the upper part, or face, of the magazine.

Dr. Maynard explained to the Board how the underside of this magazine slit is formed of a steel cutting edge, and how the under part of the face of the hammer presented another cutting edge, so that when the hammer falls, the priming lozenge which protrudes from the slit, is cut off and carried down instantaneously by the hammer to the top of the cone, which is just under this slit, and there exploded.

Dr. Maynard explained how the function of the primer itself was the same as that of the copper percussion cap; the flash of the explosion being conducted through the hollow cone to the main charge in the breech and discharging the arm. When the hammer is drawn back again, after passing the half-cock notch, it acts by a simple contrivance on a small ratchet, or toothed wheel, the teeth of which, work in the intervals between the priming lozenges. This action thus caused another of the primers to be protruded through the slit in the face of the magazine, ready for the action of the hammer again, thus illustrating how the piece could be primed by the action of cocking it.

For the facility of inserting the slip of primers, the cover of the magazine on this gun lock was made to open easily on a hinge, and when closed, it was held down by a simple spring catch. The magazine was sufficiently large to contain sixty five primers at once.

The following statement of advantages possessed by the new gun lock and priming was submitted to the consideration of the Trail Board by Dr. Maynard:

"1st – The priming costs no more than the caps now made by the United States Government; the same number of charges occupy only about one-tenth the space, and are of only about one-fifth the weight.

2nd – The hammer can be carried resting upon the cone with perfect safety, thus lessoning the risk of damage to the interior lock work, while the face of the hammer, accurately fitted by repeated blows to the face of the cone, effectually shots out water from the vent.

3rd – The priming apparatus is as firmly secured and is capable of withstanding violence as any other part of the gun.

4th – The gun, not being primed when the hammer is down, or at half cock, cannot be fired from either of those positions.

5th – By the simple motion of the hammer from "half-cock" to "cock" the gun is primed with a mathematical certainty and precision unattainable by hand, without regard to the position of the gun, or to the heat or cold, or light or darkness; in fair weather or foul, rain, hail, snow, or fog, or even after immersion in water; whether the soldier be in haste or at ease, attentive or not, skilled or awkward.

6th – The lowest degree of intelligence ever found in the soldier is sufficient to enable him to understand the nature of the priming, and to apply it to their gun for use in less time than it would take him to prick a flint.

7th – The priming requires no tools, implements, or appendages for its application to use.

8th – The priming apparatus is not liable to any perceptible wear in some thousand of discharges and when worn can be easily and readily repaired anywhere.

9th – No pieces of metal or other dangerous missiles are thrown off from the priming.

10th – It is impossible that the soldier should lose his priming, as it cannot be separated accidently from the gun.

11th – The cone, being shorter and thicker than the cone for the cap, is less liable to be broken or split.

12th – Should the priming apparatus be damaged, it may be replaced by another in a few minutes by the armorer or even an intelligent soldier, no tools except a screwdriver being necessary for the repair.

13th – The detonating matter can never, by jarring or being jolted about, get out of its proper place.

14th – The soldier applies the priming to the gun when at leisure – not when on duty or in action, unless, as is seldom or never the case, he has to fire more than fifty rounds in one battle.

15th – All waste of powder from the open cartridge will be avoided, as the cartridge is not opened until after the soldier has "cast about"; it is then "handled," "torn," and carried directly to the muzzle of the gun and inserted.

16th – A great saving of time will be effected in loading, as the whole manipulation of priming is dispensed with; thus simplifying very greatly the operations of the soldier in action, and consequently increasing the efficiency and celerity of his fire.

17th – No "blowing up" of the priming can happen from its use, as there is no fulminate or other easily combustible matter at the point where it is cut off.

18th – No jarring, such as is produced by coming to "order arms" upon a stone, or striking the hammer in getting over fences, upon any side or in any direction, or catching the hammer among limbs or twigs of trees, or trappings of horses, or dress of soldiers, or rigging of vessels, or hooking the hammer on to boats or vessels to pull alongside, or any other possible accidental disturbance of the lock can produce an explosion.

19th – The priming is so made as to be unimpaired by keeping for any length of time in climate, to as perfect a degree as any other percussion priming.

20th – The apparatus for using the priming may be placed upon the top, bottom, or either side, or in the interior of the gun."

After thoroughly examining the apparatus presented by Dr. Maynard, the Board adjourned until the following day. On January 30th, the following trails were made, in the presence of the Board, for the purpose of testing Dr. Maynard's lock and of comparing his musket lock with the ordinary percussion lock:

1) A common percussion musket and the musket with Maynard's lock were fired together, by two men of nearly equal expertness, the advantage in point of quickness in loading being first ascertained, by trail with two percussion muskets, to be in favor of the man who fired the common musket. Blank cartridges were used, and the caps for the common musket were carried in the pocket of the man who fired the musket. Twenty rounds were fired by Maynard's musket in 6 minutes, while there were 2 rounds for the common musket left and one in the barrel out of 20 charges. With Maynard's musket there was no misfire; with the common musket, 1 snap and 1 attempt to fire without putting on the cap. The slips of priming for Maynard's lock contained only 35 primers. After this, the percussion caps were laid on a table for the common musket.

2) The muskets were exchanged (after being cooled) by the two men. The result with Maynard's musket was the same as before, 20 rounds in about 6 minutes, although it was necessary to renew the slip of primers. With the common musket there were two flashes of caps, owing to the choking of the communication between the cap and the charge, rendering repeated ramming necessary. Six rounds were left when the 20 had been fired with Maynard's lock.

3) The muskets were put into the hands of two other men, with the same results as before with Maynard's lock – 20 rounds in 6 minutes; with the common musket, 4 rounds left and 1 in the barrel out of 20 charges.

4) The muskets were exchanged by the last two men. With Maynard's musket nearly the same result as to time of firing 20 rounds; 3 flashes of priming occurred from the choking of the priming canal in the cone seat. With the common musket 1 cap flashed; 1 cartridge out of 20 was left when the other musket had fired 20 rounds.

5) With the common musket once again in the hands of the man who had first fired it, 20 rounds were fired in 7 minutes; 2 caps missed fire. With Maynard's musket, it was necessary to renew the priming, and in so doing, the two last primers which did not come under the action of the ratchet, and which could not be pushed out by it to receive the stroke of the hammer, were left in the magazine and caused the new slip of primers to get choked in the throat of the opening through which they protruded when fired. This caused some delay and made it necessary to open the magazine and take out the old primers, which resulted in having 4 charges unfired after 20 rounds had been discharged with the common musket. After these 100 rounds were fired, the muskets were cleaned. Maynard's musket was then fired with ball cartridges, as follows:

6) Twenty rounds in 7 minutes; the balls of the cartridge were of irregular size, and several of them stuck and required hard ramming to force them down.

7) Twenty rounds in 10 minutes; the priming had to be removed; there was 1 snap, and 1 ball stuck in the barrel.

8) Twenty rounds in 7 ½ minutes; 2 balls stuck in loading; there were 2 snaps, owing to the priming not being forced out by the ratchet. On examination, this was found to be caused by loosening of the pivot screw of the ratchet wheel, which caused the ratchet to turn too easily. The tendency of the loosening of this screw was also to force open the lid of the magazine. The snap in the preceding 20 rounds was probably caused by the same circumstances.

9) Twenty rounds in 8 minutes; the magazine was made wet by pouring about a pint of water over the lock, the muzzle of the gun being down. One primer missed fire.

10) Twenty rounds in 8 minutes; the magazine was opened and filled with water before the firing commenced. One primer missed fire. The priming (being exhausted) was renewed and the magazine again filled with water. No more primers missed fire.

11) After cooling the piece, water was again poured into the magazine and remained about 3 minutes before firing commenced. After firing about 10 rounds, the priming appeared to be much damaged; 7 primers failing to fire. The 20 rounds were however, discharged in about 8 ½ minutes. On the last round fired, the flame communicated to the primers in the magazine caused the explosion of about 6 primers, from the throat down. From the appearance of the apparatus, the flame seemed to have entered not by the throat, but by the lid becoming slightly opened; this however, was not certain. The explosion of the primers did not throw open the lid of the magazine entirely, and caused so little disturbance of the parts, that in the heat of an action the fact would hardly have been observed immediately by the man who was firing the piece.

It is to be observed that when water was poured into the magazine, it soon passed out when the piece was being loaded. However, much moisture was necessarily retained by the form of the magazine and by adhesion to its parts and to the primers, so that the test of the priming was considered a severe one with respect to the quantity of moisture to which it was exposed, though not as to the time of exposure.

Before the tests, Dr. Maynard stated that, in consequence of defects in the varnish, he was aware that the primers were not perfectly water proof, but thought that they could be made so, or at least be made to bear a very long exposure to moisture.

After the above trails, the piece was snapped about 20 times in a high wind, turning it in different directions to the wind, upside down, etc., but the primer never failed to be carried on to the cone and to explode there.

On Friday January 31st, the Board, with all members present, continued the examination of Maynard's tape-lock. It was first tried by catching the head of the cock under the edge of a table, to see if it were liable top accidental explosion of the primers. In the course of this trail, the end of the spring which moved the ratchet became bent backwards, so as to work on the wrong side of the ratchet which, therefore, ceased to operate on the primers, and the action of the lock was consequently impeded.

The quickness of priming the gun with this lock was tried by snapping it and a common percussion lock at the same time. The caps for the latter were put in the pocket of the man who held the musket. Maynard's musket was snapped by the inventor himself. The experiment was tried in the open air, while a cold North West wind was blowing. During the time that 99 primers were snapped on Maynard's, including two changes of the charge of primers in the magazine, 64 caps were snapped on the common lock. With Maynard's lock there was no misfire; the lid of the magazine was partially opened at almost every snap, and the pivot screw of the ratchet wheel required tightening with a screwdriver on two occasions. With the common lock there was one miss-fire, owing apparently to a faulty cap lozenge, which was found to not having been properly charged.

On February 3, 1845, the Board members met with respect to Dr. Maynard's lock and came to the following conclusion: " That the principle of the lock, that of self priming, is adapted to the military service as well as to firearms for private use,, and that the mode of applying that principle which is now offered to their examination is exceedingly ingenious, and accomplishes most of the objects and advantages claimed by the inventor; but that in the details of arrangement of the apparatus, there are mechanical defects which have appeared on trail, but which it is thought may be remedied with little difficulty."

Captain Mordecai proposed as the opinion of the Board: "That Although the principle and construction of this lock is exceedingly ingenious and well adapted for private firearms, the apparatus as now arranged is too complicated to be adopted for the military service; the number of pieces in the lock being nearly doubled, and most of the new parts being very small, and therefore easily lost in cleaning and repairing the arm," Commodore Powell concurred with this opinion and other members of the Board dissented.

"The Board did not meet on the 4th, due to poor weather conditions, but they did meet on February 5th and agreed upon the following report, which they approved, signed, and forwarded to the Secretaries of the War and Navy Departments: "The joint Board of Army and Navy officers directed to examine a new percussion lock for small arms invented by Dr. Edward Maynard, have the honor to report that they assembled at Washington Arsenal on the 29th January last, and after examining the subject submitted to them, have arrived at the following conclusion: "The Board is of the opinion that the principles on which this lock and its priming are constructed may be applied with great practical utility to firearms in general, and that they are applicable to small arms for the military and naval services; that the apparatus for this purpose is exceedingly ingenious, and accomplishes most of the objects proposed by the inventor. "

"The lock and the priming effect with great certainty the primary object of igniting the charge in the barrel, even under very unfavorable circumstances."

"The priming is probably as well secured from the action of moisture as that in ordinary percussion cap, and its use appears to be attended with little risk of accident."

"When the apparatus is in good order the piece is primed with perfect regularity by the simple action of cocking so long as the supply of priming lasts; and this supply, which is sufficient for more than 60 rounds, may be renewed with little difficulty or loss of time. The quickness of firing is therefore increased by nearly all the time required for putting on the percussion caps, which is found to make a difference of about 20 or 25 per cent, in favor of the musket with Maynard's lock."

"The difficulties which present themselves in the use of the common percussion lock with respect to a convenient mode of carrying the primers, and the facilities of using them in cold weather or in the dark, are nearly all avoided by the use of this lock."

"These advantages and others attending the construction of this lock, when the apparatus is in good order, have induced the Board to entertain the favorable opinion above expressed as to the principles of the invention; but in the course of the experiments made by the Board it has been found that there are some imperfections in the mechanical arrangement of the apparatus which render it liable to derangement and impair the safety and certainty of its action."

"The nature of these defects may be seen by reference to the record of experiments which accompanies this report; they are not here mentioned in detail because they are regarded by the Board as merely as imperfections in the mechanical execution of the work, which may be easily remedied and which do not affect the principles on which the lock is constructed."

Shortly thereafter, Dr. Maynard advised the Secretary of War that he believed he had removed the mechanical defects and objections that the Board had pointed out in his percussion lock.

On February 20, 1845 Adjutant General Thomas directed Brigadier General Brooke, Fifth Infantry, in Washington, D.C., to have the Army officers assigned to the Board re-convene at as early a day as practicable, for the purpose of re-examining Dr. Maynard's invention of percussion locks for firearms. Secretary of Navy Mason assented, and on the same date gave a corresponding order to Commodore Powell, directing him to meet with the officers of the Army, and after making the proper examination, to report whether or not the defects had been removed.

The Board met at Washington Arsenal on Wednesday February 26th, for the purpose of examining a musket submitted by Dr. Maynard, to which he had adapted a priming apparatus, with improvements, intended to remove the objections made to some of the mechanical arrangements which were found defective on the former trail. The number of parts of which the apparatus consisted had been reduced by the omission of several of the small parts. The magazine for primers had been secured against the accidental opening of the lid and against the penetration into it of the blast from the vent. The arrangement of the magazine on the lock-plate had been slightly changed, so as to permit the use of a cone which could receive a common percussion cap.

The apparatus was examined by the Board, and the operation of it on the primers was tested by snapping the lock and exploding the primers a great number of times without a charge in the barrel. It was found that, in consequence of the want of due proportion between the thickness of the priming lozenges and the width of the throat of the magazine, through which the primer was protruded, the slip of primers was liable to be choked in the throat of the magazine, so as to impede the action of the lock. In order to give Dr. Maynard sufficient time to remedy this defect, the Board adjourned until 11:00 o'clock the following morning.

On February 27th, the following trails were conducted at the arsenal, in the presence of Captain Mordecai, with Dr. Maynard's musket, using blank cartridges:

1) Twenty five rounds were fired in quick succession. Four primers flashed without firing the charge, owing probably to some obstruction in the vent.
2) After cooling the piece, 25 rounds were fired without any failure or accident.
3) With the hammer let down on the cone, water was poured freely over the lock and it was found that none of the primers would burn. These slips of priming were originally too wide for the depth of the magazine, and in order to put them in place it was necessary to trim off the edges, which removed the varnish from that part and caused the paper and powder to be exposed to the water which entered the magazine through the throat. Without drying the interior of the magazine, another slip of primers was inserted, nearly all of which exploded effectively under the hammer. When the paper became moist it no longer retained the requisite hardness and stiffness for receiving the due action of the ratchet wheel by which the primers were fed up, and they consequently became choked in the throat of the magazine. This action of moisture entering the magazine was the only defect observed in the trails today.
4) Fifty rounds were fired, without cleaning either the magazine or the musket itself, and all without any accident or failure. It appeared possible that, in cocking the piece, the hammer could be drawn a little too far back, beyond the "cock-notch", by which occurrence the primers might be protruded so far as to cause an irregularity in cutting them off at proper intervals. This was considered as merely a defect in the adjustment of the tumbler, and did not constitute an objection to the mode of priming, provided the work on the lock was accurately executed.
5) The regularity of the action of the lock was further tested by firing about 100 primers without a charge in the musket. No further defect or irregularity was observed.

Having completed the trails, Captain Mordecai reported the results to the Board, who agreed on the following opinion during the afternoon of February 27th: "that the improvements made by Dr. Maynard in his priming apparatus, since their last examination and trail of it, have remedied the imperfections which were then observed in it. The slight irregularities which are now found to exist in the action if the priming apparatus are to be attributed chiefly to a want of uniformity in the manufacture of the primers themselves, which have been made with imperfect machinery; but the Board thinks that, in the present condition of the lock and priming, their operation is sufficiently safe, regular, and effective to authorize them to recommend the invention to the patronage of the Government to such an extent as may be necessary for giving it a full and fair trial in service."

Copies of this report were forwarded to the Secretaries of the War and Navy Departments on February 28th, for their information and guidance.

Another Ordnance Board met at the Ordnance Office in Washington, on the 20th of February for the purpose of planning the conversion of flint-lock muskets to the percussion system, using those muskets in storage which had been manufactured between 1821 and 1831, inclusive, and previously classified as being suitable for issuance for all ordinary purposes or for alteration to percussion. An interesting extract from the proceedings of the Board, which adjourned on March 12, 1845, had to do with substituting other primers and new arrangements of the lock for the percussion cap then in use. It read:

"The Board, considering that the efficiency and convenience of the cap, having been established by long experience in sporting guns, so as to cause its general adoption for Military Service, think the subject of a change in the kind of primer should be approached with great caution, and they are therefore unwilling to make any suggestion with regard to the ingenuous contrivance of Dr. Maynard for this purpose, except that a full and sufficient trial should be given to his plan if the report of the Board of Officers appointed to examine it should be favorable."

On March 13, 1845, Dr. Maynard made the following offer to the Government:

"As a Board of Officers of the Army and Navy have reported favorably on my patent invention of an improved musket lock and percussion priming, I respectfully offer for the approbation of the Secretaries of War and the Navy to sell to the United States the right to make and use my percussion priming and lock for –

5,000 muskets for $5,000
10,000 muskets for $7,500
20,000 muskets for $10,000
100,000 muskets for $25,000

"The right of making and using the priming, however, is not to extend beyond the necessary supply for the muskets that may be contracted for under this proposition."

On March 13th 1845, in forwarding Dr. Maynard's written offer to the War Department, Lieutenant Colonel George Talcott of Ordnance, recommended Dr. Maynard's proposals to the favorable consideration of the Secretary of War.

Secretary of War William L. Marcy wrote to Major General Winfield Scott, Commanding the Army, on March 14th, transmitting the proposition of Dr. Maynard to sell to the United States the right to manufacture and use his patent invention of percussion lock and priming for muskets. Attached to the letter were copies of correspondence between the War Department and Secretary of the Navy, George Bancroft, indicating that Commodore Charles Morris and William M. Crane were to be associated with General Scott and Colonel James G. Totten, Chief of Army Engineers, to compose a board to report to both departments as early as was convenient, in relation to the proposition and its expediency, and the extent to which contracts ought to be carried by each of the departments.

The Board convened at 12 noon on Saturday, March 15th, in the room next to the Quartermaster's Office, under the Engineer Department, diagonally opposite to the War Building. Captain William Maynadier, of the Ordnance Department, was appointed by General Scott, as recorder to the Board. After reading Dr. Maynard's propositions and the report of the trial board of the Army and Navy officers who had tried his invention, the plan of Dr. Maynard and those of other inventors for altering the flint to the percussion-lock were examined and compared. The Board, after due consultation and deliberation, adopted the following report:

"The Board of Army and Navy Officers appointed to determine certain written propositions of Dr. Maynard, submitted to them and now before this Board, respecting an improvement in fire-locks, have had the subject under consideration, and unanimously recommend that the contracts be made by the proper authorities with the said Maynard as follows; viz: a contract by the War Department for four thousand arms, and by the Navy Department for one thousand arms, making in all five thousand arms, on the conditions stated in the proposition submitted by him. But the Board suggest that a condition be inserted in the said contracts to this effect: that if, when the improvement of the said Dr. Maynard shall have been duly subjected to the second or practical test, or actual service, it shall be found as valuable as it now promises to be, on the first or scientific test, the War and Navy Departments, or either of them, shall be at liberty to apply said improvement to any greater number of fire-locks at the diminished rates of compensation, according to the written propositions of said Dr. Maynard, counting, in the payments, the number of arms before contracted for as a part of any greater number subsequently needed by the government; and, further, should the government, or either the War or Navy Department, desire to apply the same improvement in any number of firearms exceeding one hundred thousand, the rate of payment for such further privilege shall not exceed twelve and a half cents per fire-lock, including the right of making and using a sufficient supply of priming for the number of arms that may be contracted for."

On March 18th, the report of the Board was approved, so far as it came within the jurisdiction of the War Department, by the written endorsement of Secretary Marcy, who then referred it to the Ordnance Bureau to be carried into effect.

On March 20, 1845, Secretary of War Marcy and Dr. Edward Maynard drew up and signed a contract, wherein Dr. Maynard agreed to sell to the Government, for $4,000, the privilege and right to use his improvements under certain expressed conditions. Maynard assigned to the Government, the right to make, use and apply the improvements in his percussion lock to a number of muskets or other small arms not exceeding four thousand.

On March 22, 1845, a similar agreement was made between Dr. Maynard and W. M. Crane, Chief of the Naval Bureau of Ordnance and Hydrography, in which the Navy Department paid $1,000 for the right to apply the priming device to a number of muskets or other small arms not exceeding one thousand.

Both of the above mentioned contracts also permitted the respective service departments to make and use a sufficient quantity of the improved priming for these arms. In addition, the contracts set forth the provision that, in case the Government of the United States desired to apply the original improvement, and / or all subsequent improvements made by Maynard based on the same principle, to any greater number of arms than had been provided for, and to make and use the improved priming therefore, it had the privilege and right of so doing by paying Dr. Maynard at certain diminished rates, according to the number of arms to which the improvement might be applied, base upon the figures previously mentioned in the written offer of Dr. Maynard, dated March 13, 1845.

However, the payments of $4,000 and $1,000 made by the War and Navy Departments, respectively, were to be counted as part of the payment for any greater number of arms that might be made or altered to posses Maynard's improvement. It was further provided that, in case the Government wished to apply the improvement to any number of arms exceeding 100,000, and to make and use the priming for the same, it would have the right of doing so by paying Dr. Maynard at a rate subject to further agreement, not to exceed twenty-five cents for each arm so improved. It was also to be understood that the privilege of fabricating and using the improved priming was to be limited to the quantity required for the arms that might be made or altered to the United States, and was to be used in the public service only.

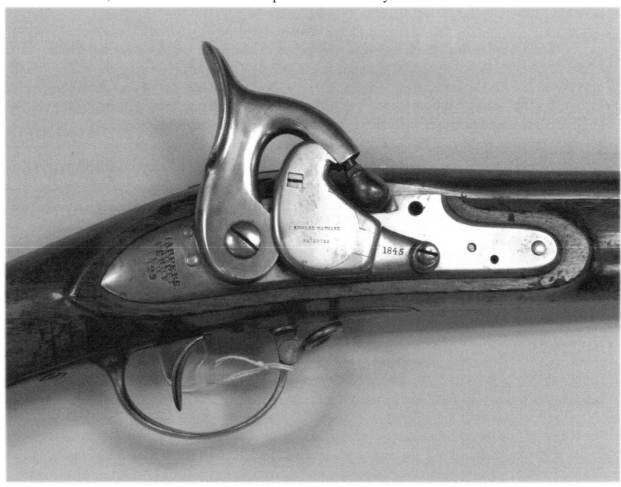

Above: Dr. Maynard's tape primer lock patent model submitted to the U.S. Patent Office in 1845 with his patent paperwork. This patent model is on a Harpers Ferry 1829 dated musket with Edward Maynard Patentee stamped on the tape primer magazine door and dated 1845 in front of door hinge.
(Courtesy of the Smithsonian Institution Museum of American History)

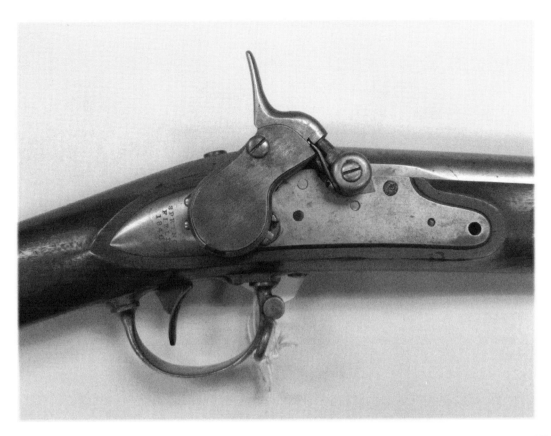

Above and below: Close up pictures of two of Dr. Maynard's Tape Primer Lock models each with a different style of primer lock. The lock above is marked Springfield 1840 and the lock below is marked Harpers Ferry 1829. These models have cut stocks and barrels for ease of travel as seen in photo on page 5.

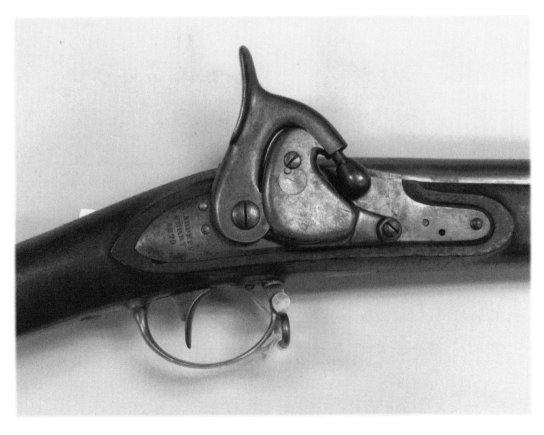

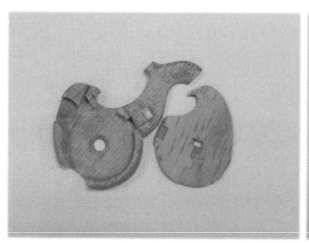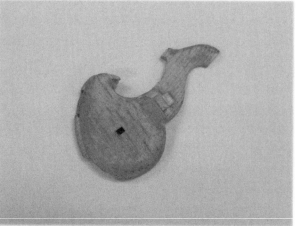

Dr. Maynard hand carved many of his preliminary gun models out of wood. Above left: Dr. Maynard's wood model of his Tape Primer Lock in the open position (door detached), Above right: Same lock with magazine door in closed position.

Above: Several of Dr. Maynard's gun model parts carved out of wood to include gun hammers, tape primer lock and several unidentified parts.

Below: Circular for Maynard's Tape Primer listing the advantages of primers over copper caps.

CIRCULAR,

In answer to the very important inquiries made at the War Department and elsewhere, respecting the Maynard Primer, the undersigned, Its inventor offers the following statement of some of the advantages over the Percussion Cap for military use.

EDWARD MAYNARD,
Washington, D.C.

CAPS.	PRIMERS
Copper for 1,000,000 costs six hundred dollars.	Paper for 1,000,000 Primers costs six dollars.
Caps cost one dollar per thousand.	Primers cost from 10 to 20 cents per thousand.
One machine will make fifty thousand caps per day.	One machine of equal cost will make fifteen hundred thousand Primers per day.
The Cap gun has to be primed by hand every time it is loaded.	The Primer gun primes itself.
The Cap gun often goes off at half-cock, and even when the hammer is down, if it gets a blow by falling or otherwise.	The Primer gun is not primed except when cocked.
The act of priming the Cap gun is the most difficult one the soldier has to perform in battle.	The Primer gun primes itself.
The Caps, being carried in a pocket separate from the gun, are liable to be separated permanently from it, rendering it useless	The Primers are carried in the gun and cannot be accidently separated from it.
Nearly as much time is required in battle to prime the cap gun as to load it: and if the weather be cold, or the time be night, more time will be required.	With the Primer gun, all this time is saved.
In drilling raw recruits, a great deal of time is required to teach them to use the cap.	With the Primer gun, all this time is saved.
The Lock for the Cap gun is the cheapest ; but ---	The Primers cost so much less than the Caps that the savings on five hundred will pay the difference in the cost of the Locks.

Below: Dr. Maynard's first Patent Number 4,208 for the Tape Primer Lock.

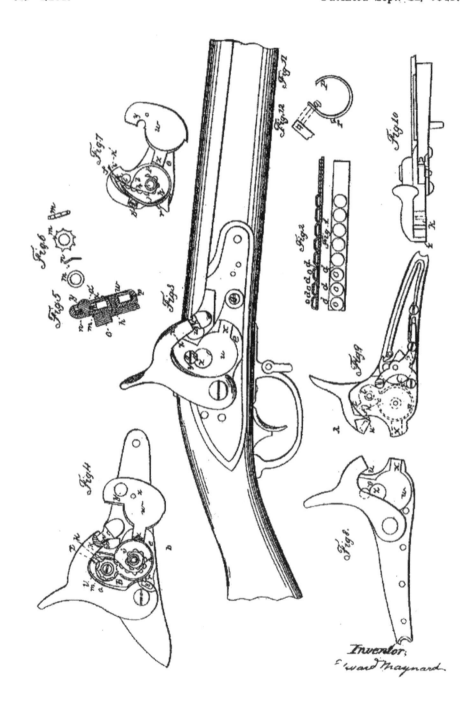

E. MAYNARD.

Priming-Cock.

No 4,208.

Patented Sept. 22, 1845.

Inventor:
Edward Maynard

Chapter 4

Dr. Maynard's Departure for Europe

Fresh from the sale of his patented tape primer and lock to the U.S. Government and encouraged by the Ministers of several European countries, Dr. Maynard had already made plans to travel to Europe to meet with the heads of foreign governments in hopes of selling his invention to them for use on the guns of their armies. He was especially encouraged by the Russian Minister to the U.S., Mr. Bodisco, and by the Russian Minister to London, Baron Brunow, into believing that his invention was something the Russian Government would be anxious to acquire.

Maynard had two partners for the overseas marketing and sales of his new tape primer lock and for his overseas trip, Major Thomas L. Smith and General J. Washington Tyson. These two men, who in exchange for putting up certain amounts of money to pay for Maynard's trip and expenses and other obligations, were made equal one third partners and were thus each entitled to share in any of the profits in the sale of Maynard's Patent. As Maynard's letters reveal, Major Smith and General Tyson failed to put any money up front, leading to a possible falling out with Dr. Maynard upon his return to America.

The Contract

This agreement made at the City of Washington, in the District of Columbia, on the tenth day of February, Anno Domini eighteen hundred and forty five, by and between Edward Maynard, of said City of Washington of the first part, and Thomas L. Smith, also of said City and J. Washington Tyson of the City of Philadelphia in the State of Pennsylvania of the second part,

Witnesseth,

That for the reason and consideration hereinafter mentioned, the said Edward Maynard, hath covenanted and agreed by these presents doth covenant and agree, for himself, his heirs, executors, administrators, and assigns, to and with the said Thomas L. Smith and J. Washington Tyson, their heirs, executors administrators, and assigns, that they, the said Smith and Tyson shall each receive one third part or portion of all profits, avails or benefits whatsoever arising or which may hereinafter arise in any quarter of the world, except the United States, from the sale of the patent rights to individuals, companies or governments to use or manufacture a self priming lock, a new form of percussion priming invented by the said Maynard, both in improvements or alterations as the said Maynard may from time to time introduce into the same.

The said Maynard hath further covenanted and agreed and by these presents doth covenant and agree for himself, his heirs, executors administrators and assigns to and with the said Smith and Tyson, their heirs, executors administrators and assigns that they, the said Smith and Tyson shall each receive one third part or portion of all profits, avails or benefits whatsoever arising or which hereafter may arise from any contract or contracts which the said Maynard himself personally or through the agency of others, made with any individuals, companies or governments in any quarter of the world except the United States, to manufacture any number of said lock or priming.

The said Maynard hath further agreed and covenanted and by these presents doth further agree and covenant for himself, his heirs, executors administrators and assigns with and to the said Smith and Tyson, their heirs, executors, administrators and assigns, that they, the said Smith and Tyson, shall each receive one fourth part or portion of all profits, avails or benefits whatsoever arising or which may hereafter arise from the sale of patent rights of said lock and priming (as well in their present form, as aforesaid, as with such improvements or alterations as the said Maynard may from time to time introduce into the same) to individuals or companies in the United States or in the government of the United States or the government of any of the States, or from contracts with individuals or companies or with any State or the general government of the United States, to manufacture any number of said locks or priming.

It is further understood and agreed by and between the parties to this agreement, that no present to the inventor from any Emperor, King, Sultan Governor or other ruler or potentate, is included in this agreement, but is retained by the said Maynard for his own exclusive use and benefit.

And the said Thomas L. Smith and J. Washington Tyson have covenanted and agreed and by these presents do covenant and agree for themselves their heirs, executors administrators and assigns with the said Edward Maynard his heirs, executors administrators and assigns, that they, the said Smith and Tyson will jointly and severally make all such efforts as may be, from time to time, agreed upon between the parties to this agreement to procure contracts from the government of the United States and the State governments, as well as from individuals and companies in the United States for the manufacture of said lock and priming and also to sell patent rights to individuals and companies in the United States, to manufacture and use the same.

It is further covenanted and agreed by the said Smith to and with said Maynard and Tyson, that during their absence in Europe or that of either of them, he will devote such portions of his time and attention as may not be required by his official duties as Register of the Treasury, to the joint interests of the parties to these presents, so far as relates to said lock and priming.

It is further covenanted and agreed by the said Tyson to and with said Maynard and Smith, that at such time during the approaching spring, that the parties here to may agree upon, he, the said Tyson will in company with said Maynard, visit Europe and take out patent for said lock and priming from such governments as they, the said Maynard and Tyson, may deem expedient, also solicit contracts from the various governments of Europe, for the manufacture of said lock and priming, as well as sell patent rights to individuals, companies and governments abroad, provided a contract or contracts be obtained in time from the War and Navy Departments, of the United States Government (for furnishing them with said lock and priming) which will afford sufficient profits to meet the current wants of the said Maynard in this country, amounting to five thousand dollars and pay his travelling expenses to Europe and back, but, if no such contract or contracts be obtained as will afford sufficient profits, as aforesaid, then the said Tyson agrees to go alone, for the fulfillment of the aforesaid objects.

It is further covenanted and agreed by the said Smith and Tyson to and with said Maynard, that if the contract or contracts before referred should not be obtained, or if obtained should not yield profits sufficient, over and above such sum or sums of money as may be required by the current wants of the said Maynard, amounting to five thousand dollars as aforesaid, and to pay his travelling expenses to Europe and back, as well as to defray the travelling expenses of said Tyson and the fees for taking out patent rights abroad, then and in that event the said Smith and Tyson agree to furnish such sum or sums as may be necessary to pay the aforesaid expenses of Tyson while actually employed in the business of the parties to these presents, as well as the fees necessary to be paid in taking out patent right as aforesaid, without in any manner, making the said Maynard responsible for the same.

It is further understood and agreed by and between the parties to these presents, that the whole of the first profits arising from said lock and priming in the United States shall accrue to and be received by the said Maynard until they shall amount to five thousand dollars – the quarter parts or portions of which five thousand dollars, belonging to the said Smith and Tyson to be refunded by said Maynard to the said Smith and Tyson out of the said Maynard's parts or portion of the profits arising from said lock and priming as well as in the United States as abroad, but if no such profits should arise, over and above the said five thousand dollars, then the said Smith and Tyson have no claim upon the said Maynard as aforesaid.

It is further understood and agreed that the said Smith and Tyson shall alone be responsible for the manufacture of the machines for making priming, and also for the manufacture of such locks as may be required to exhibit it's advantages abroad, and that they will pay for the same.

It is further agreed that neither of the parties hereto shall assign or transfer to any other person or persons his interest in said lock and priming without the consent of the other parties hereto.

Witness our hands and seals affixed the day and year first written.

Witnesses present at signing

Edward Maynard   H.E. Campbell

Thomas L. Smith

J. Washington Tyson

Below: Dr. Maynard's original signature from his 1845 contract.

27

It is further agreed by the parties to the above agreement that if contracts be obtained from the government of the United States as above described the fees for patents and the travelling expenses abroad of the said Maynard and Tyson shall be defrayed from the quarter parts or portions of the profits accruing to the said Smith and Tyson.

Witness our hands and seals affixed the day and year first written.

Edward Maynard

Thomas L. Smith

J. Washington Tyson

Dr. Maynard departed from Springfield, Massachusetts on July 3, 1845 where he left his wife, Ellen with their three small boys; Edward Jr. age five, George age three and John age two. His destination was St. Petersburg, Russia where he planned on meeting Tsar Nicholas I of Russia or his representative, where he hoped for a quick sale which would help him realize a fortune. To get to St. Petersburg, Russia he would have first made a three week ocean crossing trip by steamer to Liverpool, England then traversed to London via coach. It took him eleven weeks and five days (That is just shy of three months) of travel before arriving in St. Petersburg. His first letter from St. Petersburg describes his trip from London to St. Petersburg. After approximately five months in St. Petersburg, he would then travel to Berlin via a coach over land; a seven day trip, then on to Paris, Brussels, and London, to both try to sell his invention and secure patents in each country for his invention as it was clear to him that without a patent in each country, his invention could be easily copied with no benefit to him. Maynard took with him a number of different models with his tape primer lock invention, as well as a pistol which he carried. He left behind not only his young family but a thriving dental practice in Washington D.C. which he had built up over the preceding eight years. He took with him one thousand dollars and the hope that he would not be gone too long with an anticipated return date of sometime in December of 1845.

Below: Dr. Maynard's Dental tools he likely travelled with to St. Petersburg and through Europe.
Courtesy Smithsonian Institution Maynard Dental Collection

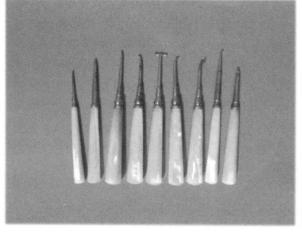 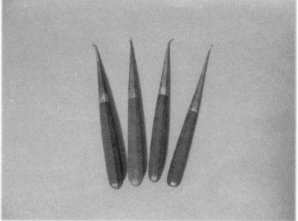

The Cast of Characters

During Dr. Maynard's fourteen month trip, he would meet and write about the following people. This list in order that each person appears in his letters serves as a brief guide and index to each person and it gives a short description of exactly who each person was.

Major Thomas L. Smith and General J. Washington Tyson; Dr. Maynard's two business partners and partial owners to the rights of Dr. Maynard's patent for his lock and priming. They were supposed to front the funds for Dr. Maynard's travelling expenses but never did. General Tyson was a Commissary General for Purchasing. Smith was a Register of the Treasury.

Major George Whistler; Chief Engineer and Railroad Engineer. In 1842 he was invited by Tsar Nicholas I of Russia to build a railroad line from St. Petersburg to Moscow. He was paid $12,000 a year which allowed him and his family to live luxuriously in St. Petersburg with many servants. His son, James Abbott McNeill Whistler was a famous American artist. His wife was Whistler's Mother of the famous painting.

Colonel Charles Todd (1791- 1871)**;** He was from Kentucky and graduated from William and Mary College in 1809. He served with the Kentucky Militia in the War of 1812 with General William Henry Harrison. He was Secretary of State under Madison in 1816, he was a member of the Legislature in 1817 and 1818, and he was Charge d'Affaires to Colombia from 1818 to 1823. He accompanied General Harrison to Washington in 1841 and was appointed to be Minister to Vienna. President Harrison's untimely death prevented this appointment and he was given the Mission to Russia by President Tyler in 1841 where he served until he was recalled by President Polk in 1845.

Emperor of Russia Tsar Nicholas I; Absolute ruler of Russia from 1825 to 1855.

George Washington Parmly; An American dentist practicing in Europe. Travelling companion and family friend of Dr. Maynard's. He travelled with Dr. Maynard from London to St. Petersburg. After arriving in St. Petersburg with Dr. Maynard he traveled alone back to other countries in Europe.

Mr. and Mrs. John Randolph Clay; Appointed Secretary of Legation to St. Petersburg in 1830, Appointed Charge d'Affaires in 1836 in 1838 became Secretary of Legation to Austria and in 1845 went back to Russia in the same capacity.

His Imperial Highness Grand Duke Michael; He was the younger brother of Emperor Tsar Nicholas I and he Grand Master of Ordnance.

Messieurs Eastwick, Harrison & Winans; Three partners in a Locomotive and railroad manufacturing firm whose firm was hired by Tsar Nicholas I to build a Russian Railroad.

Mr. Thompson; British dentist in St. Petersburg.

Mr. Bodisco; The Russian Minister to the U.S.

General Prince Dolgorouki; Close Aide to Grand Duke Michael.

Colonel Solovzoff; Interpreter for Grand Duke Michael English to Russian.

Baron Heurteloup; French inventor who designed a method for priming a gun that involved individual percussion caps held in coiled tubes of metal. The Russians claimed Dr. Maynard's invention too closely resembled this system.

Miss Sarah and Elizabeth Benson; Dr. Maynard's landladies, owners and operators of Boarding house in St. Petersburg overlooking the Neva River.

General Alderberg; A man said to be only second to one (Count Orloff) in the favor of the Emperor.

Count Orloff; see above

Mr. Sopozhnakoff; Immensely wealthy and of a very influential Russian family.

Dr. Arndt; Physician to the Emperor.

Mr. Thomas Charles Grut; An Englishman – merchant and purchaser of rights to tape primer lock for both Denmark and Sweden.

Her Imperial Highness the Grand Duchess Helen; Wife of Grand Duke Michael.

Dr. Brewster; Dentist practicing in Europe; considered the first Dentist in Europe by the Russian Imperial Family.

Baron Krudener; Master of Ceremonies to Her Imperial Highness the Grand Duchess Helen.

Count and Countess Kleinmichel; Russian Minister to operate for him and the Countess.

Mademoiselle Troubat; The lady who attends upon the Grand Duchess Helen.

Her Imperial Highness the Grand Duchess Marie; Daughter of Grand Duke Michael and Grand Duchess Helen.

His Imperial Highness the Grand Duke Alexander; The "Cesarovitch" – heir to the throne; - from this circumstance, next to His Majesty, the greatest man in Russia.

Her Imperial Highness the Grand Duchess Catherine; Sister of Grand Duchess Marie.

Her Imperial Highness the Tsarina; Oldest daughter of Tsar Nicholas I.

Dr. Wiley; The Physician of His Imperial Highness the Grand Duke Michael.

Mr. W. H. Ropes; An American merchant long settled here.

Miss Moravieff; A young Russian female dental patient.

Dr. Zdekauer; Physician to the Grand Duchess Marie and the Grand Duchess Catherine.

Countess Cheremetef; A patient of Dr. Maynard's.

Baron Seddler, and his two daughters; A Baron and one of his daughters is a Maid of Honor to the Grand Duchess Catherine.

Mr. De Hassing; Secretary to the Grand Duchess.

Mr. Gellibrand; Brother-in-law of Mr. Ropes. Mr. Gellibrand is an Englishman and a merchant.

Mr. Fay; Secretary of U.S. Legation at Berlin, Prussia.

Mr. Henry Wheaton; An American lawyer and diplomat. He was the United States Supreme Court Reporter of Decisions from 1816 to 1827. His diplomatic career began in 1827 as Charge d'Affaires to Denmark. He became U.S. Minister to Prussia in 1837 to 1846.

Mr. and Mrs. Clemson; Charge d'Affaires in Belgium, Mrs. Clemson is the daughter of John C. Calhoun.

King Leopold of Prussia; King of Prussia.

Sir Hamilton Seymour and Lady Seymour; British Minister to Belgium and his wife.

Officers Colonel Fredericks and Timmerman; Belgian military officers involved in inspecting Maynard's invention and providing advice.

The Chevalier Iobard; Director of the Museum of Industry.

King of Belgium

Dumont; Interpreter hired by Dr. Maynard in Belgium and France.

Vivario-Plomdeur; Belgian gun maker who Dr. Maynard hired to fabricate several locks and guns based on his design.

Mr. Graves of Kentucky; An ex-member of Congress.

Soliman Pasha; An Officer from Egypt and creator of Egypt's first army.

General Count Woyna; The Austrian Minister in Brussels.

Mr. Merle; Frenchman involved in helping Dr. Maynard secure patent in France.

Dr. Ricord; An American surgeon at a hospital in Paris that Dr. Maynard visited.

Mr. Ralston; An American living in London with a mild interest in Dr. Maynard's invention. Dr. Maynard met him in Hamburg.

Chapter 5
(First Letter)
Arrival and Settling into St. Petersburg

My Dear Ellen,

       With what feelings I write you from this remote quarter of the Earth I am unable to tell. Thank Heaven I may say that I have got safely as far from you as I ever expect to be, and, notwithstanding that I suffer from sea-sickness every time I go to sea, still I am well when on shore: and I trust I shall suffer less in future from the sea than heretofore. When I wrote you last I was about to sail from London for Hamburg on my way here. I did sail as proposed in the nastiest steamer I ever saw, and had the most miserable time of it crossing the German Ocean and until we reached the mouth of the Elbe, up which river, about 80 miles I think, lies the famous City of Hamburg. Contrary to our expectations we were detained, certainly not against our will, 3 days at Hamburg waiting for the time for the next steamer from Lubec to this place. We arrived in Hamburg on Saturday and on Sunday at the suggestion of a Dr. Ralston of London, an American, (of whom I shall have more to say) we next went with him by railroad from Altona (a city 2 or 3 miles from Hamburg) across the province of Holstein in Denmark (60 miles) to Kiel, (Keel) and back again the same day. Of what I saw in this excursion as in many others I must tell you but as to writing it – that is out of the question.

Hamburg, as you know is one of the most important Commercial Cities in Europe, and until within a few years was very strongly fortified and all built in the Old Dutch gable-end-to-the-street style. Since it has been a free City all of the old fortifications have been leveled down into beautiful gardens, shrubberies, plantings etc. threaded in all directions with beautiful walks, promenades and drives. And since the disastrous fire of 1843, which destroyed a large portion of the City, the new buildings and streets are such as to make it in the new part very beautiful indeed. Nothing that we had seen could compare with some of the architectural beauties in Hamburg: and I doubt if anything here will, - but of that we have not had time to judge.

From Hamburg to Lubec we travelled in what we call a diligence – a sort of coach, made in various ways, some for six, and some for three or four times that number of passengers. At Lubec, (once a City of great Political and Commercial importance but of precious little of either now) we stayed overnight and ran about a little in the morning, and then we took omnibus for our place of embarking on the Baltic Sea at Travemunde, a small town at the mouth of the river Trave – one or two hours from Lubec. From Travemunde we had very favorable winds until we reached Kronstadt when we changed steamers, taking a smaller one to run up to this place, about two hours from Kronstadt. We arrive here about noon yesterday, but did not get through with our passports and baggage until near night.

Today I called upon and delivered some letters to Major Whistler, our Countryman, who is Chief Engineer upon a great Railroad from here to Moscow – now being constructed. The Major received me very kindly and I accompanied him to hear the Episcopal services at a chapel established here by the English residents. After Church walked about a little, saw the famous equestrian statue of Peter the Great, came home to lunch and to write you; and while doing so was interrupted agreeably by a visit from Major Whistler who sat and examined my invention, admired it and advised with me for two or three hours. Nothing can be done here <u>now</u> because the Emperor is not here; and he is not expected under about a month. George Parmly and I have room and board at an English boarding house kept by two sisters, the Misses Benson, who are fat enough to be what they seem – very good people. We are to pay each about $2.20 per day; and I suppose there will be extra charges; as in England, enough to double it: - so much for candles, so much for soap, so much for washing bed linen, and so on and so forth.

It is my present impression that it will be impossible for me to return to you before spring. Had the Emperor been here I might perhaps have got through very soon so as to finish up my business in other places and return in December or January. One thing is very certain – what I don't do now I shan't come again to do – I am not quite so fond of sea-sickness and all the other inconveniences and disgusts of travelling as to wish to repeat this trip for any moderate compensation when I might be comfortable and happy at home.

Our Minister, Colonel Charles Todd, to whom I have letters resides twenty miles from here – so I have not seen him, but propose doing so in a day or two. Sunday is a general holiday here, I am told – and in Hamburg and Altona it seemed as if the whole population must have been in the streets, walks, gardens, pavilions etc. on the Sunday we were there.

We have found and engaged for a few days a fellow here, an Englishman, who has been some twelve years or so in Russia, as a sort of Valet de place (val de plas) for strangers visiting the Country – he speaking thus Russian, German and English and so being of great value to those who do not speak the former as it is the common language here – indeed one must have the language or some such person to get along at all. The very waiters of the house where we board do not seem to have, all of them put together, a dozen words of English or anything else except Russian.

Your next letter that I expect I hope to get in about seven or eight days, but the mails are so very uncertain that I may not hear from you again for a month; and as I mentioned in my last letter to you, you must not be uneasy about me if you do not hear from me for my letters may not reach you within a month of the time they should do and may not even reach you at all, or yours me.

This is a dreadful state of things for me, but it will be over sometime and I shall have learned a good lesson by it – <u>to be contented</u> – as you have so often and so wisely told me. That will be <u>one</u> of the improvements I shall make by travelling.

You may remember that a Dentist of the name of Hitchcock received a splendid gold snuffbox set with diamonds, in return for a set of teeth sent to the Sultan of Turkey. The same Hitchcock tried the same game here, sent a large box of newspapers, each containing something about himself and in a large box a smaller one containing a set of teeth, etc. etc. This was sent to Colonel Todd for him to send to the Emperor – which he never did. Afterward he came here himself, having in the meantime published a book defending the Emperor, his policy etc. etc. and expected to be presented to the Emperor and probably receive some reward for his labor: but Colonel Todd wouldn't present him – told him he <u>could</u> <u>not</u> – that it was not customary here to present any but Official persons etc. and finally got rid of him. (By the way, I was told in Boston that Hitchcock didn't see the Emperor because his Majesty was <u>not</u> here. I am told here that he <u>was</u> here.)

I shall make you another long letter I expect for I don't know when I shall have an opportunity of sending this so as to insure it's reaching America. 11 o'clock - bed time – just about <u>tea</u>-time with you – say <u>5</u> o'clock – hope you have a good cup and enjoy it. Parmly has been with Mr. Cunningham of Boston today to see a great horse-race; and on his return went to the Theatre – a very large one and very full. So much for <u>Sunday</u> – Good night and sweet dreams to you – good-night.

Monday night. September 22, 1845. – Parmly and I have been out sight-seeing all day. Visited a Museum here where they kept many of the tools of Peter the Great (the founder of the City) and many models of ships and many other things which he made with his own hands – having worked while young at ship-building in England in order the better to build up a Navy for himself. Visited also the "Church of Peter and Paul" where the dead members of the Imperial Family lie buried from Peter the Great to this time. This church is within the walls of a fortress on an island.

From there we went to a very old church, or rather the oldest here, and thence to the log-house built by Peter the Great for his residence until he could build something better. In one room of this (it contains but four including the entryway) we heard the service of the Greek Church which seems very like the Catholic "only a great deal more so". Here we saw a great many presents of cheap jewelry etc. etc., left as offerings in consequence of the givers having recovered from sickness by worshipping here – at least so we are told. Thence we went to the "Summer gardens", a beautiful plot of ground of many acres covered with trees and laid out in walks and enriched with about 60 full size statues representing the seasons, etc. etc. and perhaps twice as many busts of distinguished characters, all beautifully wrought in white marble and standing upon pedestals of granite. Two of the latter I remember were the two philosophers, Democritus and Heraclitus, of whom we read in the old English reader of our schools. One of them seems to be crying his eyes out while the other is splitting cheeks with laughter. Thence we went to the Cathedral Church where we heard part of the service again. This Church exceeds in cost and magnificence all others I have ever visited. If what I took to be precious stones in this church were really so, as I suppose, I must have seen hundreds of thousands of dollars worth. Our Valet de place pointed out one particular diamond in the head dress of one of the pictures of the Virgin Mary the light of which we easily caught while 40 feet off: and from curiosity I walked backward keeping the sparkling in my eye until I reached the wall of the church, at least a hundred feet from the stone. After service we went all around and examined critically many parts. There are in this church several paintings of the Virgin and Child some full size some less and, in all of them, all except the faces, hands and feet were covered with gilt metal – very thin – and wrought and stamped up to represent the drapery. Some of these <u>dresses</u> we were told, were fine gold, solid, and these were set about the head and bosom with diamonds, emeralds, amethysts, rubies etc. etc. and great quantities of pearls. This about finished the day and we returned to dinner at 6 o'clock. This is certainly in its design as well as execution <u>very</u>, <u>very</u> far before all other cities we have seen yet – and we have <u>just</u> <u>begun</u> to see this yet – it being a city of <u>four</u> <u>hundred</u> <u>thousand</u> inhabitants.

Every way you turn your eye here you see soldiers: - soldiers, soldiers, continually – almost every rod of our walk we meet them. Here we have a sketch of a <u>drosky</u> – the sort of carriage in use here for the same purpose that cabs and hacks are with us. The carriage is shown in profile to avoid confusion of lines.

The driver sits astride and the passenger may do the same as in the sketch or he may sit side ways. They are very funny looking things and Parmly says they are very easy to ride on. I have not tried them. The horses here are rather small but are by far the finest I ever saw as well at rest as in action. If Willoughby could see some of the perfectly jet black ones that I have seen here, with their tales reaching within a few inches of the ground and their manes half way to their knees – perfect models of beauty and all life and grace in motion he would almost, like me, go crazy because we cannot take them home; the voyage being too long. The bow which you see in the sketch over the horse's neck is to keep the shafts apart – it being a spring of wood like an ox-bow and fastened to the shafts. The object of it in this respect I can more easily explain when I come to talk of it. You will also see that the check-rein passes up over a ring at the summit of the bow and then down and is secured to the shafts – this is quite effectual in keeping the head up. (I am thus particular because the whole thing taken together is very curious to me and will, I am sure, interest Willoughby and John and Father Owen.) There are traces fastened to the outside of the shafts, opposite the belly-band, extending back to the end of the forward axle-tree where they are also fastened at the other end: but of what use they are I don't know except they act as stays or braces, as the draft is by two short straps, one on each side, extending from the harness to the end of the shafts: and here you will see the use of the bow in keeping the shafts apart when the horse pulls. With the exception of the collar, traces, pad and belly-band there is not a strap about the harness more than from ½ to 5/8 of an inch wide.* The trimmings are all either silver or silver plate and some of them are pretty; the straps being so covered with little ornaments that they look like chains or silver bands. Good night.

*The surface of the country here being almost level the harness need not be made to hold back much of a load.

Tuesday night, September 23, 1845. – Have been out all day again visiting Churches, Palaces, Monuments, and Grave-yards etc. etc. At one church we saw a silver tomb containing the remains of some Alexander. There were candlesticks, stands, etc. two figures of Angels large as men and a great display of Armor, etc. at the tomb and some beautiful chandeliers nearby, all wrought in silver, the weight being, as we were told, very nearly 5,000 pounds avoirdupois, and the labor must have cost far more than the material, I should think. We went into but one palace and that not now occupied. We were told that it was a favorite one of Catherine 2nd, or at least that it had been in her time occupied by one of her favorites. Here we were shown many large and beautiful rooms containing paintings statuary etc., but the grand thing was the ballroom of which I will attempt to give you some faint idea. First you must suppose the room to be 2 or 3 hundred feet long and then you start with a good beginning. There is a circular room of statuary from which we entered the ballroom; there are columns on each side and a semi-circular conservatory. Outside the columns on one side containing quite a forest of orange and other trees and plants and looking out upon a beautiful lake in an extensive garden or park. Between the columns, between the windows, against the walls and in many other places beside, including the semi-circle, were most exquisite marble statues, mostly of life size and naked – especially the female figures, one of which – I'll tell you more about that one when I see you. I can only say now that I expect to dream about it tonight. One of the statues, almost half size or less was placed before a mirror. As you look at the figure it represents a beautiful woman lying on a mattress, asleep, with her back toward you but turned over so her bosom lies on the mattress and her face is turned farther still so as to be toward you; a very natural position and showing the form most charmingly while she seems to be in a very sweet sleep. But what is curious about it is, that as you look in the glass under the figure, between the body and the mattress, and you see that it is a male. I could only account for it by supposing it represents her dream. (Do not suppose that I am neglecting my business to run about the city – my affairs are doing all they can do just yet.) Good night.

Wednesday night, September 24, 1845 – Went out by railroad with Parmly to the village or town where Colonel Todd resides. How the name of the place is spelled I don't know but it is pronounced, as near as I have got it, Sars-co-cells, we called upon Colonel Todd who received us very civilly. In half an hour or so his Secretary of Legation and Lady came in ready dressed for the races, close by. Colonel Todd having to take Mrs. Clay (the Secretary's wife) in his carriage to the races and we being also anxious to see them he invited us to join him after the races and dine with him. So we returned and found he had not dismissed his carriage but had it in waiting in grand style. Servants in splendid livery, to take us on a drive before dinner in the Imperial Gardens (covering hundreds of acres I suppose) and to visit the Armory in the Gardens.

This Armory as much surpasses the one in the Tower of London as that one does a gunsmith shop: even so much I can say from what I saw, and I saw only a part less than half I was told – the other part being closed for some repairs to the building. After driving about for a mile or two through grounds kept in far better order than those at our Capital and a hundred fold more beautiful – passing over beautiful and fanciful bridges, under the like arches and along before the Imperial Palace to which the Grounds belong – a most magnificent summer residence extending over I don't know how many acres of ground we returned and had a very pleasant little dinner party – Colonel Todd, Mr. and Mrs. Clay – Parmly and myself. After dinner had a private interview with Colonel Todd and found him ready to do all in his power to serve me.

At the races I saw the Grand Duke Michael (brother of the Emperor) two of the Emperors sons (some 12 or 15 years old) who are also Grand Dukes and wear uniforms, and several Duchesses, Princesses, Countesses etc. Colonel Todd told us who they were while we were at the races but their names I do not recollect. All the male members of the Imperial family, I am told, wear military dresses constantly and are all Officers. Even the Princesses and Duchesses, tis said, have each the command of a regiment of soldiers and rank as Colonels, or Generals. Such of the last as we saw today would be taken, if set down in Washington just as they were then dressed, for very well dressed ladies, and nothing more.

One of them, a girl of perhaps 18 was very pretty, but except her I did not detect anything uncommon <u>with</u> <u>us</u> in appearance; and I have seen very many at home far more beautiful than she. Here is a sketch of a carriage in which, or <u>on</u> which some of the <u>imperials</u> came to the races.

It is like two sofas placed back to back and hung upon springs. The sofas are so wide that if any of the persons happen to tumble off they fall outside of the wheels. Probably it is intended for garden drives in pleasant weather. No reins- the near horses being rode by postillions. I can only give you once in a while a sketch – just to help me describe to you. It will be midnight before I get to bed. Good night. Sweet dreams.

Thursday night, September 25, 1845. – This morning Major Whistler took me in his <u>drosky</u> to Alexandrosky, a village a few miles off, where Messieurs Eastwick, Harrison & Winans (our countrymen) are making locomotives for the Emperor. Their establishment, (the property of the Government leased to them,) is said to be the most extensive one for the same purpose in the world. They are to make 162 locomotives and 500 freight cars, for which they receive about three millions of dollars. I went all through their works or rather through the shops for the locomotives and saw much in the way of machinery that was new to me and very interesting. They have about 400 serfs or slaves, the property of the Emperor, working in the establishment besides a great many others, natives of this and other countries, - Germans, Swedes, etc. etc. All the Russians go out of the works at a particular gate and are searched to prevent their stealing. All the others go out at another gate without searching. So much for <u>Russian</u> <u>honesty</u>. My room is too cold for me to stay in, out of bed, any longer; - so good night and a pleasant meeting to us. Remember that I have you in my arms every night.

Friday night, September 26, 1845. – This morning Parmly and I went out, by invitation to see Colonel Todd again. The Colonel was very anxious we should see at the Armory the things which we could not see at our former visit; so he drove us out and procured our admission and then walked back leaving the carriage for us to drive to the Palace etc. I said that I saw but part before – in interest it was a small part, and in value a very small part indeed. Today we saw a great deal of beautifully wrought armour of all kinds – plate armour, scale armour, chain armour etc., etc. – a great many kinds of guns, swords, battle axes, etc. – several (stuffed) horses were arranged in the rooms visited carrying men in armour. Among them was the identical horse, a beautiful black, rode by Tippoo Saib. On him was seated a figure of that Sultan in his own dress etc. etc. But the most interesting things were two saddles with holsters, pistols, bridles etc. to match, presented to the Emperor – one by the Sultan of Turkey and the other by some other Sultan or Pacha or Nabob of some sort. I scarcely know how to describe these things; but I will try and see if I can give you some idea of their magnificence.

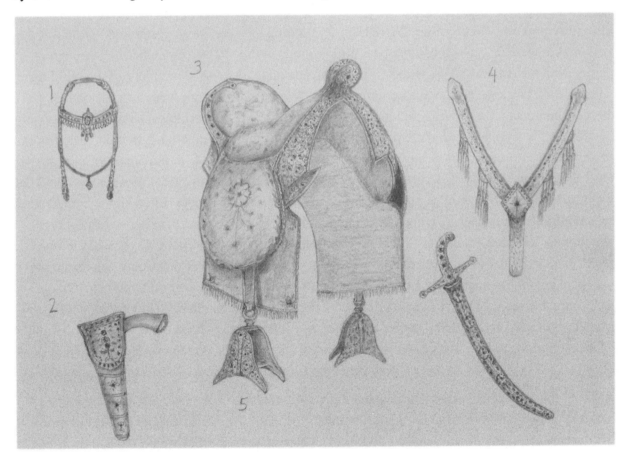

Now (I speak of one saddle etc.) if you can, suppose 1 to be the bridle front, 2 one of the holsters and its pistol, 3 a green silk velvet cover to the saddle, 4 the crupper and 5 one of the stirrups. The saddle cover has a rich heavy fringe all around. The leather of the bridle crupper etc. is plain black good leather. The stirrups and the ornaments on the bridle and crupper are of solid massive fine gold. The stirrups will weigh, I think, 2 or 3 pounds each and are most beautifully wrought. But all this is nothing. There are more diamonds on this saddle bridle, holsters, pistols and the sword and scabbard accompanying them than I expected ever to see in my life time. On the gold ornament in the forehead strap of the bridle is a diamond larger than the sketch I have made of the whole bridle; and in the same ornament, around the large stone are others of less size but of great value. The other ornaments on the face of the bridle are of the same character, as are those of the crupper. The holsters are set with diamonds and the butts of the pistols also. Where you see some marks on the saddle cloth are wrought the most exquisite ornaments in diamonds (their being just enough metal used to set them in) some of the stones being worth from one thousand to ten and perhaps twenty thousand dollars each. Colonel Todd thinks some of them worth a great deal more. The whole hilt of the sword – all but its blade is <u>covered</u> with diamonds. The scabbard is in perfect keeping with the sword. Colonel Todd thinks the value of diamonds in this set does not fall short of a million dollars. Past midnight. Must go to bed. Good night to you.

Saturday morning, September 27, 1845. – Continuing the account of yesterday; - from the Armory we were driven through the beautiful grounds to the "Palace of Catherine" through a part of which we were shown. I can give you no adequate idea of the grandeur of the building without the assistance of drawings or engravings. We passed through many rooms some 30 or 40 feet square and one dining room judged to be 40 by 200 feet. Ceilings all very high, probably 25 feet. A great deal of raised ornamental work, like carving, all covered with gold. The floors of variously colored woods wrought into a great variety of figures, forming beautiful <u>mosaics.</u> One of the rooms, about 30 feet square by 25 feet high has a beautiful floor of such work and the walls, all around, from the floor to the ceiling, are covered with <u>Amber</u>. Even all the carved work and mouldings and panels (except a few mosaics in marble) are of solid amber – the cost of which must have been immense. There is one room which we could not visit, (greatly to our regret,) in which the floor is inlaid with <u>mother-of pearl</u>. In several of the rooms we visited the walls are <u>covered</u> – not merely <u>hung</u> – but <u>covered</u> with masterpieces of oil paintings. On our way to the Palace we visited a fountain called "The lady of the pitcher". The design is this. An immense rock ten feet perhaps in diameter lies, as if it had always been there, in a sort of slight depression in the side of a very gently rising part of the gardens. On the rock is seated a beautiful girl crying for the loss of her pitcher as if it had just fallen.

After all this and much more, returned and dined with Colonel Todd; and afterward went to a ball one or two mile off at Pavlovsky or the Palace of Paul. Here we saw a great deal of the Military, some of the nobility and a good – very good share of pretty women – Countesses etc. etc. (Must go out now for the day; but will keep up the history.)

P.M. After the Ball (which was held in what, with us in America would be considered the best and the grandest ball room we could show, but is not grand here.), we returned to Town by railroad – took a drosky at the end of the railroad, some 1 ½ miles from our quarters, and soon found our driver was so drunk that we had to watch him to prevent his falling off his seat or running against other people, it being quite dark, and he driving like a mad man. However, we got home safely and have had some hearty laugh over the adventure, as indeed we had during it – for he could not understand a word that we said to him nor we a word that he said to us.

This morning we visited the museum of the "Mining Corps" (core) where we saw a magnificent collection of minerals, crystals, petrifactions, etc. etc. Among them were dozens of specimens of diamonds and many other precious stones, some in their natural state, as found, and some cut for use. In one row of cases were pearls from the smallest we see used in jewelry up to <u>half</u> <u>the</u> <u>size</u> <u>of</u> <u>my</u> <u>thumb</u>. After this sight we were taken down into a model of a mine underground – a perfect representation in all respects of a mine – the earth through which it runs being an imitation of the interior of a mine etc. and the copper, silver, gold, iron, coal, etc. etc. showing themselves just as they do in nature. In the sketch here you have some idea of it. We went down at A and walked, each carrying a candle, for I don't know how many rods, all through the galleries as they were called, and had explained to us the various minerals we saw etc. Where you see the passages stopping shows the extent to which any certain vein had been worked.

41

After this we came home for Parmly to get lunch and me to write to you; and now I must tell you what I have seen since it being now sundown or so. We have been through the principal rooms of the Palace where the present Emperor resides during winter. Not, of course into his bedroom or the kitchen, but into the <u>grand show</u> rooms, very much like those I have written about. Many of the rooms were filled with pictures – such as sometimes hear, or read of, in America, but never see there, nor probably ever will – by the old masters – Murillo, Valasquez, Guido, Reubens, Raphael, Correggio, Potter, Claude Loraine, and a host of other worthies, the bare mention of whose names sends one's blood like lightening through the heart. How then shall I describe the feelings with which I looked upon their unquestionable productions? I cannot. Nor can I tell you, so as to give you a just idea, of t he splendor of the rooms we saw – gold, gold, gold, - gold everywhere that it can be used with effect. In one room the bases and capitals of the columns, and the mouldings and ornaments would be gold (<u>gilt</u> of course) – in another the columns would be gold, and panels also, and the whole ceilings, ornaments and all, in another. In the grand ballroom there are white marble columns in pairs, with gilt bases and capitals, the whole length of each side, supporting a splendid gilt balustrade and gallery. This room we judged to be 150 feet long by 50 wide and at least 30 high. The walls (outside the rows of pillars) were white marble, and at one end was a gallery for the music, supported by white marble pillars: - all the pillars we judged to be 18 or 20 feet high. At the other end of the room was an elegant chair upon a raised platform for his August Majesty. And then <u>such</u> chandeliers – none of the jingling glass-drop concerns – but metal – gilt – and so beautiful in design and so perfect in execution – and such branches and girandoles- birds – animals, angels, men and women, in such perfection of workmanship and such profusion that one can set no limit to the wealth that procured them.

11 o'clock P.M. – Have just returned from spending a very pleasant evening with Major and Mrs. Whistler, but have only to say so much and that I found Mrs. Whistler like most of our women, very sensible and well informed and very amiable.

Yesterday Parmly received a letter from Paris directed to him in London. Tyson redirected it to him here, and wrote on the outside that no letters for either of us came by the last steamer from Boston – which is a matter of some suspense and disappointment to us both. I still hope that he may be mistaken and that I shall soon here from my dear, dear Ellen and our dear little boys – May Heaven bless and preserve you from all harm. I must go to bed – good night-good night.

Sunday night, September 28, 1845. – Not having been out today I have no new adventures or sights to tell of. The Steamer from London with my box of arms has come and now I must try to get them through the Customs House. Colonel Todd says the Government will have copies of them before I ever see them; but he may be mistaken. On Wednesday I expect Parmly will start for Paris via Riga, Berlin etc. etc. I shall not send this letter to you until I am sure of its leaving Russia without being opened and perhaps destroyed at the Post Office. The Government – that is, the Emperor, does what he pleases; and nobody is sure of getting his letters and certainly not his newspapers from abroad until they have undergone a close examination; the papers having sometimes paragraphs cut out. I shall have an opportunity before long to send this by Courier from the British Embassy here, as far as Hamburg, at least, where he will mail it safely and then there will be some certainty of your getting it. I must go upstairs to the Parlor and warm myself a little then return and go to bed. Good night.

Monday night, September 29, 1845. – Visited Colonel Todd upon my business and at his most urgent request sat down to dinner with him knowing that I should not have time to finish before the time for the cars to start back again. Got as far as the third dish and a glass of wine and left him and his company to finish – arrived at my quarters just as dinner was ready – sat down and got as far as the fish when Parmly sent up his card saying that he was waiting for me to come to his room and go out with him to dine with a Mr. Thompson, Dentist. So I broke off again and went with him and dined with Mr. Thompson and his two brothers who were very civil and seemed very glad to have the opportunity of learning something of American modes of practice which the Mr. Thompson complimented very highly. He had some European publications in which I saw a number of articles copied from our Journal. Our operation of destroying the nerve and plugging the nerve cavity as well as the decay cavity seems to have been unknown here until I told of it – so also in Hamburg – had never heard of such a thing. Near 12 o'clock – good night. I think you must have dreamed of me last night, because _ _ _ good night.

Tuesday night, September 30, 1845 – Went this morning to the Academy of Arts where I saw some more – "ever so many" good pictures some old, some modern: One of them very large, representing the destruction of Pompeii – a grand subject and treated in a most masterly manner by Bruloff, a Russian. I shall never forget it while I remember pictures. It is a modern production. After leaving this place met Major Whistler, who invited me to accompany him to Alexandrosky – from which place I returned with him after dark. Major Whistler and some of our countrymen at Alexandrosky are anxious to have me operate for them and I have promised to do so if I have time. Major Whistler is so kind and Mrs. Whistler and their children so amiable that I must do so for them at all events. Good night.

Wednesday night, October 1, 1845 – Today I have been home nearly all day expecting to hear something from Colonel Todd about my models; he having made application for them – but heard nothing. I have drawn a hundred dollars from my Banker here. – It being the first out of one thousand. I am living as economically as I can and be respectable; and have, as I think, pretty good grounds for expecting a fair remuneration from the Emperor for my expenses in coming here. If the invention strikes him as favorably and as forcibly as it does others he may do something handsome; if not, I shall have had the advantage of seeing this Magnificent City and of telling you all I learn of it. In the mean time I am making sketches of whatsoever strikes me as good and can be sketched readily, for use hereafter. Good night and a long kiss.

Thursday night, October 2, 1845 – Spent about 4 hours today in viewing the "Isaac's Church" now approaching a state of completion- having been a great many years in building, tearing down, rebuilding etc. You will recollect that I gave you an account of my visit to St. Paul's in London, and that I spoke of that as if it were a wonder of art and magnificence. Alas! That our

43

language does not admit of superlatives of a progressive order: - for this Isaac's Church so far surpasses St. Paul's in the design as well as execution that I recollect the latter with feelings of pity for the people who boast so much of its possession. Imagine a building so large that away up as high as the roof of our Capital at Washington there should be a row or rather a circle of Columns, each in a single piece of granite and almost as large (only six inches less in diameter) as the columns at the Patent Office. Above this colonnade is an immense gilded dome surrounded by a heavy balustrade, on which, one over each column, are figures of angels eight feet high. The capitals and bases of the immense columns, the balustrade, and the angels are of bronze metal. The edifice has four fronts with, of course, larger columns than those mentioned as being so high up. These also are each of one piece of granite, and their capitals of bronze. The pediments of the fronts are filled with groups of figures in bronze, of a religious character; one of them representing the Saviors rising from the tomb. The workmen were putting up the figures on one of the fronts and several pieces lay on the ground ready to be hoisted up. One figure was of a little boy perhaps two years old; I could just barely reach around his head with both arms. Another was a warrior – this required both of my arms and one of Parmly's to reach around the head. The standing men are about twelve feet high – cast in pieces and hollow, but still of enormous weight. Hundreds of men are at work on the building and I may safely say that nearly if not quite one hundred, were at work, flat on their bellies, polishing the marble and granite pavements or floors of the Porticos. Now, you have no doubt an idea that the men who work upon and build these magnificent churches and palaces must be, and must appear to be, superior to the mechanics and workmen with us. Such is not the fact. They never shave any part of their faces and seldom wash them if one may judge by their habits and appearance. Their most usual dress is a pair of thin cotton stuff pants very loose – a coarse ditto shirt outside the pants – coarse long legged boots, also outside the pants and a sort of surtout coat made of sheep skin with the wool on; so tanned as to be flexible, and so made as to be worn either side out; wool side out n rainy weather and 'tother way in all other weather. They are not superior in appearance (and certainly not so "Taste") to our Indians – have little or no schooling – but astonish all people of other nations by their aptness at learning to do things and by their ingenious but very rude contrivances. Probably no carpenter and joiner with us would think it possible to build a house without a hand saw ; yet I am told that not one in a thousand here can be induced to use one. If a board is to be cut in two, it is cut with a large hatchet; and I have myself admired the skill and precision with which they use it. I have in some places mentioned the perfection of some of the work here – I refer only to such parts as come with province of Artists – sculptors, painters, carvers etc. The work, - masonry, wood work etc. is bad, (although the design of the Architect may be good,) – in fact like apprentices work with us, or not so good: - even in the palaces this is the case – all is grand, showy , magnificent, superb, etc. etc. but must not be examined too closely. Major Whistler tells me that the Emperor is expected here in about 12 or 15 days. I ought to have told you that in Russia time is still kept in old style; that is, for instance, today is here the 21st of September with us in America and elsewhere it is the 3rd of October – 12 days difference. Good night.

Friday morning, October 3, 1845. – Parmly has just gone to the Steamer to sail for Stockholm the Capital of Sweden – On his way to Paris via Copenhagen, Hamburg, Berlin, Frankfort and Brussels. Had he been going direct to Hamburg I should have sent this letter to be mailed there. A week from tomorrow I shall have a direct and <u>safe</u> conveyance for it to Hamburg by a British Courier. I know you will feel very uneasy about me, in consequence of not hearing from me, but I am sure you will pardon my seeming neglect when you know its cause.

The navigation closes here very soon – so soon that if I wait here more than one week longer I must make a long and tedious and expensive journey to Stockholm or not go there at all. And so in going to Berlin if I wait long I must go by land – but this I do not so much mind as I can go by diligence and at a less expensive rate than to Stockholm, as, to the latter place I should have to take a private conveyance.

There is an American sea captain at the same house with me who says he has not been home to see his wife and child in <u>4 years</u>! He says he keeps promising himself that he will go soon, but something turns up to take him off in another direction. He is, I suspect, waiting to get money enough to quit the ocean altogether, for he says sea life is the most miserable life a man can lead, and I quite agree with him on <u>this</u> point, but he will find he has done very wrong when he does <u>get</u> home.

There is a new brick house going up near me and I have been all over the walls scaffolding etc. None of the partition walls between rooms are less than two feet thick and some of the walls are three feet solid brick and grouted, yet the house is to be only of ordinary size, three stories perhaps. I hear nothing about the guns yet, from Colonel Todd. There seems to be nothing like promptness in any of these European Governments. They seem to think that, if they do anything in such a manner as to accommodate those who want it done they will lose something of their dignity. Here there seems to be every possible obstacle thrown in the way of strangers particularly who chance to visit the country and desire to stay a little while. On arriving you have to go to the Alien Office and do this – and to the Passport Office and do 'tother, until you are tired, sick and disgusted with the proceedings. Finally you get permission to leave the Country for about six dollars and have some other expenses to pay besides for – God knows what – but a part for it is for advertising in the proper papers that you intend to leave the country – this you must do before you can get a passport.

I understand that the Emperor has issued an order or <u>ukase</u> as it is called that all Russians travelling out of his Empire shall pay 200 rubles (about $150) a year for permission to do so. He could scarcely have adopted a surer method of preventing the civilization of his people than putting these obstacles in the way of traveling. Night.

In every new Country that I visit I see something that I wish to take home to my dear family; but I have seen nothing that would come within my means and at the same time be so acceptable as some embroidered slippers which a lady showed me tonight. If I can find the shop where she bought them I shall venture to get you a pair I think. They are very pretty indeed. Only give me the funds and I will show you a magazine of presents as will keep you awake a week. I've got my <u>head</u> full of them for you and the boys and our friends, but can't get them into my pockets <u>until I can buy them</u>. We'll see when the Emperor comes whether I am to buy two pairs of slippers or one. Good night.

Saturday P.M, October 4, 1845. - I've got the slippers – two pair of 'em – and <u>uppers</u> for three pair besides. The temptation was too great for me. I guessed at the length of your foot, having forgotten to take the measure. You must mark the length of your foot upon the margin of a letter to me then I shall come nearer perhaps.

While out after the slippers I went into the store or show and sale room of the Jewelers to the court; and now for what I saw there. I asked the price of many things and sat them down that I might tell you about them. The price is given in paper rubles – a paper ruble being, about 22 or 23 cents. (The silver ruble is 3 ½ times the value of the paper ruble.) A diamond dress ornament, worn upon the bosom like a breastpin 13,000 rubles. Bracelet 7,700 rubles. Pin and Earrings are 15,000. Two head ornaments, one for each temple 6,597. Earrings are 8,600. A Necklace of diamonds and pearls is 29,750. Two head ornaments, diamonds and pearls 6,525. Head ornament representing a wreath, - leaves, stems and all diamonds extending from one ear to the other, 26,500. Necklace and earrings of diamonds and emeralds, 17,220. Necklace of diamonds, 25,000. Breastpin and Earrings of diamonds and opals, 6,000. Diamond Earrings, 3,000. Ditto 6,600. Diamond necklace 8,000. Head ornament, diamonds and rubies 4,300. Bracelet of diamonds and emeralds, 4,800. Breastpin, diamonds, 4,400. etc., etc. The most curious thing was a heavy bracelet of gold enameled, with a large ornament representing part of a coat of mail. This ornament was hinged so as to open. Under it was a finger ring made in joints and with a clasp so as to be put on precisely as you put on a bracelet. Instead of a stone set in the ring you see a watch face about ½ of an inch broad. Open the ring and you take out the watch and find it not only a perfect gold watch in miniature but a perfect time keeper and only 5/8 of an inch wide case and all and 1/8 inch thick! The watch is of Swiss manufacture – the rest Russian; 1,250 rubles. Another bracelet, gold, enameled and set with pearls, containing a watch only, larger than the other: 750. Watches about ¾ inch wide, gold: 425.

The shop keepers here are not only ready to show you anything they sell, but they stand at their door and very politely bow to you and take off their hats and invite you in. So few strangers visit this City – and most foreigners look so little like the natives – that they know them instantly; and I must give them the credit of being very civil to us poor devils who have the temerity to enter the country. I may have an opportunity of sending the slippers to you by a ship going to Boston. If so I'll send them as you may get them sooner and my baggage will be lighter. Only about 40 pounds is allowed with each passenger without extra charge. I paid 5 <u>silver</u> rubles for the slippers and <u>uppers</u> – probably not one quarter the sum I should pay in America – indeed <u>such</u> things are not sold in our country that I know of. The embroidery is gold and silver flowers, leaves, figures etc. on morocco – green, bronze, etc. The slippers that are made up are lined with white fur – very pretty, I assure you.

I don't think you are aware of the fact that to learn the Russian language you have to learn a <u>new</u> Alphabet – such is the fact – and such queer looking letters – 36 of them! I ought not to say they are <u>all</u> queer looking, for many of them are like the English letters, but others (to those not accustomed to them) look odd enough. I shall bring you some specimens. Night.

Major Whistler tells me that the railroad from here to Moscow, of which he is the Chief Engineer, is about 400 mile long; - and he tell me also some remarkable facts respecting the road, the face of the country, etc. There are no hills on the route, nor any greater elevations than 40 feet to the mile. – There are perfectly straight lines of the road 40, 50 and 60 miles long! – and no curves of less than one mile radius! – That is, if you were to draw the curves with a pair of dividers, the points of the dividers would be, for the shortest curve, a mile apart! He says that when they speak of railroad routes here they do not speak of what <u>heights</u> they have to go around, or through, or over, but what <u>depths</u> they have to cross. The country here may be perfectly level for 30 or 100 mile and all at once you may come to what may sometime have been the bed of a river- Perhaps is now – from 20 to 160 feet deep and perhaps some hundreds wide. There is one such place on the Major's route where he has to build a bridge for the railroad 160 feet high! - and some others not much less. So little does the road bend that it is but four mile longer than a perfectly straight line between its two ends! - a very remarkable fact when we consider its great length. Bed time here for me – near 11 – you are probably all sitting at the tea table – about 3 o'clock, wishing I had some of those good hot biscuits and butter too and so do I wish so.

Don't forget what I said about the hair of the boys – don't cut it till I come except it be the front of Edward's just to keep it out of his eyes – and not that if you can manage without. About the Office I have nothing farther to say; except that it is now so late that I shall hardly be home before spring. The Operating room I would not like to have disturbed, but the others, as I told Father, may be rented, and he may rent them upon the condition that the tenants quit at a month's notice – I shall probably know a month beforehand when I shall want them. I must go to bed. Good night.

Sunday night, October 5, 1845. – Rainy, chilly weather. I have not been out today. The stoves, (or peetch as it is called), in use here looks something like a very tall, narrow wardrobe painted white and it is generally placed in one corner of the room; if the room is large 2 of them are used. They are made of earthen ware like the old fashioned milk pans, but the <u>surface</u> is like white porcelain. Some of them are beautiful in shape and have ornamental figures in relief. The one in my room has no opening in sight: the door for the fire being made in the back so that the man who makes the fire does not come into the room. The back of the stove is against the wall between my room and the passage. Only one fire in a day and you don't begin to feel the heat of that under an hour or two or three; then the stove begins to warm your room and keeps it warm. I have not learned the interior construction of the stove but I suppose it is intended to be heated like an oven – and in such a way that it shall retain the heat for the longest time.

I flattered myself that I might still get a letter from my dear wife by the Britannia from Boston, but none has come. I shall perhaps get one in a week or two by the steamer following which must have arrived at Liverpool in time for the next mail from London to this place. This is the first, and I trust it will be the last, time I am so far from you and in such a country that no dependence can be placed upon the mails. I must not trust myself to write about it. Good night. God bless you.

Tuesday night, October 7, 1845. – Having nothing to say last night I did not write. Today I have been out to buy a pair of boots and overshoes (<u>caloshes</u> they call them here). The price of the boots – very genteel calf – better than Griffin charged me $8 dollars for – was only three rubles silver; the " caloshes", very handsome, one and a half rubles silver; Taking both I got them for four rubles. – The caloshes are such as would cost about $2 in America. If things go as I wish here I hope to bring home something more in the shoe and boot line; the Russian mode of tanning appearing to me to be quite excellent. This morning we had a little snow and the day has been quite cold. Overcoats and cloaks have been worn ever since I came here and I have not been out without either wearing mine or taking it along. Very many of the overcoats and cloaks are lined throughout with fur – raccoon generally for the cloaks and something finer for the overcoats. In some of the cheaper cloaks wolf skin (with the hair on) and in others a sort of sheep, or lamb skin, with a handsome curling, grey wool is used. It will be so cold when I leave St. Petersburg That I shall be obliged to get one of some sort. Good night. I dreamed of catching a large gold-fish for you last night. I sometimes have very clear and distinct dreams about you.

Sunday morning, October 12, 1845. – Having been out very little since Tuesday last I have had nothing to write; but now I have pleasure saying that your letter of the 8th of September is received through our Minister Colonel Todd to whose care it came from London as I had directed. I cannot express my joy and my gratitude to God for the preservation of the health of my dear Ellen and our children. May his protecting hand ever keep you all from sickness and all trouble. You are, even now, daily expecting a letter from me, probably; and notwithstanding that I wrote about the little dependence to be placed upon the continental mails still it will be very natural for you to imagine all sorts of reasons for not getting my letters. I have said that I should have an opportunity of sending this by Courier a part of the way to England. – I expected to be able to send it about this time; but the Courier from Hamburg did not come by the last steamer and will not come until next Saturday and may not return for a week afterwards; so your chance of getting this letter much before New Year's is rather small. However, it's the best thing I can do – and if the delay makes us more sensible of the advantages of our own system of Government, it will not be without use to us.

As I wrote some days ago, the Emperor was expected about this time. Since then, he has changed his route and is not expected for some time. Perhaps he will spend some time in the south of Europe where the Empress has gone for her health, which is very bad. Somebody told me she has consumption and that consumption carries off a great many people here.

I am now making preparations to exhibit my invention to the Grand Duke Michael who is Grand Master of Ordnance and a brother of the Emperor. Major Whistler gives me what I think is the very best advice – probably because it coincides with what I had previously supposed the best – that is, to state in the fewest possible words what brought me here and what I wish to do. I have my box examined at the "Ta-moj-ny" – (Custom House) and it only remains now to get it without paying duties (if I can) which amount to about $175! Fortunately for me I have the pistol and the best lock in my trunk so that I can do without the others upon a pinch and unless the Government wish to see them I shall not "enter" them and pay the duties and not then unless they choose to refund the duties. I have no money to throw away.

On advising with Major Whistler, I find that I must at once expend a hundred or a hundred and fifty dollars for outdoor clothing – lined with fur throughout – such as even the natives are compelled to wear to protect themselves from the excessive cold of the winter. Even now it is almost as cold as our Washington winters – people are putting in their inside windows so as to make double windows with a space of about 3 or 4 inches between, to keep out the cold (I have a sketch of the whole arrangement to show Curran).

It seems that when you wrote the letter just received you had not received my first letter from London – by this time you are probably aware that I am, or ought to be, here: and of course, will scarcely expect me to return this year. Had Tyson remained to prosecute our plans and furnish the funds to do so, according to agreement, or even left me with funds, there would have been no necessity for my returning for want of funds as there may, and probably will be, if I do not get some either here or at the next place I visit. Perhaps I shall be able in this letter to say something more of this.

You do not say that you have been learning French but give me to understand so. That is the language of the Court here, and consequently the most fashionable here. It is no uncommon thing – indeed it is in constant practice – at our table to speak 3 or 4 languages at every meal – French, English, Russian and German. I do not attempt anything but English, but listen very attentively to the pronunciation of all others and can generally know what, is the subject of conversation. In another place I have mentioned a Mr. Ralston of London. We had some conversation about the disposal of my invention, for sporting guns, in England and he was very sanguine in his belief that a plan I proposed would be a good one both for me and for the purchaser; - and I think he might bring it into operation. I told him that if he could and would, I would compensate him as handsomely as profits of the sale would allow. I am to call upon him on my return to London. Night. –

Here I was interrupted to allow the furniture to be removed to another house which our Landlady has been getting into for some days past; and now, having got my things together, I proceed again. I confess that I shall be much more contented to remain long enough to decide my affairs in some way than I should if you had not seemed so willing to have me take my time. I suppose you think (and justly, I believe,) that I shall be more contented when I <u>do</u> return, and you are therefore willing to give me time to get cured of my disposition to be restless. One thing is pretty certain – I shall not be very likely to come to <u>Europe</u> again. As to my own country I hope to see a little more of that when <u>we</u> travel together, in search of <u>our</u> <u>farm</u>. Good night. I shall kiss you with even greater pleasure than usual tonight. Good night.

Monday P.M. October 13, 1845. – Colonel Todd sends me a note saying that he learned that the Emperor has gone to Italy and may not return within two months. What a pity I could not have known he would be so long, before I left London. I should have then gone elsewhere first and come here next year. Now that I <u>am</u> here, I must make the best of it. Night.

One of the boarders in our house consulted me today about his teeth. He is a German, teacher of languages; and needs a great deal of work upon his mouth. I am to do it if <u>I</u> have time upon such days as <u>he</u> has time. I have spent the evening with Major Whistler. He says that Russia is the very last place for a young man to come to in search of employment; - that for everything that is to be done, there are <u>sixty</u> to do it here where there is <u>one</u> with us. He has been very much annoyed by applications by letter from our countrymen for employment here; and has been imposed upon by some <u>in person</u> who have come here and borrowed money to get away again and never repaid etc. My dreams of you are all pleasant and very frequent – I wish they were more so - Good night. I will try to be in Washington tonight.

Thursday night, October 16, 1845. – For two days I have written nothing having nothing particular to say. Having met in an English book with an account of the celebrated granite column here, erected to the memory of Alexander the 1st, I will give you much of it as it will be likely to interest Father Owen if not you. The pillar stands in a large open square and is, as you will see, a grand affair. "Shaft of the pillar, <u>in one piece of granite</u>, <u>length</u>, <u>84 feet</u>; <u>diameter 12 ½ feet</u>; <u>weight 350 or 400 tons</u>. The bronze figure on the top is 15 feet high independent of the cross, or 23 with the cross; weight 13 tons. The base-reliefs (one on each of the 4 sides of the pedestal) are in 4 plates, and the length of each 17 ½ feet, height 10 feet, some of t he figures stand out nearly 2 feet; weight of the 4 plates, 44 tons. Entire height of the monument 154 feet; weight of brass (bronze) 158 tons. Stone pedestal on which the whole stands is 28 feet square and 7 feet thick; was erected in 2 ½ years and cost 400,000 pounds." The granite is not like our gray granite but of <u>red</u> cast of gray; and the whole of the stone work where it is not covered with bronze is so highly polished that the buildings opposite, carriages, people etc. are distinctly reflected by its surface.

I am told that a family which would require 6 servants in America would require for the same work here, 30! Poor devils! – Black, sour bread and salt is almost the only food the laboring class gets here. I speak of the serfs, or slaves. Our Negroes are ten thousand times better off – better clad, better, infinitely better fed, more enlightened, more cleanly, more honest, and if not more contented, they seem to be far more happy.

When a fire breaks out here there is no cry of "fire" nor any ringing of bells. Watch towers in different parts of the City have watchmen constantly on the look-out and they give notice by signals to the proper persons at the engine stations, who know from the signals where the fire is and drive there with the fire apparatus in rather more than "double quick time". I have neither seen nor heard of any fire since I have been here; but I understand that nobody but the firemen and the proper officers are permitted to have anything to do with one when it does occur; - and that the Emperor, if in town, is almost always present. It seems to me that at least one half the male adult population one sees in the streets here are in some military uniform. You can't look in any direction without seeing soldiers, and most excellent soldiers they are said to be on parade, but how they fight I don't know.

The Courier who was expected last Saturday is not coming at all! - has sent for his wife (who boards at our house) and she, poor lady, is in great distress at his not coming and will perhaps have to go wholly unprotected by the Steamer to Travemunde where her husband will meet her if he is not ordered off with despatches before she gets there. When I may have an opportunity of sending this with a reasonable prospect of your getting it is now more uncertain than before. But it is of no use to grieve for the disappointment – thank Heaven I hope not to be compelled to stay long here and if "worst comes to worst" I can take it myself when I go. There is one consolation in the matter when you do get the letter it will be all the bigger for waiting if it is not better. Good night. At the table, I write your name with the handle of my knife on the table cloth – and so have Ellen by my side to dine with me. They have a good way of serving at the table – the meats are cut and put on a dish, nicely, and the dish (with a knife or fork or spoon or all) is carried to each one, that he may take such piece as he pleases. Good night.

Saturday night, October 18, 1845. – Contrary to expectation the British Courier has arrived – greatly to the joy of his wife and friends an her account and especially to my satisfaction as he is to return on Tuesday next and will take you this short note as far as he goes towards America. – Certainly as far as Hamburg and perhaps London. Today I called upon the General to whom I brought a letter and am to do so again on Monday next – I am now waiting for the Emperor's brother (The Grand Duke Michael), to return, that I may send him a paper which I have prepared; (with good counsel from Major Whistler) upon the subject of the invention. It will be as well to keep the particulars I give you in the family: - when enquiries are made you can say where I was when you last heard from me etc. and that in consequence of the absence of the Emperor from St. Petersburg I have been delayed etc. When I write you next I hope to have something better for you to tell them. Near midnight. Good night – sweet dreams.

Sunday night, October 19, 1845. – I today received a letter from Major Smith dated 20 August and have been until this time tonight writing an answer to send with this on Tuesday – past 12 o'clock – Good night.

Monday night, October 20, 1845. – Had a very bad dream about going home last night – found you had lost all affection for me; was as cold as if I had been a stranger – whereupon I cried and couldn't sleep any more. I have learned today that so far from Mr. Bodisco's letter being of service to me it has put my matters into the very worst channel. Now I am to go to work and get the matter out of that channel; but as I must close this letter tonight I shall have no further progress to report regarding the gun.

I am as you will readily suppose not in very high spirits just now, but perhaps better things than those promised are in store. "All for the best" –"serve him right" – "stay home next time" – "let well alone" 'and so on'. By the same Courier I write to Major Smith saying that so far I have accomplished nothing here.

Those slippers I hope to have an opportunity to send by ship to Boston from here, but may not. What do you think my name is <u>in Russian</u>? <u>Dimitri Moisaivitch Maynard</u>! The 3 i's in the first name are like an <u>e</u> in sound, as are also the two first in the middle name.

Major Whistler is very kind indeed to me – seems to spare no trouble or pains to put me in the right way – for there are <u>so many</u> ways here – bribery, corruption etc. are so common among Government Officers that it is common talk I'm told.

I have been operating a little, and have more business for the same person, to do. My charges are 5 rubles for plugging (about $3.75) and other charges in proportion. My <u>manner</u> of operating has got me the title of <u>magician</u> – people are astonished to find that Dental operations are not so very horrible necessarily. Remember me to all our friends who enquire for me. I shall use all practicable haste to get through my business in Europe and return to you; and I <u>may</u> be compelled to return soon for want of funds to enable me to accomplish anything - I think I should do so at once but for the sake of Smith and Tyson who ought to have furnished me with funds, according to contract: but I am willing to go to the utmost limit to show them my disposition to do my part.

Kiss Edward and George and John for me; tell them I shall have a great many stories for them when I come – all about the muzjiks and the bootchniks and other queer folk; and show them how to build a bridge with boats, and what odd looking wagons they have here for carrying merchandise, grain, etc. and all sorts of things I shall tell them about. My kindest feelings for Father, Mother, and our brothers and sisters. I shall imprint a good long kiss upon the seal for you. I shall write by the very next safe opportunity. Direct yours as usual.

Forever yours,

Edward.

Chapter 6

(Second Letter)

A Small Gift

Mrs. Ellen S Maynard
Washington City
D.C.
United States of America

St. Petersburg, Russia   **Page 1**

October 11/24 1845

My Dear Ellen,

     Having an opportunity to send the slippers of which I wrote you in my first letter (sent a few days ago to be mailed in England) I do so and, although of no great value, trust you will get them for curiosity sake. Should I find anything to enclose with them before the vessel sails I will send it also: but, inasmuch as you will have other news from me by mail of what I am doing long before you get this I will defer writing a letter. This will go to Boston and be forwarded to you from that place, in the package of slippers.

Forever yours,

  Edward

P.S. I send you also as a sort of basket covering to the slippers a pair of such shoes as are made and worn by Russian peasantry. The contrast will enhance the value of the slippers. Edward

Chapter 7

(Third Letter)
Grand Duke Michael, Brother of the Tsar, Inspects the Gun

St. Petersburg, October 17 / 19 1845- (Wednesday)   **Page 1**

Wednesday night, October 22, 1845

My Dear Ellen,

      I received your dear letter of the 27th of September this morning just as I was about to leave my quarters for the Palace of the Grand Duke Michael, who had expressed his wish to see my models and had sent for me to show them to him. I was presented to His Imperial Highness by General Prince Dolgorouki, (to whom I had been previously introduced (by letter) by Colonel Todd), and who has been very civil to me shaking hands familiarly, joking, etc. – (Say nothing about this, as it will seem like boasting.) The Grand Duke made some remarks about the difficulty which Russian soldiers would have in managing the new lock, and the difficulty which there might be in repairing it (if damaged) by such workmen as accompany armies. As he does not speak English and not French he had a Colonel to interpret, and as there were at least 50 people waiting their turn to see him, he gave the arms a very hasty examination lasting perhaps five minutes and the Colonel and I withdrew and waited for the Prince who informed us when he came out that a Commission would be appointed to examine it and I should hear from them in 2 or 3 days – informing me of the time and place of examination etc. and so I came home – no, not <u>home</u> – but back again, to commence this letter and tell you how overjoyed I am to hear of your safe return to Washington – of your continued good health and that of the family.

You say nothing – not a word – about Father Owen and Mother, but lead me to suppose they are not at Washington as you say you would be very lonesome without George and John who are with you. I am sorry to hear of George's illness but as I don't know <u>what</u> it is I cannot say anything about his returning to Mississippi. I should be glad if he could find employment near his friends. You have my most perfect acquiescence in bringing John to stay with you until my return, which I hope will be in early spring. If I succeed <u>grandly</u> in Europe he will not be forgotten; and if I do not he shall suffer nothing by spending his time for our sakes. You delight me by praising our boys so highly for their good looks and I trust the drawback produced by the crossness of the baby will not last long. When you are in trouble do as I do – thank Heaven you are not sea-sick. Let that beautiful hair grow till I come, as I wrote before. I expect I shall be so enraptured with it as to go to sleep with a lock of yellow hair – (a-hem!) Your great anxiety to see me and your continued assurance of love make me happy in the anticipation of many, many happy days to come spent in the society of my dear Ellen and our children – God grant that no evil deeds, thoughts or dispositions may prevent the fulfillment!

Your miniature lies open before me as usual and it seems that I almost hear you speak to me. It has been a great comfort to me to look upon so true a picture of my dear wife when I am ill or troubled by the innumerable annoyances of travelling – it reminds me more forcibly that you at least are free from all such evils – for travelling in America is to travelling in Europe, so far as my experience is concerned, as paradise is to purgatory. But I have had only notoriously bad routes yet – there are better ones no doubt. At night to your miniature is the last thing I look at before putting out the candle and the first thing I see in the morning. It has gained you some very handsome compliments, and Parmly used to say in England that it was the only good-natured face he had seen except those on board a ship since he left America.

By the way, speaking of Parmly I wrote you that he had gone; and I suppose you will be sorry when you hear it, but I assure you I was not at all anxious to have him come here with me, nor at all sorry to have him go without me. And why? - you will ask; - because he was too fond of telling and acting Negro stories, dances etc. and Yankee stories etc. etc. all of which, though he did them very well, were always out of place and gave a character to us which I did not choose to share with him. I am, and he knows it, grateful for his good offices but he was very greatly in my way often. I get along much better without him here, but shall miss his French when I come to travel again. A year or so in Europe will subdue his noisy manner and perhaps improve him in other respects and then his excellent disposition and principles will be of greater value.

Poor Mr. Dyer! He was an excellent man I believe; and I can easily believe that his death, occurring suddenly, should procure quite a sensation where his character was so well and so generally known at Washington.

I have enclosed the slippers mentioned in my last letter in a strong paper envelope, put the package including a short letter into a pair of peasants basket shoes – put the whole again into a strong paper addressed the package to you and fastened on to it a letter to Harnden & Co. Boston, asking them to pay charges and send the bill with the package to Washington where all would be paid. If either pair of the slippers suit you of course you will wear them – that is if they ever get to you, and the others you will keep, or dispose of among your friends who have been so kind to you, at your discretion. A pair of uppers, at least, I should like to have sent to "Sister Celinda". Were my finances and the opportunity of sending things such as I wish, I should send instead of these at least a dozen pairs for your friends.

Tyson advised that if I could not sell the invention here to return to Brussels where he had made some preliminary arrangements (but concluded nothing) – leaving me to finish the business; and if I could do nothing there to return home; - he thinking it useless to expend any more money upon what would then have proved so unpromising. He went home with very little confidence in the speculation and would have been, I think, very glad to have sold his share for what he had expended. He should not grumble, nor Major Smith, for, as you know, they made their own terms; - I am only sorry they have not fulfilled them by furnishing the funds for my expenses and giving me the aid of Tyson's services. Legally I consider that they have forfeited their rights to the invention; but they have in some measure been controlled by circumstances which, if not unavoidable, were at least natural – such as Tyson getting married and taking his wife with him and then her having to come back again to be confined, and of course he must come with her – and then Tyson not having money enough to do what he contracted to do – he expecting to make money to pay with etc. etc. As for <u>my</u> course, if I do not get something for the invention here <u>I must return</u> because my funds will be exhausted before I can effect anything with any other government – and so I shall lose all <u>my</u> European interest through Smith and Tyson's failure to comply with the agreement. However, I shall have one very great consolation; indeed, several consolation; but <u>the great one</u> is, that I shall embrace my dear, dear family all the sooner for the failure. Good night.

Thursday night, October 23, 1845. - Ground covered with snow this morning. Accepted an invitation to visit the great bridge now being built across the Neva just above my quarters. This is the first one upon piers ever built across the river here – those now in use being built upon boats. In the spring and autumn the ice from Lake Lad-o-ga (accent the first syllable) comes down the river with such force that the bridges have to be removed. The one now being built will have 7 or 8 or 9 arches of iron resting upon immense piers of granite; - some of the stones which must be, I think, 5 or 6 feet thick and 15 or 20 feet long. The river is wide and rapid but not deep, ships do not come to the city, but discharge their cargoes into "lighters" at Kronstadt, a few miles below. This bridge of which I spoke is in fact across only one (the largest) of several arms of the river here which forms several islands.

You have seen those pictures of sphinxes in our Geographies – there are here two of them from Egypt, a present to the Emperor from the Pacha – each some 10 feet from head to tail, made of Syenite granite and very well preserved. They are erected on pedestals facing each other nearly opposite my windows, on the other side of the river and in front of the Academy of Arts. Today I made a sketch of one to show you. You will suppose from the above that my windows look upon the water. They do – giving me a fine view.   Our boarding house is upon what is here called the <u>English Quay</u> - a street with houses on one side and the river on the other. This street is a fashionable one; has several grand houses, or rather palaces belonging to the Government, the nobility etc. The method of building houses here is very different from ours in plan and construction. The partition walls are so thick that fires do not spread rapidly from one house to another or even from one room to another; and <u>all</u> the floors are of brick laid upon boards, upon very heavy round (natural shape) joists – logs a foot or more thick – so that a roof may burn and fall in and not burn through the floor it falls upon. These brick floors are covered with boards so as to be like the floors with us; in the better rooms, however, of dwelling houses, the floors are laid in figures – generally some regular geometric pattern – several of which I have sketched for you. Some of them, as I wrote you about at the palaces, are very beautiful inlaid of differently colored woods wrought into foliage, vines, scrolls, stars, and every imaginable pretty form of the sort.

Major Whistler is very kind to me, comes often to see how I get along; advises me, gets information that will be of use to me about the invention, etc. He says that so much of what he has heard about what Americans have done in Europe is false that he looks with suspicion upon all such big stories. You may remember seeing a statement in an American paper that the Emperor of Russia had conferred the Order of the Black Eagle upon "Professor Risley" the gymnast. The Major says that not only is this not true but that Risley attracted no notice whatever here – could only get an engagement in night in a week to perform, etc. and that he was an exceedingly vulgar, illiterate fellow. May we have pleasant dreams of each other tonight. Good night.

Friday night, October 24, 1845. – Didn't see you last night. There is one author in our little library at home, whose works, if you have not read the yet, I wish you would read and studiously: - <u>Downing</u>. You will recollect his "Landscape Gardening" and his "Rural Architecture": and read also some of those excellent things upon Villa Architecture in the big book of Loudon upon "Cottage, Farm and Villa Architecture and Furniture". A great deal of interest and enjoyment I have had in <u>seeing</u> have been caused by reading those works.

I learn that Colonel Todd has been recalled. His valet told me so today. The Colonel sent for me to go and visit him and examine his teeth etc. but said nothing about his recall. I couldn't go today as I was expecting to receive some notifications from the Government about where the trail is to take place etc. I must wait patiently for it. It is my present opinion that if any trail is made, the report will be that the lock is not adapted to the Russian Service, for the reasons mentioned by the Grand Duke Michael. If I had known what clumsy guns were used in Europe, I would have 'got up' one to match. I have (of course) taken particular notice of the arms of the soldiers wherever I have been and I have seen no muskets so well made as the American. Good-night.

Saturday night, October 25, 1845. – Having really nothing to write, I'll save my paper and say – good-night.

Tuesday night October 28. – So little have I seen since last week that I have not written. No news from the Government yet. They are proverbially slow. It seems pretty certain now that I shall be detained here until sledging – which, owing to bad roads, will be 6 or 8 weeks hence. Perhaps I shall go as far as Berlin with Colonel Todd – I hope so. Yesterday I operated for a fine boy of 8 or so years, son of Major Whistlers. Today being a fine, clear, frosty day I went out for an hours stroll – saw ice three quarters of an inch thick. Stopped to look at some prints etc. at a shop window and had my pocket picked of its handkerchief – first thing I have lost since I left home, I believe – a fact which it is well worth the handkerchief to know – and so I congratulate myself.

One of the first things that would strike an American if taken up at home and set down here would be the difference in color of the buildings here and at home. Instead of his red brick he would find yellow, white and many different shades of <u>clay color</u> – reddish, bluish, yellowish, <u>pinkish</u> etc. The next thing perhaps would be the great number of ornaments – indeed some of the buildings, as for example the Winter Palace, are so covered with ornaments that the eye can scarcely find a quiet place to rest upon. This same Winter Palace, by the way, (one of those I wrote you that I had visited) is built all around a square larger than the one upon which our house stands. It is upon the site of the former Palace burnt down a few years ago; and is said to have been built in 14 months from the fire of the old one. In the South or main front of the Palace is the entrance to the court-yard. It is of three arches, - divided by columns – the middle arch nearly large enough to admit our house to go through whole and the others a little smaller. There are also two main entrances to the Palace on the same front and others on the other fronts. The north front looks over the Neva which is but a few yards from the building.

When I left you last I expected as you are aware to have sent you some funds – the proceeds of sales of my Patents in Europe before this time. I have hitherto said nothing to you about economizing with the money left you, as I was disposed to trust entirely to your good sense, and am so still; but I think I ought to say that the delays I have met with so far are not indications of making a fortune very speedily with the guns. We expected more from Russia than from any other Power, and if we get nothing here after waiting so long and having encouragement from Mr. Bodisco and Baron Brunow, it will be as well to go home and relinquish the enterprise; - especially as I shall have only money enough to get home and <u>none</u> to <u>send</u> home <u>for use of my family</u>.

The case is perfectly clear to me; my course is one of necessity and results from no fault of mine inasmuch as the expenses of visiting the European Powers were not to be paid by me. It is a very provoking thing altogether if all the other chances in Europe are to be lost for want of the funds which were to pay for Smith and Tyson's share in the Patents.

By advice of Major Whistler, I have got an overcoat warmer than the one I had made of the cloak. It is loose sack lined throughout, sleeve and all, with the black, shining, wavy hair or fur, known in America as the <u>Russian dog</u>. Here these skins are known as <u>Astrakhan sheep</u>. Another and much warmer covering is necessary in traveling in winter here – a cloak lined with raccoon skins. This fur when very dark in color is very dear here and very fashionable because raccoons are not found in Russia. Astrakhan sheep skins are <u>not</u> fashionable here nor costly because the sheep are not far off. I suppose the <u>skins</u> in my "polto" would be worth in America more than the <u>garment</u> cost here. I have confused dreams of you very often but seldom remember the particulars as well as I used to. I suppose it is because I see and hear so much that is new to me.

Good night my dear Ellen.

Wednesday P.M. October 29, 1845. – Today I have been operating for the Major a little and after much conversation and turning my matters over, he coincides with me in the opinion that if I cannot accomplish something pretty soon that I had better not wait. I told him my "circumstances" about not leaving funds for a long absence etc. Tomorrow I am to visit Colonel Todd to get a letter that will procure me another interview the Prince Dolgorouki at which I shall tell the Prince that I cannot possibly wait beyond a few weeks, nor leave my models for trail after I am gone, etc. I am pretty thoroughly discouraged and dispirited with the <u>one sided</u> way of doing business – <u>if I could talk</u> to the authorities here I might do something – but no – they have their fixed, slow, plodding, never-get-done way of doing all such business, and if you manifest any impatience or dissatisfaction you are sure to suffer for it.

I dreamed last night of going home in a stage coach. You lived in a shabby country house and when the coach stopped in the middle of the road for me to get out little George and 2 or 3 other boys that I did not know, all very dirty and ragged, stood by the side of the road. George recognized me and said Pa come home! And was very glad to see me and I was so distressed at his appearance that I awoke. I sometimes think I did very wrong to come away upon this expedition and leave you so little for support. Certainly I had strong inducements to come – everybody thinking I should be sure to make a great fortune by it; and that the European Powers would not delay a moment to avail themselves of my invention; so that I should be able to send you some more money very soon after arriving in Europe. You must imagine my feelings then upon contemplating the <u>possibility</u> of your having to call upon your friends in case I should be unavoidably detained and not be able to relieve you myself. I expect your next letter in a few days and hope to gather some comfort from it as I did from the last. Oh how I long to be in our quiet little house again and to show how much better I shall love you and our children for having had this opportunity of comparison, and how much more contented I shall be. You may say I have no reason to complain – that even if I make no money by this visit still the invention has been of great service to us enabling me to pay my debt for <u>our</u> home (dear word!) - : this is perhaps true – but still that would have been paid without this expensive trip. I must get what consolation I can for the dispersion of my practice by supposing that the fact of having visited and practiced in Europe will do more than bring it all back again. People will think I will have improved a great deal professionally I dare say – while, <u>in fact</u>, I am instructing the most eminent Dentists I find on the Continent – they being ignorant of some of the most common and well established operations with us. Of this say nothing. Good night.

Thursday, Midnight October 30, 1845. - Although so late I write to give you an account of my day's work. Went out to Tsarskoe selo (sarsko sello) – saw and dined and talked a great deal with Colonel Todd and got the letter I went after – addresses to the Colonel who acted as interpreter between the Grand Duke and myself. This Colonel, by good luck, happens to be an acquaintance of Colonel Todd. Colonel Todd's chasseur (shas suer) will take the letter to its address Colonel Solovzoff tomorrow morning and I may expect to see or hear from Colonel

Solovzoff at Colonel Todd's town residence before noon. Colonel Todd having to attend a party tonight came in to town with me; and to pass away the time until the hour for this party (11 o'clock or so) he proposed going to a French Theatre. There were no tickets to be had for that – all sold - so we went to the Alexander Theatre – Russian – and saw some very capital acting. During the performance the <u>polka</u> was danced and encored and danced again very well indeed. The Colonel brought me home, and then I found that two Officers had called to see me, but as they left nothing for me, nor stated the object of their visit, I can only suppose they brought the information for which I have been shutting myself up at home and waiting a week for – that is to know in what way and where the Government pleased to act in my matter. So good night - and better information for tomorrow.

I had Eddy and George both in my lap last night and gave them such hearty kisses. As for you my dear girl I dream of you <u>all</u> the time <u>by</u> <u>day</u> and very much by night. I hope I shall never be so far from you again. Sweet dreams.

Friday November 7, 1845. - 8 days from my last writing. My interview with Colonel Solovzoff resulted in a visit to see Prince Dolgorouoki; - didn't see him – out of town; - went next day – didn't see him, but Colonel Todd did and told me that an examination would be made and a report given if I wished, but advised me to present the gun for trail first in <u>France</u>, assuring me that this Government would not adopt it until it had been adopted <u>there</u>. I arranged with him that I would either decline an examination or present the gun within a few days. Next day a summons came in haste for me to present the gun at half past 1 o'clock etc. etc. – but as I got the notice <u>after</u> that time I didn't go - sent an explanation and afterward called in person and arranged that I am to have notice a day or two in advance when the board meet again; and so the matter stands – I waiting still; and I had concluded to write nothing more in this letter until I could record the conclusion of the board; but Colonel Todd visited me tonight and brought me your letter of the 12th October – so I was compelled to bring up the history. Again I do thank Heaven for the continued health of our family. I see by this last letter that Father and Mother are with you – I hope you will manage to enjoy yourselves as well as possible upon the means you have; but it may be necessary to economize rather rigidly, as there is little or no prospect of my sending money home; - indeed I have already made arrangements with Colonel Todd to the effect that if I travel with him to Berlin he is to pay my share and I am to refund on my arrival home. In fact I consider the trip a failure; but would not have even Smith and Tyson suppose I think so as I shall still try my best for their interest as well as ours. This is my last sheet of paper.

Good night.

I don't know when I shall be able to send this to you.

Saturday morning, November 8, 1845. – The weather has been already as cold here as we have it in Washington in winter but so far I have not suffered from it. The ice from lake Ladoga has been running in the river for 2 or 3 days – making it necessary to remove the bridge of boats of which I wrote you; and yesterday there was sufficient snow for the curious little one horse sledges (like our cutters somewhat) used here. I have made a sketch of one that took my fancy.

A few nights ago an officer of the army at the request of a friend of his, boarding with Miss Benson (my landlady) brought about 20 soldiers to the house to sing national Russian songs for the amusement of the boarders etc. How much I did wish you were present – (always my wish if I see or hear anything curious or good). The soldiers (in uniform – they are never out of it) stood in a knot facing each other, and at the conclusion of each song the time was quickened – one struck in with a tambourine, a little circle was formed, open on one side to the view of the audience, and another commenced a peculiar sort of noisy, shuffling dance – then another joined him, holding in each hand a stick a foot long on which were arranged little bells and red bits of cloth so as to make them look like 2 bouquets of flowers at a distance – these he flourished about as he danced – the two moving about in the circle and dancing not merely with their feet and legs, but all over, and putting themselves into queer and amusing attitudes – very greatly to the gratification of those who had the good luck to see them.

Colonel Solovzoff, when I saw him last, again told me that the Committee (Board) would not report in favor of my invention – that the Prince (Dolgorouki) would be present and he would tell the Committee what the Grand Duke said, and the Committee would not report in favor of it when the Grand Duke had expressed his opinion against it. Liberty of opinion, or rather the liberty to express an opinion is not known here – what those in power say is never contradicted – that power being supreme - above and beyond any and all appeal – entirely uncontrolled – without any limits - in the hands of one who is aware of the necessity of inflicting terrible punishments to keep his people in subjection. Judge then of the probability of my success here where it is known that the brother of the Emperor is prejudiced against the gun – that, as Grand Master of Artillery he has active control (under the Emperor) of the arming and equipping the army – that those who are to form the Committee are interested in keeping on the 'right side' of him, and that, finally, this state of things exists among a people to whom, I am assured, moral honesty is an unknown virtue. You will think perhaps that there must be some mistake – that all cannot be false that we hear so often in America about men of science being so well received here – their inventions, and discoveries, so well paid for – themselves honored, and all that – the Russians such a noble people – so friendly to foreigners, especially to our people etc. etc. etc. – but I assure you there is very little foundation for all of this, if I may believe the foreigners themselves, or even some of the Russians.

As you may be anxious (it is so very important a matter) to know how I am lodged, I have made a sketch of my room and here you see me now, writing this line.

On my left in the corner is the "peechky" or stove – following around toward the left, comes next the door from the passage – in the corner the wash stand, - towel stand – bed with its two pillows one atop the other, by the head of which is the candle stand where I lay your picture that I may see it the last thing every night – a closet in the partition wall (2 feet thick) made by closing the door that leads through to the next room and hanging another so as to enclose the 2 feet depth – bureau and in front of it my gun case and trunk; - then comes 3 windows toward the quay with 2 pier glasses and tables – an operating table and chair before the centre window – a sofa behind me, (closing another doorway) and chairs in various places. The walls you see are very thick – yet such is the marshy nature of the ground that the passage of a carriage rapidly on the pavement in front of the house will make the whole house vibrate and the dishes rattle on the table. This house had, like many if not most houses here, no passages like those in use with us at home; and the thin partition between my room and the passage now existing , has been recently made by the present occupants and account for this partition being so thin. Before the fire is a yard and a half of common carpeting, and under my feet some 6 by 8 feet of carpet in one piece something like a Brussels carpet but not so rich – woven with a border all around. There is another yard or so of ingrain before the bed, and the rest of the floor is naked and polished with wax every week by fellows who wax all the floors in the house (except the kitchen etc.) at so much a month or year. My floor is one of those figured ones of which I wrote and of which I have made sketches.

The Gold Rogers who called to see me, or you, is I think, an old school mate of mine – sometime since appointed Charge d'Affaires to Sardinia. If it be the same he is very tall, large boned and rather good looking for so large a man. I have understood that, like his father (and I think his mother also) he has been insane – and that he returned from his mission to Sardinia on that account. He embraced the profession of his father - Law – and from his indolent good natured disposition led me to think he would not succeed very well. I was greatly surprised therefore to hear that he made a very brilliant speech at Harrisburg in a Convention to which he had been sent to assist in revising the constitution (I think) of Pennsylvania. If I recollect aright I operated for him before he went to Europe. Father knows the reputation of his father, Judy Rogers of Madison, who was in Congress some year ago.

Monday night, November 10, 1845. - Today I visited a furniture warehouse, said to be one of the grandest establishments of its kind in Europe. The furniture, consisting of tables of every description, bookcases, candle-stands, map cases, music stands, desks, bedsteads, sofas, divans, chairs (about 200 patterns of chairs I understand) mirrors etc. etc. without end to either the number, style or cost. Nothing common there – all rich and so beautiful. How I wish you could see that furniture! The wood is chiefly dark – rosewood, walnut, etc. and beautifully carved; inlaid etc. One bookcase which was priced – How much do you think its price was? Now all of you guess. About three thousand dollars! I concluded not to buy it. Centre tables for from 50 to 500 dollars and all other things equally costly, but not dear if you consider the labor and material. One of the proprietors told us that the establishment employed <u>500</u> workmen – that they sent furniture to various parts of the world, and that they were compelled to refuse to fill many orders because they could not well manage a larger number of workmen. I wished to make sketches of some of the articles but it was not permitted. I don't blame them – their designs must have cost a great deal of time, talent and money; and they are right in considering them <u>property</u> and not to be given away.

Colonel Todd has removed to town for the winter, (or so much of it as he spends here). I called upon him today and learned that the British Courier arrived yesterday and will return a week from next Saturday (I think) when I can send this letter. In about 6 weeks more you will probably get it. Well, well – I hope to be nearer to you before spring – though not so near as I could wish. Good night.

Thursday night, November 13, 1845. - Today I have been to "The Marble Palace" to see the Imperial collection of <u>Cameos</u> – said to be the best in Europe and numbering <u>fifteen thousand</u>! They are all sizes and cut in a great variety of stones – some as small as ¼ inch diameter, and some – 2 or 3, as large as 4 or 5 or 7 or 8 inches. I suppose the fifteen thousand includes the stones having the figures sunk, as well as the cameos – there being a great many of those, by the side of each of which was an impression or cast in plaster or of other material so as to show the figures raised, like the cameos. A great many of them were mounted in fingerings – very old; - and some of them – a great proportion, were of exceeding beauty. A small case of about a hundred is kept covered in a room apart – they being such as ladies do not like to examine – when gentlemen are present. I saw also an immense collection of coins of all countries and all dates; also one of medals and another of seals; but these I paid but little attention to as time was short and the stones interested me infinitely more.

Last night I paid a visit of charity to a sick women at the Soldiers barracks nearby. Ah Ellen! Such misery, such a filthy, crowded, hot, stinking place – but I am glad I saw it – I wish to see both sides of the picture. Good night.

Saturday night, November 15, 1845. – I have been writing a long letter to Major Smith detailing my operations here and telling him that I should give instructions to Father Owen to go to him for money if the funds I left should fail before I return; - that this would not be necessary if I returned as soon as I expected; - but that if, by month's delay, I had a reason to think I might effect something for our mutual benefit, I should not like to return without making the trail; and that with this view of the case I felt assured he would not fail to meet Father's demands, which would not be heavy. I assure you my dear Ellen that the possibility of your being without money before I return gives me a great uneasiness. Sometimes when I have been reflecting upon it I have almost concluded to abandon everything that I came abroad for and get home as quick as I possibly can, regardless of everything but my family. Then I go over your letters and you seem to be so easy, and comfortable, and to say nothing about money, and then I feel more quiet.

I learn from a note from Colonel Todd that the Courier starts on <u>Tuesday</u> next, so I must finish this letter tomorrow. He writes me also that he expects letters on Monday that left Boston on the 1st. – but that is hardly probable I should think. If anybody enquires how I am getting on with my business tell them I am waiting for the return of the Emperor – which is fact for I calculate to travel with Colonel Todd who cannot take his leave until the emperor returns. I think of nothing to write concerning home affairs – office etc. No doubt all goes on right – and that Mr. Johnson has not been unjust to me as to let my neighbor have the office. He must not have it; - and beside my lease is not out for some time yet. Ah! The dear old place! How I should like to be in it again quietly earning our bread, as please God, I will be before many months pass. I have fixed upon April to be home – which will bring it, let me see – into January – ahem! What's the matter? No? Very well - we'll see about that. Oysters are good in every moth that's got an <u>r</u> in it, and there's an <u>r</u> in April, <u>any</u> – <u>how</u>. D. says he don't care anything about them – he's quite independent; and looks forward with pleasing anticipation of a snug resting place at home. Last night I dreamed that I went home and you addressed me in French – Good-night – good-night.

Sunday night, November 16, 1845. - Your letters after receiving this until further directions from me should be directed to me, "<u>care of the American Minister, Berlin, Prussia</u>". On one corner you will write "<u>via Liverpool</u>" and mail them and pay them as usual. It is probable I shall write you one or two, perhaps three letters still from this city, as I shall not leave it probably until the middle of January (new style). You will not, I think, receive this before after new year's day; so that your next letter would arrive <u>here</u> too late for me if sent here; and will reach Berlin if sent there about the time I do. After that I shall have no difficulty in writing you by every steamer. Remember me to the family – Father and Mother, big George, little George, Big John, little John and Edward - Mrs. Haag and Amelia.

Colonel Todd comes for my professional services tomorrow and <u>possibly</u> will bring me a letter from **<u>home</u>** – from my dear wife but if he does I shall not be able to answer it with many lines as he will take this with him to put with his letters to be sent by the courier to England.

You are aware that the days are very short here in winter. Even now it is scarcely light enough to see to dress without a candle at 9 in the morning; and at half past 3 or 4 it is too dark to write by daylight. Breakfast is on the table at our house from 8 to 10 or 11. Lunch at 1 or half past, dinner at half past 5, and tea about half past 9 or 10. Go to bed somewhere between 11 and 2 and get up in time for breakfast. The good custom of having a cup of coffee about 10 minutes or so after dinner prevails here; with the coffee, Turkish pipes or cigars – quite after the manner of the Asiatics from the Russians branched off, preserving many oriental habits.

Don't fail to tell me all about your funds, how long they will probably last and all that I ought to know about such affairs – and don't lead me to think you are better provided for than you are in reality – let me know the worst and I can do the best for us. Father Owen will be gratified perhaps to learn that the famed Russian stove so much in use here is almost precisely, in principle, the same as <u>his</u> plan of making the whole chimney breast a heating surface. The greatest difference is that in the Russian stove (which is of white glazed earthen ware and generally placed against the walls in a corner of the room and is as big as a good sized wardrobe, but not quite so wide) and the fire is made in a sort of oven in the lower part; the heat and smoke rise to the upper part in a flue then down another, then into the wall in which is the flue or chimney leading to the top of the house. The oven is nearly filled with wood in the morning early, fired and allowed to burn out with the oven door open. When all smoke and gas ceases to rise from the coals, the flue leading from the stove is closed – the door also, and the stove continues to give out its heat for 24 hours. Sometimes it is necessary to heat the stove twice a day, but very often in winter, as I am told, they are only heated once in two days. The walls being of great thickness (2 to 3 feet, solid brick work) and the windows all double and every crack and crevice caulked and pasted up, the most intense cold <u>out</u> is not heeded in-doors nor the fiercest wind heard; and when the inhabitants go out they are so well defended by furs from head to foot that after a ride of half a dozen miles, with the mercury at 40 degrees of Fahrenheit below freezing point, they throw off their furs and sit down to write with supple fingers and as comfortable as if they had not been out of the house.

Father Maynard desired me to write him on the first of every month but I have not written him since I was in London – much to his disappointment I am sure. I told him then what I had heard about the difficulties in sending letters from the Continent of Europe. I wish you to write him Ellen – say that I requested you to do so and that I have not written him for reasons that will be satisfactory when he hears them – that, thus far I have not succeeded in doing anything with my invention and have no prospect of reaping any reward here; but that I hope to write him more favorably from Prussia or France.

You can tell him when I shall leave Russia, where I go to and so forth and make out as much of a letter as you can about my affairs and the family etc. and remember me to him most affectionately. It will warm his heart to see you sign yourself his Daughter – Heaven knows he needs every evidence of regard we can show him and I know he is very anxious to have your good will and affection as I know you have his – most truly and sincerely. The apparent coldness, apparent even to me, that he met with at our house last winter nearly broke his heart and went far toward confirming an opinion which I then held but changed most happily at Springfield, - never to be held again I trust, and not to be farther talked about now. I will leave the remainder of this page for tomorrow and bid you now, for the last time in this letter.

Good night.

Monday P.M., November 17, 1845. - The Colonel has been here and tells me that if I send the letter to him tonight it will be in time. He had not yet received his expected mail from America.

Should you have occasion to apply to Major Smith for funds and he should refuse, perhaps Mr. Baily will advance you sufficient and take your or Father's note at interest. I have written to our Counsel in London to send my letters that leave Boston in the middle of December to Berlin.

Give our dear children an extra kiss each for me. Your daily kiss you get at about 7 P.M. – being 12 o'clock here. As you sit by the side of your work-stand before the fire – perhaps with the baby in your lap – perhaps just resting yourself after jolting him up and down until his belly aches so that he can't cry and sinks to sleep from exhaustion and has been laid in bed – then I step up behind you, reach over your shoulder and give you a kiss as you turn to see who it is. Sometimes (pretty often) I fold you in my arms after you go to bed and give such a – kissing and hugging as you may expect on my return.

You must not expect to see me very stout when I come back; I do not think I am as fleshy as when in London, but I shall soon recover my lost weight when I get once home again – and you will regain your too, probably, as you will then have less anxiety and care.

Tell Mrs. Haag to tell enquirers that I am expected home in April – Father and the rest of you can say the same thing. So far I have suffered less from the cold than I should have done at the same season in the state of New York, and I entertain no apprehensions for the winter – I have already learned much here that I intend to put in practice for making our house more comfortable.

Yours, my dear Ellen, forever,

Edward

Chapter 8
(Fourth Letter)
The Russian Military Committee Examines the Gun

St. Petersburg, Russia

November 22nd. (December 4th) 1845 – Since the last of my last letter I have been waiting for a good starting point for this one – thinking I might begin it with the report upon my invention; but as the next British Courier starts for England on Tuesday next I will delay no longer but begin by telling you that, in accordance with the arrangement mentioned in my last letter the Committee of Examination met and I was present with my models. There were I believe twelve persons at the table. Colonel Solovzoff, interpreter (as before at the Grand Duke Michael's). The room was so dark that it was impossible to examine the models carefully even if they had been taken to pieces, which they were not – nor even the locks taken off – nor even the slips of priming taken out. The President and perhaps half of the other members of the board took the models into their hands, opened and looked at the magazines, and snapped some of the guns two or three times. All retaining their seats during the examination. Enquiries were made and answered about the cost of altering from flint lock to the new one, and how to remove the primer projected by cocking in case it should not be wanted at the time. The whole "examination" lasted about ten minutes. I was then informed that the examination had closed – that it would not be necessary to leave the models for further examination – that the Committee would now talk over the matter and that in the course of a few days I should receive their report. This was last Saturday and I am now waiting for the report, which, as a matter of course will be against adopting the invention. The "examination" was a mere formality – the opinion of the board or rather the <u>decision</u> was no doubt dictated, (as I had been told it would be,) by the Grand Duke Michael before the board met.

The old Negro preacher says "blessed am dey what don't 'spect nuffin', kase dey ain't guine to be disappintide". You know from my last letter that I expected nothing from the Board; and I have had plenty of time and cause to prepare myself for an adverse report – so that I attended the meeting without excitement; and now even anticipate some sport from reading their decision after such a laborious investigation. Almost every day since writing the close of my last letter I have been busy from about 11 till 1 or 2 o'clock professionally. Before 11 and after 2 at midday, it is so dark that I can't see to operate. The Sun is so low, even at midday, that the shadow of the 2 ½ story house in which I live extends nearly across the Neva- 30 or 40 rods I should think. Those for whom I have operated are very anxious to have me remain here – assure me that I should rapidly make a fortune – etc. etc.

Today I have an engagement to operate for a daughter of General Alderberg – a man said to be only second to one (Count Orloff) in the favor of the Emperor. The day is so dark that he lady will not come probably- that being the reason why I did not operate for her when she came to consult me last week – with her governess, in a coroneted carriage, four horses, and three servants in livery. Twice since my last letter Colonel Todd has taken me to plays – once to the French theatre and last night to the Italian Opera, where I heard Madame Castellan, with the same sweet voice she had years ago at Washington. The Great Theatre where the opera is performed is said to be next in size and magnificence to the celebrated one at Milan – the grandest in the world. So that if I had seen this structure, its scenes and "properties" and decorations only I should have been amply repaid for the outlay. A part of the ceiling represented in one of the scenes was so beautiful that I sketched it upon a scrap of brown paper on the spot, to get the pattern, and revised it for you after I came home. You will only have a very faint idea of it however from the sketch. How I did wish you could see it and all the rest of the beautiful representations. I will remember as much of them as I can for you, begging that you prepare yourself by imagining all possible beautiful combinations of shape and color and substance.

Night – Lady didn't come. I see by the American papers that the Anti-senters are getting their deserts. They should have a few Russian lessons in keeping <u>order</u>. Old Father McLeod who says (on his sign-board) that "order is Heaven's first law" would be in ecstasy here, the most orderly city perhaps in the world. I am told that if you sing in the streets a policeman tells you "it is not ordered to sing in the streets' – if you whistle or otherwise amuse yourself audibly or smoke – you are told that such things are not ordered.

At the theatres an armed military police superintends the arrival and departure of carriages. Mounted policemen are on duty constantly and in addition to the usual police of cities there is what is here called "Secret Police"; and spies are so numerous that strangers are cautioned against conversing upon even mentioning many topics. Punishments for official misconduct or mistakes are such that every device is used to keep clear of individual responsibility. To give you an instance; - a Macadamized road, some 15 or 20 miles long, was ordered and built. The Emperor inspected the road – gave the Officers who designed and the Department that sanctioned the design to understand that he thought them all a set of dam fools, and ordered that the Colonel who had charge of the work should be imprisoned a month, and all the Officials who had anything to do with the <u>work should pay for it</u> – which order was enforced. There are some great advantages however as well as disadvantages in this strict and orderly country. Speedy detection and prompt and severe punishment are great safeguards against many crimes. Goodnight and happy visions of future happiness.

Sunday night, November 23, 1845. – Nothing from the Committee yet. Since Thursday I have been very busy "keeping my hand in" and refilling my purse, or at least keeping it from being exhausted. I have been daily expecting for more than a week a letter from you but get none – at which I am not surprised – the mails are so very uncertain. If I do not hear from the Committee tomorrow I shall not be able to inform you of their decision in this letter. In my last letter I spoke of one of the entrances to the Winter Palace; where I say that the centre arch is large enough (or something like it) to put our house through, just take your pencil and cross <u>that</u> out – the remainder may stand. This P.M. I took a sledge ride about the city. Curious sledges – got a sketch for you; and when we live on our farm in New York, we'll have a nice one built.

There have been a few inches of snow here only this season and the Neva is still open – quite unusual I am told, for the time of year. Good night.

Monday P.M., November 24, 1845. – I must close my letter without giving you the report of the Examination of the Guns and without having received your expected letter. I shall send by some Courier a letter to Major Smith giving him an account of the examination; and by the next Courier (2 weeks hence) I shall be able to give the report. Give my best wishes to the family and kiss Eddy, George and John extra for their Papa, who never fails to kiss them before he goes to sleep. Make yourself and family as contented as you can as comfortable as your circumstances will permit. Should I continue to practice for a week or two longer I may not have to borrow from Colonel Todd to get home. My health is good yet, thank God! And promises to continue so, - may this find you all well. If you are a little disappointed at the length of this letter you must recollect that I have scarcely been out since writing my last one, and as for any news – you might as well enquire at the North Pole. I have just finished my letter to Major Smith and have repeated my request that he will furnish you funds if you need them; and have told him that any obligations signed by Father Owen or Brother John for money for my family I will pay. This subject gives me a great deal of anxiety – and although I am perfectly sensible that fretting is of no use, still that does not prevent it.

I don't know whether I am getting corpulent or not but it certainly is very agreeable to unbutton my waistband after dinner. Remember me to Mrs. Haag and Amelia. Tell Perry I shall want him again if he keeps a good character.

Forever yours,

Edward.

P.S. Father may give my respects to Dr. Hall and tell him I am practicing here with success and credit to my country, while I am waiting for the return of the Emperor – and that I shall return in the Spring.

Chapter 9
(Fifth Letter)
Dental Work and Delays

My Dear Ellen,

Since the conclusion of my – (here I stopped to operate, and now – at night – I go again) – my last letter, less than a week ago, I have been constantly occupied professionally during such time as I could see to labor – and after business each day have taken a walk or a sledge ride for air and exercise. While I think of it – here is a most capital soup – such as we have here. Take beef soup strain it through a fine hair or wire sieve and put the liquor into the tureen; - take then some boiled potatoes rub them through a fine sieve and put the product into the soup and stir the up the compound – potato soup. There's one good thing for you – almost worth coming after. I think beans and other vegetables may be and probably are treated in the same way with good effect, so of chickens – have 'em so here sometimes – and perhaps other meats. Another good thing to eat here is the Russian cucumber; - cured in salt and water and sweet herbs – no vinegar; - intend to get some seed and see if the vegetable will thrive in a free country – they say 'twont in England – where the people have somehow got an idea that they are freemen!

Of course I have heard nothing yet from the Military Committee, as that would have else been the first thing to write about. They were engaged so long, and so attentively, and spent such a vast amount of science in the investigation that they probably require at least a month to make out their report. Let's see how the new steel pen goes – ah – this is better – broke the old one and had to use a quill. My landlady has presented me with half a dozen new ones; so I shall "get on" as the English say.

Last night Colonel Todd called for me on his way to the circus – took me in his carriage and at the circus pointed out several Princesses, countesses, noblemen etc. present. The circus was such, very nearly, as were common in America ten or fifteen years ago – except the horses which were not so good as ours. There were more female than males among the players – but only 3 or 4 of the girls did more than gallop about, sitting as ladies should. The others dressed in flesh colored tights, rode side-wise, astride, standing etc. including the ordinary feats of female riders in the circus with us and some others extremely well calculated to show off their beautiful legs and – bodies. House crammed and highly pleased – applauding vociferously. One of our circuses would completely distract the Russians.

Mr. Eastwick tells me that if the Military Board had spent a week examining my guns they would know no more about it then they do now – because they can't comprehend anything of the sort – they merely know what it does – but the means – the how and why – in fact the science of the thing is beyond their comprehension. He has a great deal to do with Military Commissions – everything is done in a military way here - roads and bridges built – works surveyed and inspected, etc. etc. – everything according to military usage and rules, and especially according to some <u>system</u> – everything goes by a system, whether the system is right or wrong is not for those who design or execute the work to attend to. For instance; a certain building having a dome is to be constructed; the weight and size and thrust (if any) of the dome are calculated and then is required the thickness of a wall to support it which wall is to be itself supported by another wall outside.

A Russian Architect <u>takes</u> <u>his</u> <u>system</u>, makes his calculations, and says, <u>7 feet</u>. An American Architect says he erected 5 years ago, (and it is now standing) a dome, 30 per cent heavier, upon a wall, having no outside or inside support, and only 20 inches thick; - no matter, says the Russian – it <u>ought</u> to fall – because it is not according to <u>his</u> system – which is based upon mere theory.   It seems a very curious thing that this should be one of the most remarkable countries for showing and teaching everything by models in order to make everything as practical as possible and yet it produces very, very, few men as Engineers or Architects who are really skillful beyond pictorial representations.

The <u>outsides</u> of things here are very pretty – except the women – who are not – to my tastes, at least. The exterior of the houses here can be made to look far better than with us, from the fact that they are so much larger. The houses of the nobility of the 1st Class (there are 12 classes of nobility here) are some of them much larger than the President's House at Washington – and the streets are composed of houses of immense extent, occupied by many shops below and many families above. One house was pointed out to me in which lodges 800 persons, residents, shopkeepers, servants etc.

Many years ago in the time of Emperor Alexander, the Jesuits were getting numerous and troublesome here – using great efforts to convert young noblemen etc. from the Greek to the Catholic faith. One morning a complaint was made, <u>at 5 o'clock</u>, to the Emperor, against the Jesuits; - <u>at 7 o'clock</u> there was not a Jesuit in the City – an ukase (u'-kas) was issued for them to leave the country <u>instantly</u> – each one was furnished with a fur pelisse to protect him, and their debts (about 200,000 silver rubles) were paid by the Emperor. Rather prompt.

A few years ago the present Emperor sent a messenger to his brother with orders to go and return with an answer <u>as</u> <u>quick</u> <u>as</u> <u>he</u> <u>could</u> (the case was urgent) – the man returned so soon that the Emperor would not believe until he read the answer brought back, that the man had been. I should have said that the roads here in the country are <u>very</u> <u>bad</u> (the country being thickly populated) and the method of traveling for messengers in very crude wagons without springs and on horseback. The man was brought into the presence of the Emperor by two men who took from him his wagon – his abdomen so ruptured that his bowels hung in sacks supported by his clothes. 5000 silver rubles and a pension for life were his reward; - rather less than I have thought <u>I</u> should take to have <u>my</u> "guts shook out."

How often I have thought I should like to look in upon our dear little snuggery at home and catch you all by surprise. I should, at night, about 8 or 9 o'clock, see the babe in our bed, George and Eddy in theirs in Mother's room, and Father sitting near, reading the Intelligence; Mother sitting before the stove in our room, next the wardrobe; - you next, sewing at the work stand which is between you and John who is reading a book which lies on a table. Whether George sits beside Mother or is upstairs in his room, writing, or has made a trip into the country to preach I can't see distinctly.

Sunday night, December 14, 1845. – Sometimes I am interrupted at night and can't write 'good night' to you – but I have the disposition to say it, and you are <u>sure</u> of your <u>kiss</u> "any how". I expect to get in the habit of kissing you that I shall continue the practice on my return – "shouldn't wonder" – as John says.

About the story of the Jesuits – I find there are conflicting accounts – one, - that their debts could not have been great as their establishment here was very extensive and the order <u>very</u> <u>wealthy</u> and that their property <u>was</u> <u>confiscated</u> – so that Alexander made a tolerable speculation out of it.

Last night the ice which has been coming down the Neva for some days, closed; and in a day or two will probably bear to be crossed by people on foot. I heard a report today that the Emperor was expected on the 22nd of this month (old style) – but nobody knows when he will come – he seems fond of surprising his people by appearing unexpectedly. It is said of the Emperor Paul that he used to compel ladies to get out of their carriages in the street and make their courtesy as he passed, and that all men were obliged by him either to wear the Russian dress (according to their station) or else, cocked hats, breeches etc. etc. He died rather suddenly one night from taking, involuntarily, a little too much – <u>cold</u> <u>steel</u> - - administered by some persons who thought he had lived long enough.

With the use of a few words of Russian one may ride all over town. "Pashon" – go on; "Preamo" – forward-; "Na prava" – to the right; "Na lava" – to the left; "Poskarce" – faster; "Stoy" –stop. When you have done with the driver you give him what you please – if he don't like it he'll ask for more, and if he can't get it he'll call you a great sausage, (in Russian) and look out for you next time. The usual compliments and answers are quite poetical "Solaroveli" – (how are you) The answer is "Slavo bogo" – (God be praised) – quite Asiatic you perceive. The letter <u>a</u> in most cases having the sound of our <u>ah</u> – same as in papa. Good-night.

Tuesday morning, December 16, 1845. – Last night I was too much fatigued and suffered too much with a headache to give you an account of yesterday's occurrences. Having perfectly recovered – broken fast and smoked my Turkey tobacco in my long Turkey pipe, (which is cheaper than cigars) and having a little time to write before my next Patient comes, I will commence by saying that I accepted an invitation to visit (with a party of Officers and one of our boarders) an extensive looking glass Fabric (all manufactories are called <u>fabrics</u> here) where I saw the various operations of melting the glass, - rolling it out into thick plates 3 or 4 by 6 or 8 feet, - grinding the surfaces of the plates, - polishing them – silvering, etc. In another department of the fabric the most beautiful glassware I ever saw is made; - saw some made, and went through and examined the different processes of grinding, cutting, painting etc. etc. I saw many things which I thought would suit you exactly, but I had neither the funds to buy nor the place to carry them. I must give you a more minute description on my return.

From this fabric we went to the Locomotive fabric of our countrymen at Alexandrosky – met Colonel Todd and Major Whistler there – went all over again and remained there after our party left the place to dine – Colonel Todd and Major Whistler doing the same. After dinner they left for home and I came in with Messieurs Eastwick, Harrison & Winans and Winans brother and two others to the Opera – they having politely offered me a seat. Heard Madame <u>Garcia</u> the celebrated and Mr. <u>Salvi</u>, ditto and one or two other dittos whose names I have forgotten already.

Our Countrymen have <u>1653</u> men employed at the locomotive fabric – speaking <u>13</u> <u>different</u> <u>languages</u>. They turn out, <u>finished</u> and ready for use, one locomotive every week and are doing a great deal of other work (making freight cars, etc.) besides. Their contract is very large, and now the Government wish to increase it by adding another for passenger cars – amounting to two or three hundred thousand dollars more. Here comes the Patient – Mr. Harrison.

Tuesday P.M. - While I was operating there came a letter from you and one from Father Maynard. As I expected – your funds are getting low – but "Slavo Bogo" I am able to send you a draft for two hundred dollars in this letter and perhaps in another, soon, a little more. This I arrange most unexpectedly through Mr. Harrison whose partner, Mr. Eastwick has some business transactions with Mr. Andrew Hoover of Washington. Mr. Eastwick will send a letter with this and also there will be a draft for the money which letter and draft Father or John will present to Mr. Hoover and you will have money at once. I am very, <u>very</u> glad that I have this opportunity for as you know I have been greatly distressed about your necessities in this way. Mr. Harrison tells me that he can also send this letter through his agent in London so as to help it to Boston and insure its going by the Steamer of the 4th January. You must pardon me for mentioning business matters first – but really I have been so uneasy and am now glad to send you this little sum out of my earning that I nearly lost myself in the excitement. This is your letter of the 6th November (6th to 10th) in which you say that two months have elapsed since my last that you had received was written. This long time of not writing I explained in the first letter I wrote from this place – so that I need not repeat the explanation. Since the first I have sent you 2 or 3 letters and shall send oftener in future – now that I have learned <u>how</u>. I'm sure my Dear Ellen that the time does go slowly with you – would to God I were with you instead of being six thousand miles away. If Heaven please I shall return ere long; in April I hope. I am so delighted to hear that you are all well that I almost wish myself sick so that I might have a more perfect realization of the blessing you enjoy. You say nothing of Eddy, the dear little boy, but I am sure he is well or you would have mentioned it; same as Father, Mother and Brothers John and George. In this last letter you hope soon to hear from me and that my proudest wishes are fully realized – alas!

What a disappointment you had when the next letter reached you! The fondest wish I have <u>now</u> is to get home and embrace my dear wife and children as soon as I can – and the guns may go to the _____ people who will buy 'em – and if they won't buy 'em they may go to the devil.

If I don't get that precious report before I close this letter, Father may tell Major Smith that since writing him last I have heard nothing farther about the examination. If I do get it I will say so in this, tell you what it is, and write the Major also. I think little George must have got the idea of my bringing him a carriage and horses from my letters as I said something about them and liveried servants etc. (By the way the young lady who has come to have some operation was taken sick and is still quite ill.) Your continued assurances of love render me as happy as I can be without your society and under the existing circumstances. I have been a <u>long</u>, long time away and am sure it must seem much longer to you than to me because I have had so many things to see that were new to me and therefore interesting; - but you, dear Ellen, - I can imagine your loneliness and your anxiety about the welfare yourself and children and me when so long a time elapses without hearing from your natural protector and provider. Do not believe that I will neglect you; while I have life it is yours by <u>right</u> as it is most sincerely heartily by <u>inclination</u>. You give me a more cheering account of little John – I pray he may compensate you by his goodness for the trouble you had when he was so cross and required so much attention. The great ladies here, I'm told see their children once a day, enquire of the nurses or governesses how they are, etc. but very few give them any personal attention.

I shall send you as much money as I can from here should I be so fortunate as to get any more to send; my last month's bill I paid this morning – between 75 and 80 dollars – out of my earnings; and I think this for which I send I send draft will about pay for the services for the Alexandrosky people; - but I have not finished with them yet and perhaps I shall be able to send 50 or 100 dollars more before leaving Petersburg. I think it will be well for Father to ask Mr. Johnson <u>as a favor</u> <u>to me</u>, which I shall acknowledge, to let the next quarter's rent remain due until my return – I think he will do it – for I once paid him a long time in advance, telling him that the time <u>might</u> come when I should ask him to wait for his pay a short time. He will recollect it, I am sure.

Father Maynard merely acknowledges the receipt of a letter from me dated in London – states that the families are well, but <u>his</u> affairs not prosperous; and that he had met with a very painful accident, of having the end of one of his fingers <u>bruised</u> <u>off</u>! God help him to bear his reverses and troubles! – his children, I am sorry to say, cannot be of much service to him pecuniarily – but we can do much perhaps to comfort his old age, and I trust we shall not fail to do so. My expenses here have been and will be as small as I can well have them and hold my head up amongst folks – quite as small, I am certain, as you could wish them; I feel that every dollar that I can send home will be enjoyed five-fold more than if <u>I</u> use it.

How I long to see those dear children again; they will have grown so much that I shall scarcely know which is John and which is George; - how amusing it will be to see the little fellow, that could only sit when propped up as I last saw him, running about the house and <u>talking</u> – I'm sure he <u>will</u> talk by April next – he is so <u>cute</u>. And then – won't we have such good times talking over my adventures, and travels, and sight-seeing, and about the queer people and queer costumes, and how they tricked me at one place and I <u>yankee'd</u> 'em at another "and so on".

Ah Ellen! I've learned a good many lessons since I saw you last – lessons to be remembered and practiced upon to make us happier by making <u>me</u> better, as I hope; at least I shall be more <u>contented</u>, and that will be something gained.

This morning the mercury by Fahrenheit's scale was 37 degrees below freezing point – (5 below zero) – pretty cold weather; but the people are said to feel it very little, because they know how to dress so as to keep warm. Great expense is sometimes incurred here in furs for cloaks; - at diner today a gentleman was telling of a friend of his in Moscow who gave his wife a fur coat that cost six thousand paper rubles – about twelve hundred dollars. The fur was of the <u>black</u> <u>fox</u>- very valuable. Mr. Harrison has one lined with <u>wolf</u> <u>fur</u>; and advises me to get one like it when I go to Berlin inasmuch as I <u>must</u> have something of the kind and I can get on like his for 25 or 30 dollars. He says it is as warm as a feather bed and so thick and soft that it is a great protection against the raps and bruises of traveling. Besides this "schube" I must have a pair of fur boots – things that look as if made for an elephant lined with some cheap fur and reaching above the knees – and a cap, also a fur. Altogether I think I shall make quite a "sizable" man – only picture me at least twice as thick, legs and all, as now – with only the tip of my delicate nose visible – nothing else to tell you whether it is a man or a young elephant standing on his legs! Good night, my dear Ellen. May your dreams all be sweet.

Wednesday P.M., December 17, 1845. - I shall send you <u>two</u> bills of exchange for the money I mentioned yesterday; one (the "first of exchange") will be enclosed in this letter and the other (the "second of exchange") in my next letter. You will probably receive both – in which case you bill burn one of them after having received the money for the other. Father will first see Mr. Hoover before you make it payable to his (Hoover's) order. If Mr. Hoover will cash it at once Father can return to you with the bill and you will make it payable to Hoover's order (as I have to yours) and then Father will get the money. Should Hoover refuse, or be out of town, or dead, then Father had better ask Mr. Bailey to get you the money through some friend of his in Philadelphia to whom he can send the bill for collection; or Father may ask Mr. Sweeney, at the Bank of Washington, to have it collected through that Bank. My next letter will be sent by the British Courier of next Tuesday but will probably be half a month or, if the Steamers run monthly, <u>perhaps</u> <u>a</u> <u>month</u>, later than this in getting to you.

Although it is so cold out of doors that horses and beards and fur collars are white with frost, yet it is my room like summer and from a small fire in one corner – the room larger, considerably, than our bedchamber. We'll have a more comfortable house next winter; and little or none of that mournful sound of the wind which is unpleasant to you. I more and more every day think with the wise old Solomon that "there is nothing better than to eat, drink and be merry" and of course <u>comfortable</u>. At least half my time since I left home has been spent in observing, studying, inquiring and planning how to make my <u>home</u> comfortable and cheerful; and if I don't succeed in making it so it will not be for want of a disposition to do it. I have been thinking about getting now some furs for you and the children next winter; but your more immediate wants are of more consequence, and should I have the ability I can send next summer for them. You tell me of Amelia's indiscretion – I am sorry for her but I can hardly blame her, for only think how hot <u>she</u> must have been in summer – much masses of flesh to keep <u>it</u> hot too! – but, all joking aside, she is to be pitied, as all chance of a decent marriage for her is out of the question.

11 P.M. I have just returned from dining with our Minister – had quite a good French dinner, and a good <u>American</u> <u>talk</u> afterward. He will probably sail from Liverpool for Boston on the 4th of March and it is <u>possible</u> that I shall do so likewise; but if there is any probability of success in any of the countries I pass through I feel I ought to present my invention for examination. Major Whistler tells me that if a gun was presented here for adoption that was – no matter <u>how</u> perfect – even if it would load itself and go off itself when you wished and required nothing to have nothing done for it – still the Russians would hesitate and delay and put off its adoption perhaps for years – I have not more than others to complain of – all or nearly all inventors who come here as I did fare as I have fared; - and they say of one man who had some business with the Government that he waited and waited and waited – a year or more – for some matter or other of great consequence to himself, until finally he became crazy from vexation, want, etc.

Tomorrow is a great holiday here – great ball at the Winter Palace – Colonel Todd tells me that he will ask of the Grand Master of Ceremonies, as a special favor, that I may be admitted as a spectator. He is not sure of the favor, as it would be one of no mean importance <u>here</u>. If I go you will have some account of the ball in my next letter.

Last night a fire broke out and greatly damaged the famous Assembly Rooms of the Noblesse – said to be the finest ball room – or suite of rooms including the ball room <u>in Europe</u>. I hope to be able to give you a description of the place as I intend to see it soon. May we meet in our dreams again, Good night.

Thursday morning, December 18, 1845. – Mr. Harrison has just come with Mr. Hoover's letter and I must close this at once to be in time for the mails. Remember me most affectionately to the family and measure my love for yourself by your own for me – Be as cheerful as possible and "hope for the best" – there is positive certainty of our happiness if we do but justice to ourselves and each other. Kiss our dear children for me again on receipt of this from me. My next letter will start next week. Good bye- Forever truly and wholly Your own, Edward.

Chapter 10

(Sixth Letter)

Russian Bureaucracy and Gun Invention Rejection

My Dear Ellen,

At last the report has come and, as I expected, is against the adoption of my invention. This I should care less about than I do were it not that the objection is founded upon the similarity between my gun and two others which have been tried and have failed here; when the <u>fact</u> is that there is but <u>one</u> point of similarity between them and that is not an objectionable one – in every other particular they are entirely different; - but the Grand Duke Michael did not see or comprehend the principle of mine, and so condemned it unfairly; - and of course the Committee must condemn it too.

The report is in the Russian language and I have not yet had it translated having received it this P.M.; but it was accompanied by a note in English from Colonel Solovzoff, giving me its substance and informing me that it had been approved by the Grand Master of Ordnance (Michael). If I can get it translated in time I'll send you a copy in this letter.

Yesterday I mailed a letter to you enclosing a draft for $200 – the draft being the first of a bill of Exchange from Eastwick & Harrison upon Charles E. Lex, of Philadelphia. The bill was made payable to your order, and was enclosed together with a letter from Mr. Eastwick to Mr. Andrew Hoover (near 7 Buildings, Washington) asking him to cash the bill. Should you not have received the other when you receive this let Father take it to Mr. Hoover and if he can cash it at once then you can make the money payable to his order (as I have yours) and so get the money; should Mr. Hoover be absent, or dead; then Mr. Bailey, or Mr. Sweeney at the Bank of Washington will give Father any assistance he may need by collecting the bill. In the event of <u>both</u> of the bills reaching you, you will burn the "second" <u>after</u> payment of the "first". Having a bad cold in my head.

Good night.

I have had the document from the Committee translated and here you have a copy.

Staff of His Imperial Highness

_____

By Order of the Master General

Of Artillery

_____

4th Division

_____

St. Petersburg

6th December 1845

_____

No. 4711

To Colonel Solovzoff
Of the Artillery;

The Committee for the improvement of small arms after examination of the percussion gun invented by the citizen of the United States, Doctor Maynard has recorded in its journal upon this subject that this arm similar in its principle to the system of the Baron Heurteloup and Mr. Nobel cannot be acceptable for the use of the army on account of the inconveniences of this system proved by experiments tried for a long time and upon a large scale.

Therefore by order of the General of the Staff informing your nobleness* I most humbly beg to make known this decision of the Committee of fire-arms to Doctor Maynard with the addition that it has been deemed worthy of the approval of His Imperial Highness, the Master General of Ordnance.

Officer of the Day

1st Aide de Camp.

*(This word nobleness comes as near as anything to the meaning of the original. M.)

In order not to lose space I will fill this part which is left blank in the document. You will see that the objection is on account of the invention being like one or two others which have been tried here. Had the "examination" been a proper one, all the faults of which they had to complain in the other guns, would have been found to be obviated in this; - while all the advantages aimed after in the others would have been found to have been attained in this; but there was a prejudice in the way – too strong to be overcome without more influence than I possess. The only appeal is to the Emperor; and he is probably quite as much prejudiced as his brother. Whether it will be possible or expedient to make this appeal remains to be decided after His Majesty's return. Whether this report is made as a pretext for not purchasing the invention while they intend to use it if other nations do I can't say. I am told that no trick or meanness is too low for the Russian Government to practice when either money or power is to be gained; - and if this be true I could not reasonably expect to be paid for my invention when it might be used <u>without</u> being paid for by <u>merely</u> violating the law of honor; - a law of very little, <u>if</u> <u>any</u>, consequence in dealing with Russians.

Monday morning, December 22, 1845. – Last night I was too much fatigued by a sort of frolic among the boarders, games, dancing, etc. to take this paper out of my trunk and write good night to you. Yesterday I was visited and professionally consulted by a young gentleman – Mr. Sopozhnakoff – said to immensely wealthy and of a very influential family. He has been suffering very greatly for months from a tooth which he says has broken 7 times by some of the most celebrated Dentists here in their attempts to extract it; and he is now threatened with effects of the diseased tooth (or rather the jaw) that will, if not prevented, disfigure him for life. He is to come again at 11 this morning. I relieved him a little yesterday, and hope to improve him farther today. Should I succeed in relieving him altogether the influence of his family may be useful to any American Dentist who may come here to practice and the fact of the cure it will be my reward to know.

I send by same mail (per Courier) with this a letter to Major Smith giving him the report etc. It will be well not to talk of this decision out of the house – except that Father may do so with Major Smith when no other person is present. When all the facts can be known there can be no harm in telling them all; but a partial statement of them might prejudice even our own Government. There is a good probability that I shall be able to send you a bill for 50 or 100 dollars soon – perhaps by the next steamer after the one that brings you this. Remember me to all the family; kiss the boys again for their papa and don't let them sleep between a door and a fire unless you would have them suffer with earache. Adieu my dear Ellen;

Forever yours,

Edward

Ellen Sophia Maynard,

I have written to Major Smith that I have sent you $200 of my earnings here; money that I hoped would save me from borrowing from Colonel Todd to get home. And I have renewed my request to him to furnish you with funds if you send to him for them – (as I wrote to you in my last). My bad cold is better, and will be gone, I hope, in a few days.

Monday P.M. Mr. Sopozhnakoff called and could scarcely find English enough to express his gratitude for the relief he felt after he got home yesterday – for the first time in a long while he slept quietly last night. I find his teeth nearly all suffering and he expressed a great desire that I should operate on them; - seemed to be glad that he had got out of the hands of the Russian Dentists etc. etc.

I have requested Major Whistler to write (and he has promised to do so) to Captain Swift of the U.S. Army, at Washington and give him the facts of the "examination", decision, etc. for him to communicate to Colonel Talcott; this will keep everything right at Washington as Major Whistler is perfectly aware of the injustice of the proceedings – I must close.

Forever yours,

Edward

Chapter 11
(Seventh Letter)
Denmark Patent Sale

Legation of the U.S. St. Petersburg
Mrs. Ellen S. Maynard
Washington City
D.C.
United States of America

St. Petersburg, December 26, 1845   **Page 1**
January 7, 1846

My Dear Ellen,

      I have two sources of pleasure with which to commence this letter; - first and greatest is that I am able to send you a draft for a hundred dollars and the second is that I have partially recovered from a rather threatening illness – brought on by a cold in the head – during which I have had the best of care from my land ladies Miss Sarah and Miss Elizabeth Benson. I am now so far recovered that I go out every day for a short walk or ride and manage to earn some money for you. For our countrymen I operate at my Washington charges – for the first patient I had here (as I believe I wrote you) I charged for plugging – 5 rubles, silver, (equal $3.75) and other charges in proportion. Lately my fame has so extended that I have gone up suddenly to <u>ten</u> rubles silver at which price I have had only one patient, who paid me fifty rubles. I have still much to do for our countrymen – 2 or 3 of them and something more for Mrs. Harrison, one of our pretty and sensible women from Philadelphia. I have also one or two engagements with other foreigners resident here. As for the Russians – that young Sopozhnakoff of whom I wrote you is said to be a good specimen of their way of viewing such matters. You recollect that he was very grateful for being relieved, etc. etc. – well – he was very, <u>very</u> anxious I should put all his teeth in order – appointed a time etc. –etc. – but didn't come. Some days after the time, one of our boarders was at his mother's house and was asked to request me to send in my bill – that her son was not now suffering from his teeth and declined to have anything more done – at the same time expressing great pleasure and gratitude for my services etc. etc. - 'Tis said there is no dependence to be placed upon them – the Russians – they never hold to a resolution 24 hours. Some days – 6 or 8 – ago a gentleman called and made particular enquiries about me – as a Dentist etc. – enquired what time of day I would be most likely to be found at home etc. – etc. adding that a Grand Duchess was suffering from her teeth and I might be sent for to visit her. I did not see the man nor did he say <u>what</u> Grand Duchess it was who sent him to make inquiries. It seems from what he said that she heard something favorable of my practice. Dr. Arndt, Physician to the Emperor, having heard from Colonel Todd about our American operation of destroying the nerve and filling the tooth and got my address of the Colonel and said he should call upon me for farther information in the matter; - this was a week or less, since and he has not called yet – perhaps he is waiting till the Christmas holidays are over. While I have been writing tonight I was requested to go up stairs (where the boarders usually spend the evening) and see a Russian custom – went up and saw five men in masks and fantastic dresses – one played a guitar while four danced a simple but peculiar figure and step – for about five minutes, when they bowed to the company and withdrew. Miss Benson tells me this is one of the ways in which the Russian servants amuse themselves at this time of year, - they mask and go about from house to house where they have acquaintances in the kitchen and so amuse themselves, each other, and the company.

Yesterday being Christmas day <u>here</u> (Old Style) we had a Christmas dinner – champagne etc. – etc. at which your health was most cheerfully drunk by the company, for which I thanked them in your name. I have tonight read the message – Mr. Harrison having very kindly brought it to me. I must say that I am glad of the fine tone and high ground the President thinks proper to take respecting our claims in Oregon; and his remarks about the National Treasury and the Tariff seem to be very good – but of these matters I should like to talk to Father Owen before forming my opinion to act upon.

Not having been with you to wish you a Merry Christmas or a Happy New Year, you must take my good wishes in writing. May this and every succeeding New Year only make you all more happy than ever. Give the boys each a hearty new-year's kiss for their father and ask each to give you one for him.

Colonel Todd has such information about the Emperor's return that he has fixed the time for our departure, - on the 1st of February (new style) some twenty five days hence. Had I known that I should be here so long I might have received one or two more letters from you before that time but now I shall find them, perhaps three or four of them, at Berlin where I shall arrive probably in eight days from this City; passing through part of Poland on the route.

Colonel Todd tells me he can get a good carriage, have the wheels taken off and lashed on somehow to carry them and have the body of the carriage put upon runners so as to make a close bodied sledge, in which if we please, and the wolves will let us, we may sleep. As we shall have my models with us and plenty of ammunition we shall be pretty safe from such enemies whether they have four or only two legs. The carriage to be sold at the end of the journey for whatever it will bring – the loss to be divided between us. He thinks this loss will not be greater than the extra charges for baggage – etc. – if we were to take any other mode of conveyance. I need not tell you of my suspense until I get your next letters in Berlin – you will I am certain much better imagine it.

Good night my dear Ellen.

Monday December 31, 1845. – having had nothing to write I have saved paper for some days. Yesterday morning "His Majesty" returned to his capital and was welcomed by grand illuminations last night – to see which we (boarders, landlady etc.) filled four sledges and took a nice ride about the city so as to see the lights etc. <u>Tis</u> <u>said</u> that the Emperor paid about three millions of silver rubles for bones and relics of Saints etc. while in the South of Europe, to bring home – he being the head of the Greek Church, as the Pope is of the catholic. Being above all responsibility and one of the most influential monarchs of the world he might do something more than he does for the <u>moral</u> improvement of his people; and especially as he is the head of the Greek Church, he ought not to set the example of keeping a mistress - but perhaps his religion allows that – I ought to have thought of that before I expressed an opinion. One would think from what one hears in Russia that almost anything was tolerated in society here provided it were done by people of "<u>rank</u> <u>and</u> <u>respectability</u>".

For these 2 weeks I have been operating very little. Last night another company of masks, not servants like the others but respectable people, probably some acquaintances of the Bensons, but <u>who</u>, nobody knows, came in and danced. It is customary now in such cases to admit the masks unless at least one of the number is known, as a voucher for the rest – some robberies having taken place for want of this precaution. Last night there were 3 men or 4 women – one woman played the piano while the rest of the party paired off with some of us and danced quadrilles.

Tuesday January 1, 1846. - This is New Year's Day <u>Old</u> <u>Style</u> and a great holiday here. Last night according to the custom here we had a great merry-making. First of all, in a separate room there were privately arranged several tables covered with presents of candy, bon-bons, jewelry, and all sorts of things usually given away at such times. The presents were divided into parcels or lots and the name of the person for whom it is designed written upon a label and placed by the side. In the centre of the room is a pine (or other evergreen) tree, like those in our door-yard for size, the branches all hung with candles, kisses, bon-bons, fruit, etc., etc., and on the branches are placed a dozen or two little wax candles of various colors, all burning and lighting up the tree most beautifully. Some of the presents last night were of considerable value – sets of silver table spoons, ditto gold-band china plates etc. – made to the Misses Benson by two brothers who visit them frequently. Having been of some service professionally to three of the family, gratuitously, I came in for a liberal share of their favors – the more valuable for having been, most of them, wrought by the hands of the givers with a feeling of gratitude. My presents were – from Miss Elizabeth Benson a black velvet Greek hat, elaborately worked with a pattern in chain stitch (from a design I gave) lined with pink silk, and decorated with a splendid variegated silk tassel. From Miss Sarah Benson a pair of purple velvet slippers wrought in chain stitch and bound with the fur of the gray Siberian squirrel; - From Mrs. Flood an elderly lady, a pair of red woolen knit cuffs to draw over the hand above the glove to keep the wrists warm. From Miss Lucy Finley (cousin of the Bensons) a gilt morocco case or box to hang against the wall and contain matches; - the front of the box being a running flower piece beautifully wrought in fine worsted. Beside these I had a plate full of little sugar bon-bons, etc, etc. After the company was admitted to the room and the presents had all been admired, thanks given, congratulations received, jokes passed etc., etc. we returned to the dining room (it being large) and there we danced until about 2 o'clock; stopping just before 12 long enough to fill our glasses with champagne all around and as the first stroke of the clock announced the new year, wishing each other a happy new year and many return of it - touching our glasses with those of the ladies etc. – etc. – etc.- etc. – we drank bumpers. I ought to have mentioned before that from another lady, a boarder, a Miss Spershott, I received a present of a purse at Christmas as a token of gratitude for services in saving some of her teeth and taking out half a dozen others.

P.M. – Mrs. Whistler called today and had two teeth filled. Yesterday while walking out I got a glimpse of His Majesty as he passed in a sledge; and tonight at 11 o'clock Colonel Todd is to call and take me to a masquerade at one of the theatres where it is supposed the great Autocrat will be, and where I may have an opportunity of seeing him to better advantage. As I shall return late I will bid you good – night now – so good night my dear wife.

Wednesday morning, January 2, 1846. – Went to the masquerade at half past 11 and returned at half past 2 – Emperor not there while I was. The theatre (one of the largest class) was so arranged that the stage and the area in front within the circle formed one immense room in which the people promenaded. Nearly all the women were young and wore black silk cloaks and black silk, satin, velvet, etc. and masks, covering the forehead and nose, having holes for the eyes and black lace for a sort of veil over the mouth and chin something like this sketch – which ugly as it is, looks quite as well as a majority of the masks.

The whole person is often so disguised, and the voices also, that it would be impossible for a man to detect his own wife if she were only cautious in her expressions. It is understood that a great deal of immorality results from this practice – the women may say or <u>hear</u> <u>said</u> anything she chooses without anyone knowing her – thus appointments, assignations, declarations, seductions and other things usually called gallantries follow as a matter of course. His Majesty gives his countenance to this custom so it is fashionable, and what is fashionable is proper of course. The men were not masked, except a very few – half a dozen perhaps while the others were many hundred perhaps 1,000 or 1,500 with half as many women. Today I have been operating a little ($12-) and have engagements for several days to come.

Thursday night, January 3, 1846. – Busy all day ($25.00) with one of our countrymen from Alexandroffsky. (By the way, heretofore I have spelled this word without the <u>double f</u>. It should be as here written or else with a <u>v</u> instead of the ff.) For some days past we have had a Russian Count, Countess, their daughter, and her governess as fellow boarders. The Countess sleeps in a room adjoining mine (N.B. - <u>door</u> <u>locked</u> and key on <u>her</u> side.) while the Count, her husband, sleeps in a room on the other side of the house. She is pretty and he is not, and is in bad health. The governess also is not bad looking and <u>she</u> sleeps in the room on the other side of me, with the key on <u>my</u> side; but whether the door is locked or not I don't know – I have not (nor she) ever opened it yet since the room has been occupied.

I think it would be well for me to get to Paris as soon as I can and present my letter to the Minister of War there before trying even Berlin. There seems to be such a disposition to adopt French plans and do as the French do that it seems to me this will be the best course. Today Miss Sarah Benson filled a little box with sugar toys for Eddy and George and asked me if I would take them home from her. She wrote something in the lid and I sealed the box and shall try to get it home safe; but for fear I do not succeed it will be best not to mention it to the boys. O Ellen! How I do long to see you all at home. I am afraid you will think me very old when you see me again – it seems to me that I am 10 years older than I was last winter.

O this horrid country! When shall I get out of it? – here comes a note from Major Whistler – with a request from Colonel Todd to tell me that he is making arrangements to start for Berlin – for <u>HOME</u>, glorious word! – On the 26 of this month. O my dear Country – happy – happy – thrice happy America! Let me but once set my feet upon thy shores, and – dam me if ever I leave them again. Good night.

Saturday night, January 5, 1846. – Very cold day – coldest yet this winter. Having no proper fur-lined cloak or "schube" to wear over the fur-lined coat of which I wrote you, I have not been out. I am to have a schube lined with wolf fur – very cheap and very warm – to travel in.

I am now negotiating with a man who proposes to buy the right to my invention for Denmark. Should he not "fly off the handle" before the papers are made out he will pay me in cash two thousand five hundred dollars and guarantee to give me in addition ten per cent of all he receives from the Government of Denmark for the use of the invention; he taking all the risks and paying all the expenses and using all his exertions to bring the matter before the Government of Denmark as soon as possible. I have been making him a set of drawings and shall let him have one of the models, some priming etc. and such other papers and documents and instructions as he may need if he adheres to our present arrangement. I hoped to be able to say positively that the money was paid, and indeed to send you some of it in this letter, but I must close it for the mail of Monday in order that it may reach you by the 4th of February steamer.

Colonel Todd expects to take the next steamer after – viz. 4th March – and perhaps he will bring you my next letter. The endorsed letter and bill of exchange you will use as you were directed to use the other to get the money.

Father may tell Major Smith what I have said about Denmark, and that as soon as I conclude my arrangement I will write him. Give our little boys extra kisses from papa and as usual take at least a dozen from me for yourself. The hope of soon being on my way toward you cheers me, and although not very well, still I feel determined to be so, and to get home as soon as my duty to my associates and myself and you will permit. Possibly I shall cross the Atlantic with Colonel Todd in March but you must not expect me then.

Remember me most affectionately and gratefully to Father and Mother for giving me such a good wife; and tell Mrs. Haag that I have not forgotten her coffee and hope to taste it again soon. Tomorrow is the great day here – being the 6th of January (Old Style) the day for blessing the water of the Neva. I hope to give you some account of the ceremony in my next letter. May all comforts you can enjoy be yours – I'll come home as soon as I can. God bless you all.

Forever yours,

Edward.

Chapter 12
(Eighth Letter)
A Patent Sale to Sweden and a Dentist Introduces His Craft

Via Ostender

Care of Harrison, Winans & Eastwick
No. 1, Crooked Line Chambers,
London
S. Hibernia
Mrs. Ellen S. Maynard
City of Washington D.C.
United States of America

St. Petersburg, Friday 11, January 1846.   **Page 1**
23, January 1846.

My Dear Ellen,

You know 'tis said that the first impression of anything is seldom easily obliterated; I wish it may be so with the letter provided you will take your <u>first</u> <u>impression</u> from the fact that I have concluded the sale of my right for Denmark and have this day received Bills of Exchange on London for the payment – five hundred pounds Sterling – say, two thousand five hundred dollars. By the terms of the sale I am to receive, in addition, ten per cent of all the Government of Denmark pays for the use of the right. All the costs, risks, charges etc.,etc., about the Patent are to be borne by the purchaser; who is Mr. Thomas Charles Grut, an Englishman – merchant – having extensive connections in business with various parts of Europe. He has purchased and sold (to be delivered this year) about a hundred ship loads of Russian lumber for English railroads – this lumber operation brought him here, and so brought us together. He talks of buying a farther interest after he has secured his right in Denmark provided it promises well. He speaks and writes several languages, - French, German, Danish, Swedish etc. besides his own and is evidently (from his letters) an upright, businessman. I have given him one of my models (a musketoon) a set of drawings – 200 or 300 rounds of priming and of the <u>entire</u> <u>process</u> of making the <u>priming</u>; and also I have given him samples of the paper to be used and have, in fact, satisfied him perfectly that he can not only have a machine made but that he can make the priming without any trouble.

Now, if this good impression is so good to console you for not leaving Russia within one or two weeks, at least, of the time I set in my last letter, then it will be of some use. How do you think <u>I</u> feel at not hearing from you for so long a time? I should have stayed at home until Professor Morse joins the opposite sides of the Atlantic.

There is a ballroom or rather a suite of Assembly rooms, including a ballroom, here, said to be the most magnificent in Europe. It is the place where the Nobles have their balls – where the diplomatic corps and the Imperial Family etc. attend. Perhaps I have mentioned the place before – it was damaged by fire lately but shows no trace of the element now. Last night by favor of my excellent friend Colonel Todd, I had the distinguished honor of attending a Ball there which commenced at about 10 and lasted <u>as</u> a <u>ball</u> until about 12 and then it became a masquerade, like the one I wrote about in my last letter. The dancing continued during the masquerade, a great many ladies being not masked. At about 12 His Majesty the Emperor, his son the heir to the throne, and his brother, the Grand Duke Michael arrived and they remained an hour or two the latter indeed was so much interested by one of the masks that he remained until after I came away – about 3 or 4 o'clock. I had a very good opportunity of seeing these great personages, and on my return will give you some ideas of them by comparison with people whom we may meet in our walks. (Here comes my hot water, so I must bathe and go to bed, Good night)

Saturday evening, January 12, 1846. - Today have done little or nothing except accompany the ladies to do some shopping. Saw many pretty things for the boys but have no place to put them; and besides, I should have to pay heavy duties at every frontier I passed going home. While out we called upon Mrs. Flood whom I mentioned in my last. I call her mother – (she is about our Mother's age) and she gave me a little paper box of toys for her grand children <u>Eddy</u> and <u>Dorzh</u>.

To continue my account of the masquerade; - It is the custom for the <u>lady</u> to take the <u>gentleman's</u> arm but not for him to ask her to promenade with <u>him</u>. She seizes hold of anyone she pleases and says what she pleases – sometimes telling a man things he don't like to hear; for which his only remedy is to get away from her – if he can. At this masquerade two masks seized me by the arm (one at a time) and each walked with me for some time – they pretending not to understand English very well and speaking it so brokenly and so mixed up with French and with voices so disguised that I could only guess from the matter of conversation who they were – till now I don't <u>know</u> them. Some very amusing intrigues are thus carried on – the same mask meeting and intriguing a man a dozen times without even making herself known to him. In this way third persons are very often employed to let the gentleman know what feelings exist for him in some lady's heart – this third person thus acting the go-between without exposing herself etc.

It is said that the Emperor was so greatly interested once by a mask who intrigued him that he promised to grant her a wish if she would tell him who she was; She complied – unmasked herself – and demanded the release from imprisonment, or exile, of one of her relations who was then suffering for some offense against the Majesty. The order was given immediately for the release.

This, before I inked it looked a little like Nicholas, the Emperor, but the eye is blotted and now the expression is spoiled.

The Grand Duke Michael is something like this – isn't he a beauty?

A Staircase by which you mount to the second story of the building in which are the rooms. B reception room. C D E F G H I J K rooms, all forming parts of the establishment, H I J K were not apparently <u>public</u> so I did not enter them. L the dancing floor, some 3 or 4 or 5 feet lower than the promenade M which it and is on a level with the other rooms. N a place screened off with drapery for the imperial family. O music. P steps leading down to L. All around L extends a colonnade in imitation of polished white marble. Q stairs leading up to the Gallery and some other rooms. F and G refreshments rooms tables being set where you see dotted lines. Suspended over L were 8 chandeliers, very large and very grand; and between the columns about 50 more of the same character but smaller. Around L and between the steps are seats for those who choose to sit and covered with scarlet cloth. (Sketch missing)

Mr. Grut (he pronounces it groot) wishes to have the right for Sweden provided he pays to my credit 500 pounds sterling within about a month, at Copenhagen or Berlin – to which I agree, and have made a draft of an agreement; he is to have the right provided he pays within the time. He cannot say <u>now</u> that he will take it, because he does not now see how he may be able to arrange his business so as to devote his time to <u>this</u> matter; but if he can arrange it satisfactorily and can induce his brother-in-law at Copenhagen (who is very rich) to join him perhaps he will not only take Sweden but a <u>large</u> <u>part</u>, or perhaps <u>all</u>, of Europe. He even talks of buying the entire right for the world, except that part sold to the U.S. I have convinced him that if he can <u>control</u> the business, the profits will be greater than if he has <u>competitors</u> in other parts of Europe – inasmuch as the greater the number of arms made by one establishment, the greater the profit upon <u>each</u> arm; and so of the primers, - one establishment being sufficient to supply the world. Sweet dreams to you.

Good night.

Monday P.M. January 14, 1846. – Yesterday I went with a party of ladies and gentlemen to see the "ice-hills" at Catherinehoff – 2 or 3 miles out. Here is a sketch which may assist in giving you an idea of them.

Imagine this to be an artificial hill – being in fact a flight of stairs on one side leading up to a floor about 40 or 50 feet from the ground, and a steep hill of ice on the other side – with a level continuation of the road that leads down the hill, as you see by the line, for some 20 or 30 rods- the road being made of thick ice, smooth as glass. At the end of the road is another just such hill with another road by the side of the first one, so arranged that you slide from one almost to the stairs of the other, both ways, having only to go up stairs at each end. There are men employed there who sit upon pretty little cushioned sleds, take a lady on before them and down they go as if falling from a precipice and then away over the level road at the rate of a locomotive. There are also large sleds for 6 or 8 persons. I tried both kinds and found the sport very good, perhaps from its novelty and excitement. You see a couple on the road – the man behind guide the sled by touching the ice behind on each side with his hands. Those who are accustomed to the sport go down alone.

The Count Bouterliny who rooms opposite me has just called to ask me to visit with him, the Princess – somebody - I forgot the name already – this afternoon – and I am to go as soon as I hear from or see Colonel Todd who is to send or come to me at 3 o'clock. The Princess wishes to consult me professionally having probably learned something of me from the Count.

If I let my beard grow in its present cut until I get home I may expect to be a stranger to my old acquaintances – we shall see what we shall see.

About that purse given to me as a Christmas present and a sort of token of gratitude for services – the giver is rapidly acquiring a very bad reputation – almost everyone in the house suspects her of improper intimacy with one of the boarders – I for one suspect her very strongly, and am humiliated that I should have been so taken in by appearances as to pity her for not having friends and advisors in a country where everybody – and everything that ought to be held sacred in woman – is the subject of scandal – and so being led, through a wish to serve her, to giving her many hours of labor that might have been bestowed upon some more deserving person. I do not wish to make an enemy of her by returning the purse <u>now</u> – but I intend to return it when about to go away. – I do not wish to have any such remembrances from <u>such</u> people. God forgive me if I do her injustice.

If Major Smith and Tyson are entitled to <u>any</u> part of the sum received for Denmark then their part is two-thirds – perhaps enough to cover expenses I shall have paid with <u>my</u> <u>own</u> money by the time I return, but which <u>were</u> to have been paid by <u>them</u> according to the written agreement. So of course they cannot expect me to send <u>them</u> any part of the proceeds of this sale. I shall write them about it.

Good Night.

Princess Volkovsky was the lady whose house the Count drove me to; - but it was a young widow, a friend or relative staying with her, who needed my services. "Swelled face" etc. etc. Is to come at 1 tomorrow and see if I can do anything for her. The Volkovsky's are said to be in very high favor at Court.

I have just concluded the arrangement about Sweden with Mr. Grut. He is authorized to take out and use the patent for that kingdom and its dependencies for five hundred pounds sterling, provided he deposits the money subject to my draft by the first of April next. This will enable him to go on and patent the invention at once should his friends at Copenhagen think proper to join him. Should they wish to take a greater share, they will make an offer with that view. Good night.

Tuesday night, January 15, 1846. – True to the Russian character for good faith and punctuality, the lady who engaged to come today neither came nor sent any message. I am leading a very stupid sort of life now – no business, no amusement, no exercise except at the risk of freezing my nose – the mercury being today 22 degrees (Reaumur's scale) below zero – equal to about 50 below the freezing point at Fahrenheit scale. Men's beards look as if they were lathered and ready for the razor. I rode out nevertheless, wearing 3 coats, with one of the Miss Bensons; she to make some purchases and I for company for her and occupation for myself.

If I were to stay here much longer without something to avert my mind from my home and family I really think I should go mad – have a brain fever or some other calamity. I must get home as soon as possible – I feel that truth more and more every day. I feel fully ten years older than I did a year ago – at least I think so – perhaps it is because I am so tired and sick of Russian life – made up as it is of mere out-side show and despicable intrigues – dreadfully demoralizing- nothing like truth, sincerity or faithfulness being credited. O my head my poor head! Why the devil did I ever come to this state of feeling? Well – never mind – time – new countries – home – family, and the love of my dear, dear Ellen – shall I find the same dear girl in you that you were when I left you? But why ask the question? I must – I will believe it – you will love me so tenderly – O Ellen! Would to God I had never left you! – but we shall be happy together again – I am sure of it – and I shall love you all the better perhaps – if that be possible. – How happy I was that week at Springfield! – Such a change! – And shall we not be so always when I return? Yes, yes, - we will- forever-forever. Heaven help you my dear wife. I have not failed to kiss you and our dear boys for a single night since I saw you. Ah! How pleasantly you look upon me from the locket – that sweet smile, and that look of love – how they have cheered me for these many, many O how many, long days!

Good night – good night

Wednesday 23rd January 1846. - I have been waiting since a week ago yesterday to get out of the humour in which I then wrote before I should go on. I have, thank God! Rather better spirits as the time approaches for my departure, which is now fixed for next Tuesday, Wednesday, or Thursday – Colonel Todd seeming to have had as clear an idea of his exit from St. Petersburg as of his exit from the world.

I have for the last week tried to shake off my ennui as much as possible by dining with the Colonel – attending masquerades, riding and walking out etc. One day, having learned that, as usual in winter, some Laplanders or Finlanders had arrived with their reindeers and sledges for amusing such as chose to ride by such conveyance, I went and took a turn for the novelty of the thing.

This rough sketch may give you some idea of the affair provided you imagine 4 such animals abreast, each having a wide strap for a collar from which passes a string, between the legs, back to the sledge. The heads are tied together, leaving 2 or 3 feet between, and one line to the near deer completes the harness. With a long light pole the driver ever and anon doth deal the dear dreadful digs in diverse delicate places; whereupon the scamper off at full speed.

Today I filled 6 cavities for Mr. Clay, who <u>was</u> Secretary of our Legation here but is <u>now</u> Charge d'Affaires, since Colonel Todd is no longer minister. Tomorrow I am invited by Major Whistler to dine with him and meet there some of our countrymen – of whom there are half dozen in and near St. Petersburg. Good night – sweet dreams – I had such a happy dream of home a few night ago that I was vexed on waking. Good night.

Sunday P.M. January 27, 1846. - This morning Colonel Todd sent me word that the Emperor's Physician would call upon me at 12 or 1 o'clock – and fortunately for both him and me he did come just in time to witness the performance of the operation he came to inquire about, - I having a patient in the chair one of whose teeth I had prepared for plugging, the nerve of the tooth being dead. I had an interpreter also for whom I plugged 2 teeth in the same way several months ago and at the same time about twenty other cavities all of which I showed and explained to Dr. Arndt; and so he seemed highly delighted – regretted that I was going away soon – desired to know if I would return – would tell the Emperor of the operation and me, etc., etc., etc., etc. He had been gone just a little time when I received a letter from Parmly (who is at Paris) informing me that the Grand Duchess Helen had written to Dr. Brewster to know if he could recommend me, and that Brewster had written an answer giving me a "character" and had asked him (Parmly) to write me about it. As it is understood that I am to leave town with Colonel Todd this coming week, I may not hear anything more of the matter. It would require a very large offer to induce me to live here.

I have ventured upon a little purchase – a beautiful fur lining for a cloak for you. It is such as you never saw, I think – the beautiful, rich, gray fur of the Russian squirrel. In order to avoid paying duties I am having it put into a morning gown for my use.

Yesterday Mrs. Whistler sent me a little basket and a note; the latter of which will perhaps gratify you as much as the contents of the former will please you. The basket contained 2 children's dresses for George and John, a satchel for Eddy and a bag for a watch to hang on the wall – the bag being a beautiful slipper to hang by the heel. I have also bought you a pair of beautiful velvet and morocco Turkey slippers, - perfect gems – but perhaps I ought not say much of these things as I may lose them before I get home. There are many things here that I want, and which I have made arrangements to have procured and sent to me next summer, if I send funds to buy them with. The Miss Bensons say they will procure anything for you or the children that I may direct and have all packed and shipped in order. It is now high time for bed, Good night. God bless you.

Friday night, February 1, 1846. – Yesterday Colonel Todd wrote to Baron Krudener, Master of Ceremonies to Her Imperial Highness the Grand Duchess Helen informing him that it was understood by me that she had expressed a desire to avail herself of my services; - that my departure from this Capitol was fixed for Saturday of this week; but if it was her wish to employ me professionally I would delay my departure to enable her to do so – etc. To which the Baron replied that it was Her Imperial Highness's wish that I should visit her and that she would address me upon the subject – or something to that effect. We have postponed until Tuesday of next week our time of starting; and, if necessary, Colonel Todd will wait a week for me to get through with the Grand Duchess. Major Whistler advises me to stay if the Court wish to employ me, as it will be a compliment to me and to the Profession in America.

I have another inducement for staying to operate for the Grand Duchess; - she is the wife of the Grand Duke Michael, who condemned my gun, and who may be induced, perhaps, to change his mind if I can have an opportunity of conversing with him upon the subject.

I must now close my letter for the mail of tomorrow. You will find in it the "second of exchange" of a bill for $100. – the "first" I sent by my last letter. If you have not received the "first" you can get this one cashed; if you have received the first only one of them will be of use to you. You will also find enclosed the "first of exchange" of a bill for $500 which you will easily get collected as I have before directed. I hope to write you another letter by the same steamer in which I will enclose the "second" of this last named bill and perhaps to tell you how I get on with practicing as "Dentist to the Court of His Imperial Majesty the Emperor of all the Russians".

I think of nothing to say about our affairs at home – it is so long since I have heard from you that I can have no idea of the present condition of things with you. I trust all and fully to your good sense – do what you think best in all things and I feel sure I shall be satisfied. Take a thousand kisses for yourself and the dear children. Remember me affectionately to Father and Mother and George and John and May and Zebulon; and give my respects to such as inquire for me. I think it will be well to continue to retain the office until I return or, direct otherwise. I still hope to return in April, with Colonel Todd who will be a month later than he expected. I trust this remittance of funds will maintain the family comfortably until I do return or send money. I shall write to Major Smith by same steamer advising him of the sale of Denmark and that I have thought proper not to send him any part of the proceeds inasmuch as I shall require perhaps more than the whole sum for necessary expenses in travelling. That which I send you is of my earnings, and part of that which I brought here as my private funds. Instead of Smith and Tyson paying my expenses I have so far paid them all myself; and it was understood that I was to have them repay me out of the receipts of sales. God bye for a little time longer. I dream of you and home often and long to be with you again.

What do you think of coming here to live for five or ten years provided I am requested to take a permanent situation as Dentist to the Court? I'll come home after you and the children and you will have almost as many acquaintances here as at Washington. Of course I will not take the place unless it shall be made very profitable – so profitable that I can retire in five years. More of this in my next letter. God bless you my dear girl – you deserve all and more than all the riches and honors I can bring you. Good night.

Forever yours, Edward.

Chapter 13

(Ninth Letter)

Her Imperial Highness Grand Duchess Helen Needs a Dentist
Via Ostender

Care of Harrison, Winans & Eastwick
No. 1, Crooked Line Chambers,
London

S. Hibernia
Mrs. Ellen S. Maynard
City of Washington D.C.
United States of America

St. Petersburg, Sunday 3/15 February 1846   **Page 1**

My Dear Ellen,

Yesterday morning I sent off my last letter to you enclosing the "first" of bill for $500 and the "second" of one for $100. I shall enclose in this the "second" of the 500 bill so that if you have not received the first you can use this. The "first" of the 100 bill I sent in a previous letter.

I had neither time nor space in my last to tell you that on Friday last I visited what is here called "The Hermitage", - a Palace appropriated principally, I believe, to paintings and other objects of art. I wrote you in a previous letter of my having seen many pictures by the old masters of Painting – Ruebens, Rembrandt, Correggio, Salvator Rosa, Dolci, Gerard Douw, Loraine, etc., etc., etc. Well at the Hermitage are many rooms filled with the works of these and a host of other celebrated artists. Some of the pictures were such as one might study with pleasures for hours together and others were merely interesting on account of their authors and as showing some peculiarity of style or management of color. More about them when I see you.

Yesterday morning came a request from Her Imperial Highness the Grand Duchess Helen that I attend her at the Michael Palace at half past 12. I went – I was received and conducted to her by one of the Ladies of the Court. The result of the interview was that I am to go again tomorrow at 12 to commence operations upon Her Highness's teeth. What is required I don't know; but I have promised to stay a week if necessary, for the completion of the work. She tells me she is very nervous – can bear but a little pain or fatigue without exhaustion etc., etc.

Above: Grand Duke Michael's Wife Grand Duchess Helen.

Monday night, February 4, 1846. - Today I commenced operating upon the teeth of the Grand Duchess Helen. She urged me very hard to remain a month, and <u>two</u> months if I could do so. She will require my services for two weeks probably and she is anxious that I should operate for other members of the Imperial Family. She has removed one of the obstacles by saying that my extra luggage (box of models etc.) shall be sent to Berlin. (These I could not take by any public conveyance over land.) She seems so well pleased with my commencement, and is so very amiable that I entertain a hope that I may yet have her influence to induce the Grand Duke to re-examine my gun. This is s great inducement and one that Smith and Tyson will, I am sure, consider a sufficient justification for my remaining here a little longer. And if she <u>does</u> exert that influence it will not be limited to Russia, for she is a woman to have great weight in the German States, she having been, at the time of her marriage, a Princess of Württemberg.

It must also be considered that, more for Smith and Tyson than for myself, I have lost nearly a year's time from my practice, and the consequent loss will not be more than repaid by the very distinguished honor I now receive by staying a few weeks. I have, however, not trusted to my own sense of justice and propriety in this matter but have taken the advice of Colonel Todd (who is a personal friend of Tyson's) and of others who all justify me in staying. Major Whistler says "it will pay" - that is to say I shall be compensated; So that perhaps there will be no pecuniary loss. The lady who receives me at the Palace and who does much of t he talking for the Grand Duchess, asked me about what would be considered a compensation for my services etc., etc., so that Her Highness might have some idea of what ought to be paid etc., etc., etc. telling me that I was not to take into account what the Grand Duchess might be disposed to do afterward – by which I suppose she meant some present in addition or something of that sort. She did not seem to be altogether satisfied with my telling her that my time was worth 50 silver rubles ($37 ½) per day. – and we are to talk more about it tomorrow at 12 at which time I am to visit and operate for the Grand Duchess again. From the very great desire manifested by Her Imperial Highness to have me remain I have no doubt that I shall be induced to do so for a month; and I think that even my dear Ellen will pardon and justify me for staying away from her and our dear little boys so much longer when she reflects upon the probable profits and the certain honor of having her husband reach one of the highest stations to which one of his Profession can aspire.

As this letter must go to the Post Office before I go to the Palace tomorrow I am obliged to finish it without telling you of the final arrangement; but I shall give you a full account in my next. Colonel Todd is fully determined I believe to go by the 4th of April Steamer so that you may expect to see him about the 20th and that will be better than a letter to you. I do not think I will send anything by him for you, for fear he will be careless and lose something; and it will be of less consequence because I shall follow so soon. I shall write to Berlin to have my letters forwarded to me at this place so that I may say that I shall from you in about 2 weeks; - but the date of your letters will be, some of them, 3 months back.

 Kiss Eddy and George and John for me – for their papa – and do not let them neglect to kiss you for me every night. Dear little fellows – I write as if they were all alive; yet – they may be all buried - and my dear Ellen too she may never read this except she look down from heaven to do so – but I must not allow myself to think of such a possibility. God grant you all long life and great happiness.

My affection to Father, and Mother, and George, and John, and May, and Zebulon, and to Marcia, if you write her. By the way, she will be delighted to hear that her <u>beautiful</u> brother-in-law is "Dentist to the Imperial Court of Russia".

Father may give my respects to Dr. Hall and tell him that the Emperor's Physician has visited me for information about some of my operations - that he expressed his gratification at witnessing the operation of plugging the cavity of the nerve and of the appearance and result of many of my other operations; that I am now operating for the Imperial Family and have been invited to remain here and practice for his Imperial Court; and that I have consented to remain here a month or two for that purpose.

I must close this letter with my most earnest wish that it may find you all well and happy. Try to be as contented as possible and receive all the consolation you can from my present prospects of honor and fortune. Keep up your spirits "be a good girl" and take good care of our boys – I shall expect to see great things in them on my return home. D. is quite as anxious about returning as I am; he says very often that he won't stand it any longer; but I encourage him with promises of extra compensation if he remains faithful until we return to America. Good bye.

Forever yours,

Edward.

Chapter 14
(Tenth Letter)
Dr. Maynard Receives Approval for His Dental Techniques

Via Ostender
Care of Harrison, Winans & Eastwick
No. 1, Crooked Line Chambers,
London

Mrs. Ellen S. Maynard
City of Washington D.C.
United States of America

St. Petersburg, 7/19 February 1846   **Page 1**

My Dear Ellen,

Since closing my last letter to you (on Monday last) (it is now Thursday) I have operated every day at the Michael Palace for Her Imperial Highness the Grand Duchess Helen (excuse me for writing the title so fully – I do it to give you an idea of the way such people are spoken of here). Her Imperial Highness has deigned to compliment me very highly upon my operations thus far and upon my manner of operating – "never had a Dentist operate for her who was so delicate and easy in his operations etc., etc., etc., etc." – the same that you and I have heard a thousand times before; but still very gratifying on account of the complimentor. While I was operating for her yesterday the Emperor came to the Palace and she had to go out of the room to speak to meet him; and on her return she told me she had taken occasion to speak to him of me, etc., etc. and afterward said she would send immediately for Dr. Arndt (the Emperor's Physician) and talk with him about the way, if any, in which a school of Dentistry can be established here, under my direction.

We had a good deal of conversation upon the subject of my returning here in summer or autumn with my family, (and such things as I should require for the practice of my profession) to have for, say five years) the appointment of Dentist to the Court. I told her I could not think of leaving a full practice at home to come here unless I came as Dentist to the Court, so that I might step into a full practice here at once; and this not only an account on pecuniary consideration, but also, because unless I were known here as Dentist to the Court, I should forfeit a high rank in a respectable and useful Profession at home to be classed with charlatans here – thus doing not only myself, but my family great injustices. This view seemed to please her. She had not learned yesterday when I was at the Palace, whether any other members of the Imperial Family required my services now, but she was to let me know in the course of the day. No answer has come yet and she is probably waiting to tell me tomorrow when I am to visit her again – she wishing to rest today while I go to the Palace of one of the Ministers – Count Kleinmichel – to operate for him and the Countess, to whom the Grand Duchess wrote yesterday, recommending me to them, and to whom she requested me to go yesterday afternoon when I left her. I did go –

examined the Count's mouth – am to operate for him today from 1 to 4. I have promise to remain for Her Imperial Highness until Tuesday next; and, if other members of the Imperial Family wish it, to remain a month or so. Colonel Todd cannot remain longer than Tuesday. Major Whistler seems to think that if <u>I</u> <u>stay</u> <u>now</u>, and have an office etc., etc. the fame I have already acquired would lead to a capital business for a time at least – and that If I found after a month or two that the prospect for future business would justify it, it would be better to <u>send</u> for you than to <u>go</u> for you, as the fever might abate during my absence etc., etc. He is very anxious to have me stay, I am sure, and I have had a great deal of talk with him about how much more it costs to live here than at Washington - what difficulties I should encounter from not yet speaking French of Russian etc., etc.

There are many things you would like here better than their substitutes with us in America; and first of all, the houses are very, very far superior to ours in point of comfort and elegance. True, there are few families in circumstances like ours who occupy a whole house – there may be a dozen families in the same house; but they have nothing more to do with each other than our family has with Mrs. Hill's. Each family has its complete suite of rooms, kitchen and all, and is independent of all others. In fact the great passage and stair case running up through the house may be considered as merely part of the street enclosed to protect it from the weather and warned for the comfort of those persons whose doors open upon it. And then the furniture is beautiful and cheap and in much greater variety than with us. A thousand things of necessity and luxury may be had here that were never heard of with us except by those who have seen them here and described them. You will think I have changed my mind about Russia – I have written so much about its dullness etc., but you must reflect upon my being here almost without employment for 4 or 5 months after having been very industrious for ten years; and worse than all, separated from my family and not even <u>hearing</u> <u>from</u> <u>them</u> for 2 or 3 months!

If this is not enough to make one discontented and anxious to go away and be where he can at least hear of his friends then I have something yet to learn about "blue devils." As for the excessive cold here – so much dreaded by those who contemplate coming here – I assure you I have suffered much less this winter from cold than I do every winter at Washington. I do not say that I suffer less than I shall after my return – because I have learned how to avoid suffering from cold so much as we do, but I do mean to say that, for one whose business does not require him to be out of doors much, the "cold of Russia" is a bug-bear. For instance, at the moment there is perhaps a peck of coals burning in the peetch in my room and the temperatures in my room and the temperature is delightful while horses, coachmen's beards and all things upon which any moisture rests, are white with frost – the mercury being this morning a little over 40 degrees below freezing point by Fahrenheit's thermometer. So far from dreading my ride of 2 or 3 miles to the Count's this morning, I look upon it as a pleasure. And now I must go and enjoy it.

Thursday Midnight, February 7, 1846. – The Count was so much engaged with business that he could not sit today; but had his little daughter do so. Removed the tartar from her teeth and filled two cavities. When I returned home to dinner I found a note from Mademoiselle Troubat (the lady who attends upon the Grand Duchess when I am with her) asking me to come and see her (at the Palace) so went at the hour appointed and learned that the Grand Duchess – something- wife of the Hereditary Grand Duke, wished my services, and that it was probable that some others of the Imperial Family would also require some operations; but that during next week none of them would be disposed to sit for me as it is the week of the Carnival.

Great preparations are making here now for the sports and festivities of that week. So it is now settled that I am to remain here for a short time longer.

The Colonel starts for Berlin tomorrow night; and regrets very much, apparently that he is not to have my company. He has incurred some expenses for us both which he would not have incurred had he not calculated upon my going with him so I t will be no more than justice that I relieve him of fair proportion of the expense of the trip when that can be ascertained, - not of course until the trip is made and the vehicle sold, etc., etc. Good night – but I should have said that I also learned from Mademoiselle Troubat (Troo-bah) that Dr. Arndt had given to the Grand Duchess a most flattering description of my operations – indeed had said quite as much to her as he did to me about them; and that he was to talk with His Majesty about the school etc., etc., etc. Good night. I shall write for your letters tomorrow.

Friday P.M., February 8, 1846. – Today I filled three cavities for the Grand Duchess Helen. She seems more and more delighted both with the operations and the manner of performing them. She told me today that she wished me to operate for her children next week. She is extremely amiable – no nonsense – not being offended at being addressed as "you" instead of "Your Imperial Highness" – she has too much sense not to perceive that my manner of speech is the result of a republican education and she seems too kind not to make all due allowance for it.

While I was at the palace Dr. Arndt called to see me (at Miss Benson's) and left a message for me to prepare me for another visit he is to make tomorrow morning. He has evidently been sent to "feel of me" so as to have some idea of what offer should be made me before they make any. He told Miss Benson that the Grand Duchess Helen was nothing less than enchanted with my skill. Etc., etc. and wished her (Miss Benson) to ask me to consider upon the conditions on which I would stay here and practice my Profession.

After dinner I have to go and take leave of Colonel Todd (who will have my letters sent from Berlin) and I shall try to see and talk with Major Whistler whose advice is worth more to me in this matter than Colonel Todd's.

Sunday Morning, February 10, 1846. – The Colonel has gone and will probably see you about the 20th of April and tell you more about my matters. (N.B. Say nothing – but if he asks you for a loan of money or asks you for a sum which will be due him as being my share of loss on the carriage he bought to go to Berlin in – tell him you are not provided with the means of doing so.) Dr. Arndt called yesterday morning and wished to know upon what conditions I wished to come here to practice and upon what footing I wished to be placed. Whether I wished to be attached to the Court at a fixed salary, and so, be compelled to go with the court wherever it might be traveling for pleasure or health or other purposes – or would I rather have a private practice and still be Dentist to the Court, but without the fixed salary – the Court paying according to the service they receive. Dr. Arndt recommended the latter – having tried both ways as Physician. After he had stated the object of his visit he wished me to write down an answer after reflecting upon the matter etc. – to which I answered that I had not come here to practice – that other business and a desire to travel brought me here – that being detained unexpectedly I was induced to practice for some of my compatriots and a few friends – that I had not sought for practice at Court but rather had been drawn into it by the urgent request of the Grand Duchess Helen; - that my practice at home was ample for all my wants there; and that to leave it – break up my establishment and come here would subject me to much loss of time and money. That I was fully sensible of the honor conferred upon me and not without professional ambition; but not prepared to make any proposition as he wished. Should His Majesty be disposed to make any proposition to me, I should be happy to consider it, and if the inducement to come was sufficient to justify me in complying with His wishes I would be glad to arrange the matter to His satisfaction. This he was evidently not prepared for – but as he saw that it was perfectly fair and honorable he could make no objection. Of course I will not consent to come here at all without great inducements and if any proposition is made I shall have all the advantage of the compliment of <u>being</u> <u>asked</u> rather than <u>being</u> <u>accepted</u> – quit a difference. And then I shall conclude no arrangement, however advantageous it may seem, until I hear from home and learn how my dear Ellen may view the subject of our living here for the next five years.

Fearing that Colonel Todd may be detained on his journey to Berlin I have written to our Minister there to send me all letters he may have now, or receive for me up to 2 weeks after Colonel Todd's arrival; This will give me a month to stay here – quit long enough to ascertain if anything can be done with the gun. Yesterday the Grand Duchess Helen was too unwell to sit for me but requested me to examine the teeth of one of her daughters – the Grand Duchess something – haven't learned the names of the children yet. From there (the Michael Palace) I went to that of Count Kleinmichel (Kline-mik-el), and continued my operations for his daughter. On Monday I go to Count Kleinmichels again; and shall on that day learn when the Grand Duchess Helen wishes me to operate for herself or children again. This being the week of the Carnival everybody will be disposed to enjoy the sports of the time rather than suffer the inconvenience of having their teeth operated upon.

Monday night, February 11, 1846. – Have been operating at Count Kleinmichel's for his daughters – young Countesses*

Here a Count's sons are all Counts and a Count's daughters are all Countesses; and so of a Prince; - all the sons and daughters are Princes and Princesses. Have received no message from the Grand Duchess Helen today, so don't know when I shall go tomorrow. I may yet hear from her tonight. Good night.

Tuesday night, February 12, 1846. – Have been all day at Count Kleinmichel's operating for the young Countesses. Tonight there came a message for me to go to the Michael Palace tomorrow at 10 to operate for Her Imperial Highness the Grand Duchess Marie (Mah-ree) – daughter of the Grand Duchess Helen. My friends are congratulating me upon my good fortune in being called to practice for the Imperial Family and Court; - they consider my fortune as already made, and I think I ought by all means to stay here if I intend to follow the practice of Dentistry. Good night. Pleasant dreams to you.

Wednesday night, February 13, 1846. – Went as requested and removed tartar from the teeth of the Grand Duchess Marie; and at about 1 P.M. to Count Kleinmichels and continued operations for his two daughters. Tomorrow at 11 I go to the Michael Palace again to operate for another Grand Duchess – sister of Marie. Next week I am to operate for His Imperial Highness the Grand Duke Alexander – the " Cesarovitch" – heir to the throne; - from this circumstance, next to His Majesty, the greatest man in Russia. Good night.

Thursday night, February 14, 1846. – Went to the Michael Palace today. Grand Duchess Catherine who was to sit was prevented by other business from doing so. Went thence to Count Kleinmichel's and continued operations for one of the young ladies and finished with the other. Tomorrow am to go to the Michael Palace again.

This P.M. I visited some of the temporary structures for amusements during the carnival. Saw some very good pantomime playing – very like what we saw at Niblo's by the Ravels. Most of the amusements, however, are such as American children 10 years old would be ashamed of; yet here men and women as well as children eagerly crowding to see such contemptible trash. – Riding around a ring, cider-mill fashion, behind or on a little wooden horse – or ditto in a boat – or shocking imitation of a railroad car – or ditto in a sort of swinging box. Of course these are not the Gentlemen and Ladies of Russia; but still they are of a class that <u>we</u> should not expect to see in such places.

(* March 30, 1876. Several years ago I was told that these young Countesses were natural daughters of the Emperor Nicholas, by the sister of the Countess Kleinmichel. E.M.)

Friday night, February 15, 1846. – Went to the Michael Palace today. Removed tartar for Her Imperial Highness the Grand Duchess Catherine, and plugged one tooth for her mother the Grand Duchess Helen. Am to go again on Monday next to same place and continue operations. Today the Grand Duchess Helen <u>again</u> told me she was very anxious that I should come here and settle. This daughter Catherine is a beautiful woman – such eyes, and such lips! – O how happy she might be if she were <u>not</u> a Duchess and compelled to live such an unnatural sort of life; - yet for aught I know she is happy now; - but I was led to that expression by the thought of how little liberty of choice people of her rank must have. Now that I have the excitement of business I am in better spirits and better health. Good night.

Saturday P.M., February 16, 1846. – Today finished at Count Kleinmichel's; - the Countess Kleinmichel being frightened at my charge, declines having her own teeth operated upon. "Could not pay my bill today, but would send for me to come and get my pay some day next week" – to which I replied (through the lady who brought the answer) that my time was so much occupied that I might not be able to come when she should send for me, and that it would be better, as it would be less trouble to her, to send the money to me. The lady said she thought that would do, and so I came away.

This morning a Colonel somebody sent for me to come and see him, professionally. But learning that he was sick and confined to his room and had nobody in the house who speaks English, I sent word that unless he was suffering pain it would be useless for me to visit him; and that it would be better for him to come and see me when he recovered his health so far as to ride out – which he hoped to do in a few days.

Tuesday P.M., February 19, 1846. - Yesterday morning received notice that I was not to go to the Michael Palace until <u>this</u> morning, - (their Imperial Highnesses were up late at a ball the night before – so couldn't sit.) Today I plugged 2 cavities for the Grand Duchess Marie. (N.B. Don't say <u>what</u> or <u>how</u> <u>much</u> I am doing with the teeth of the Imperial Family; - only say that I am operating for them. There may be some teeth to be inserted for someone and it is not pleasant to anybody to have their teeth talked about unless they are particularly good. You might say that I was operating for several of the Grand Duchesses, but not say what ones.) Tomorrow I have no engagement except one at home at 4 P.M. to apply medicine to a tooth for our countrywoman Mrs. Harrison. Day after tomorrow I go to the Michael Palace again.

About this Palace; - imagine our <u>Capital</u> to be converted into a dwelling house and you will have some idea of the <u>extent</u> of this Palace; but there is nothing in Washington, nor probably in America by which to give you any idea of its <u>interior</u> magnificence. I will try to tell you something of it when I see you. I have been compelled to get some new clothes. My coat that I got in N.Y., (just before I left America) has been mended once or twice, and now it needs it again; and as I have to operate in a dress coat at the Palaces it became necessary to get another.

Thursday P.M., February 21, 1846. – Today I have been at the "Michehielovsky Dvoretz" – Michael Palace. Commenced preparing to plug a large molar tooth in which the nerve has been dead so long that all the inside of the tooth has to be cut out – being decaying so extensively. I told the owner of it – the Grand Duchess Catherine – that she might have a great deal of pain and swelling of the face etc. as the socket of the tooth was diseased; but that this operation was the only one that offered any hope of saving the tooth – which tooth by the way has been plugged twice before in the same place – once by Brewster and once by a Mr. Waite, of London, who was here some years ago. The Grand Duchess tells me she had a great deal of trouble from the tooth after the operations.

Friday P.M., February 22, 1846. - Today I plugged the fangs of the tooth above-mentioned; and tomorrow at 11 I am to go again and finish the operation unless I receive notice that there is pain about the tooth. Again today I explained the operation - repeating what I said yesterday about this being the only possible means of saving the tooth; and that, however well the operation might be performed, still it might not save it – as the disease around the tooth might be so far advanced that removing the original cause might not <u>now</u> succeed. I have been thus particular with explanations to the Grand Duchess because this is the first operation of the kind ever performed for any member of the Imperial Family, and is performed under not very promising circumstances. Should <u>this</u> fail, all confidence in the operation performed under <u>any</u> circumstances, would be lost; notwithstanding that I have performed it here under even worse circumstances than attend this; - and simply because they will not take the trouble to enquire. I expect your letters will arrive next Monday; and you may imagine my anxiety about them when you reflect that the last letter I received was closed on the 10th of November, almost four months ago! God grant that I may hear that you are all well and happy.

Saturday P.M. February 23, 1846. – Today I finished the plug commenced yesterday – there having been no uneasiness about the tooth since yesterday. Also removed decay in two places – same mouth – for both which operations Her Imperial Highness, the patient, deigned to compliment me in a very flattering manner; - whereupon, of course, I made my best bow. Am to go to the same place again next Tuesday unless I am sent for to go on that day to operate for Her Imperial Highness the Tsarina; for whom by the way I was to operate <u>this</u> week; but her sickness interfered with that arrangement. Today Mademoiselle Troubat enquired what my prices would be for operating for persons not of the Imperial Family; - saying that there were some ladies who wished me to operate for them.

Monday P.M., February 25, 1846. - Yesterday I received a request to visit His Imperial Highness the Grand Duke <u>Michael</u> this morning at 10 – and before seeing <u>him</u> to see and talk with Dr. Wiley, his Physician. I went – saw Dr. Wiley and learned that the Grand Duke wished me to examine his teeth – but that first he wished me to examine the mouth of his favorite valet-de-chambre of his who, two months ago, had a tooth extracted or broken off and had suffered greatly ever since. The man was called in and I found that to make a proper examination it would be necessary to cut open the gum; to which he objected – saying that it might increase his sufferings which were now abating under the effects of some external applications; - but that if the pains continue he would have done whatever I thought proper. Dr. Wiley acquiesced in this proposition, and then conducted me to the Grand Duke who was so busy that he postponed the examination, merely taking time to thank me for visiting his servant.

This is the day on which the post is to arrive with your letters according to my calculations. O how I long for them. I will not allow myself to anticipate bad news – but so long a time – so many things may have occurred to give you uneasiness or great anxiety or you may, some of you – but why write this? Enough – I must wait.

I am to dine today with Mr. W. H. Ropes, an <u>American</u> <u>merchant</u> long settled here; that is to say, he is in the <u>American</u> <u>trade</u>; and he is also an American by birth and education. I believe there are only about half a dozen or perhaps ten, including women Americans in Petersburg all counted. Children <u>not</u> counted, of which there are perhaps many more. One great advantage children have here is that they may easily acquire all modern polite languages, English, French, German, Italian, Spanish, etc., etc., etc.

Tuesday P.M. February 26, 1846. – This morning I found <u>that</u> <u>tooth</u> of the Grand Duchess Catherine doing <u>perfectly</u> <u>well</u>; not the slightest uneasiness since it was plugged – last Saturday; - so I plugged it in two other places. Go again day after tomorrow. Several persons are waiting for me to send them word that I am at leisure. One of them, quite a young girl, I have sent for to come tomorrow – a Miss Moravieff. Yesterday I dined with Mr. Ropes and never felt at such a time so much at a loss what to say or do in order not to appear stupid. The fact is the only things they talked of were such as were only known to themselves and of no earthly interest to me. There was one Englishman present and Mr. Rope's brother and Mrs. Rope's sister. Mrs. Ropes and Sister (Englishwoman) play and sing delightfully. Mr. Joseph Ropes (the brother) sails from Liverpool for Boston on the 19th of April – to return in autumn. Of course your letters have not come – as their reception would be the first thing to write about. I may yet get them today.

Thursday P.M., February 28, 1846. – Yesterday I operated a little for Miss Moravieff and today I have been at the Michael Palace, extracting part of a tooth for the Grand Duchess Marie. She was very "nervous" – never had a tooth extracted – had a prefect horror of the operation; and had consequently suffered some of her teeth to become so much decayed as only to be extracted with much pain and difficulty. This operation today was so painful that she chose rather to let the tooth remain in its present state than have the part left extracted; satisfied as she said, that I had done my duty, and thanking me for taking so much care etc. in performance of it etc., etc., etc. – after which the Grand Duchess Helen (her mother) appointed half past 12 tomorrow for me to continue operations for <u>her</u> mouth. I understand they are not very liberal; so I expect nothing more than the sum I named at my first visit at their request as being the value of my time if I were to operate at my office – namely 50 silver rubles per day ($37.50). Mademoiselle Troubat told me today that the Grand Duke Michael was highly pleased with my operations and was very anxious that I should stay here, or come back and remain. As the steamers between England and America make only monthly trips I shall not have many letters from you – and it seems as if I should never get any – what can be the reason I can't imagine.

The letters in the Russian alphabet are more numerous than in ours. Some of them are like ours, having the same sounds, and some like ours having entirely different sounds. And then there are some letters which are really not letters as they only tell what sort of a sound the preceding letter has. For instance; Doctor Edward Maynard is written thus; - Dokmopr Edyapdr Meureapdr. Now that terminal letter which is so like our r (r) merely signifies that the letter next before it has a hard sound. In other word <u>Doctor </u>you will see that the first syllable is like ours, with the substitution of k for c hard – then t (like our m) – o, -r (like our p) etc., etc. So much for this philological lecture. By the way of addenda to it – that chap riding on the reindeer sledge is calling out "Poskarce!" – Which signifieth <u>go</u> <u>faster</u>. "Kak mozjnoi skarce" – as fast as you can.

Friday P.M., March 1, 1846. – Still no letters from you; and now I must close this and send it by tomorrow's mail to be sure of its going by the steamer of the 4th of April. While operating today for the Grand Duchess Helen the Emperor came to see her; and when she returned to the operating room she told me she had been telling him about me, and that he had made no objection to her proposition that I have the title of "Dentist to the Imperial Court". Tomorrow I go again. Other applications are coming in for my services; I am to send the applicants notice (when I have time for them) to come and sit.

As I wrote before – not knowing anything of the state of affairs at home I have only to say, do what you think proper in everything. Perhaps by the time I write again I shall have collected some funds for you; and I trust that the amount already sent will keep you from want until I send more.

My letters will henceforth be more frequent, there being hereafter 2 steamers per month. My health is quite good now. Remember me to Father and Mother and all our Brothers and Sisters. Kiss our dear children for me and tell them their papa never forgets to kiss them at night. And have Eddy write a few lines, at least, in your next letter; which direct "To the care of the American Minister, London". Don't forget, don't write <u>Consul</u> – but <u>Minister</u> because if you send it to the Consul he will send it to Berlin – whereas the Minister will keep it until he has orders to send it somewhere and so I can get it myself from him, if as I suppose, I shall be in London in time.

About my coming here – I do not think any offer will be made that will satisfy me and you too – and if it does not do both I shall not accept it. At any rate there will be time enough to talk about that when the offer is made. My great wish now is to get my gun before the Grand Duke

Alexander, for whom I expect to operate next week. Without this inducement I should not have been justified in staying to operate for the Court. I have written to Major Smith by this same point saying that I hoped to bring my gun before the Hereditary Grand Duke (Alexander) for whom I expected to operate next week; and that Colonel Todd would explain fully to him the inducements I had for remaining a few weeks longer than himself. If John is with you, and is not married, and don't intend to get married, tell him I shall want him to come here with us if I come back – which is not at all probable. – "So his chance of seeing Russia is not <u>very</u> great" just now.

I suppose little John say <u>pa</u> and <u>ma</u> and has turned out a much better boy than he gave promise of when I saw him last. I am so sure that they all have the best care taken of them that I have not a word of advice to give about that matter. I hope to see you and them in April or May certainly – as there can scarcely be anything to detain me longer unless it be something for which you would be glad to have me stay. Good night and good bye for this time.

Forever yours,

Edward

Chapter 15
(Eleventh Letter)
The "Ring Letter" and "Dentist to the Imperial Court"

St. Petersburg, 2/14, March 1846. Saturday   **Page 1**

My Dear Ellen,

      The letter to you which I closed last night I sent off this morning (Saturday). Today I have been at the Michael Palace operating for the beautiful Catherine. Have finished with both her and her sister Marie – not because all is done that should be done but because they don't choose to let me operate as I think proper, and I don't choose to operate if as <u>they</u> wish. I dare say they would be better pleased at first if I would comply with t heir wishes; but I do not choose to forfeit my self-respect to please <u>anybody's</u> fancy. The Grand Duchess Helen, however, seems to appreciate my course and to be more and more anxious that I should settle here. I was told today that Dr. Arndt would come to see me tomorrow to talk with me about coming here to practice and teach students my Profession.

Sunday night, March 3, 1846. – Slavah bogo! – all well at home a month and a half ago – say 28th January, - the date of the last of the 3 letters received today from you. The other two are dated, one 26th November and one 25th December. I cannot express to you my satisfaction at hearing that no more serious illness than slight colds afflicted any of you; and that you are not likely to be distressed for want of funds for family expenses. What you must have received in addition to the sum you acknowledge the receipt of, by this time, will, I hope, keep you all comfortable until my return. You must see from what I am daily writing that it is utterly impossible for me to set the precise time for my arrival at Washington or even for starting on the journey. I must be governed entirely by such circumstances as will affect our pecuniary interests, unless something more serious takes place in the family. Depend upon it Ellen, I shall consult <u>your</u> welfare quite as <u>much</u> as anybody's in all I do that may detain me longer than I know expect.

Dr. Arndt did not come today – but Dr. Zdekauer (Zed-e-kaw-er), (Physician to the Grand Duchess Marie and the Grand Duchess Catherine), was sent instead, as he speaks English. It would be a long and tedious story to read all that passed between us – pretty much same, <u>but rather stronger</u>, than the interviews and conversations between Dr. Arndt when he came some time ago twice at the Grand Duchess Helen's request – and the same also as some of the conversations with the Grand Duchess Helen and, by her direction, with Mademoiselle Troubat. They (the Imperial family) are devilish anxious to have me settle here, but they wish me to name the inducement for which I will do so. I reply that I do not wish to come here - that I have no propositions to make, but will take into consideration any proposition or offer which may be made to me, and if it should be satisfactory I should be happy to comply; but that nothing less than a very great inducement would satisfy me of the propriety of leaving a good and sufficient practice at home, breaking up my establishment there, and removing, for years, from kindred and friends and country. It is now past midnight and I must go to bed. Good night. God bless you!

Tuesday March 5, 1846. – Being very busy yesterday operating at my lodgings, and out last night until late, I did not write. Operated for a Madame Touchoff (too-choff). Night. – Same lady interrupted my writing just as I had written her name. Operated again for her today and am to touch her off again tomorrow. Good night.

Wednesday March 6, 1846. - Not having time last night I did not tell you that the Grand Duchess Helen sent Dr. Zdekauer to me again yesterday to make me a proposition – she having talked with His Majesty about the matter. They offer me the Title of Imperial Dentist, or Dentist to the Imperial Court; to be the <u>actual</u>, and not a mere <u>honorary</u> Dentist to the Imperial Court – as some others are who never practice in the Imperial Family. To be employed by the Imperial Family whenever they employ any Dentist and to be paid for each operation instead of having a salary – so as not to interfere with a private practice. To have the privilege of practicing without any examination or paying any license. I sent my acknowledgement for the compliment paid me by Her Imperial Highness and said that I would consider the matter and would be glad to talk with herself personally about it when I next visit her. A good deal has been said on their part about giving me some rank of Nobility – about which Dr. Zdekauer was instructed to enlighten me, as I had told them before that I was wholly unacquainted with that matter <u>in Russia</u>. Something very flattering was intimated in this way, but nothing distinctly proposed, last Sunday, by Dr. Zdekauer. I am led by Dr. Zdekauer to expect that the Grand Duchess Helen will give me a souvenir of some sort – perhaps a ring – (I hope it will be a ring if anything because then <u>you</u> can wear it) as a token of her estimation of my skill and her sense of its usefulness in her family.

I am now waiting for a request to visit her or some other of the Imperial Family; and while waiting am operating for others, with profit, my charges being such as to pay very well. I may say that you would be gratified to hear the praise I get here for my operations; and there is no harm in telling you, <u>only</u>, that the Imperial Family places me considerably above Dr. Brewster, whom they have heretofore employed and whom they considered the <u>first Dentist in Europe</u>.

I think, and others think, that if I would come here I could have a most brilliant career of practice, and make a large fortune in a few years. What say <u>you</u>? Shall I come after you? – Or shall I stay when I get home, and be content with my old practice? If you come you will have to bring a nurse who is young and healthy, and she will bind herself to stay five years at a certain rate of wages, and I shall be glad to have John come for the same length of time also at good wages to be the family "Charge d'Affaires" as Father Owen has been at Washington. In five years John would acquire a good knowledge of French and Russian and probably German, which with his English, would enable him to command good pay in many situations on his return to America. And then I must bring somebody to do my mechanical work – <u>Daniel Ormsby</u> would be just the man if I could get him, but he could not bring his family. Chauncey Warriner (who was horologist at Masi's) would answer my purpose very well if he would come upon a salary or for a share of the profits of the work he did for me. I should like to have Father speak to him about it if he is still at Washington. Father may ask him if he would like to come to Europe and work for me for 5 years for good pay provided I should want him. He need not say more than this except to ask Warriner to say nothing about it, as it may lead people to suppose that I have settled here.

Friday, March 8, 1846. - Yesterday I had another visit from Dr. Zdekauer from the Grand Duchess Helen, who directed him to tell me that she was obliged to me for the trouble I had had, that she would see me that afternoon if I would come to the Palace or today at 12 to talk farther about my settling here etc. , etc. I went in the afternoon as she wished and she gave me to understand that she was very highly pleased with what I had done for her; that there would be nothing more for me to do at present at her Palace; that the Grand Duchess, Tcezarevna was very anxious to have my services but was too ill now to have any operations upon her teeth; and advised me to write her Secretary to have him enquire whether she wished me to remain until she should so far recover as to be able to sit for me. She was so kind as to say that she would send me her own Secretary to accompany me to the other to "facilitate" matters; and when her Secretary (Mr. de Hassing) came I found that to go at the hour he wished would interfere with my engagements so I proposed that he go without me and make the enquiry and give me the answer – to which he consented. I have been touching them up a little to make them more attentive to what I am doing for them, by telling them that I had received letters urging me to go elsewhere – as soon as I could.

The Grand Duchess Helen repeated to me yesterday what she had previously said through Dr. Zdekauer; - and as to my sending a Dentist of whom I could approve, from America, she could not say that the same offer would be made to him, but that if he should be found, after practicing here some time, to be such a person as they would like for a Dentist then he would be employed. I had had Dr. Rich in my mind for a long time for this place, and intended to get the place for him if possible, if I did not think proper to take it myself; as a moderate inducement would suffice for him and not for me; - I having such great inducements <u>not</u> to stay here. The more I think of it the less <u>by comparison</u> seem the advantages of coming here over those I enjoy at Washington. Yesterday I operated again for Madam Touchoff, and am to do so again today, if the nerve be dead in a certain tooth of hers which I am treating.

Sunday morning, March 10, 1846. – No answer yet from the Tcezarevna. On Friday I finished Madam Touchoff's teeth. This is perhaps a tiresome sort of letter, inasmuch as all these particulars may be without interest to you; - if you find them troublesome just skip over them and pardon me for writing them on the ground of having nothing better to write and being anxious to say as much as possible to you. I have given up all hope of ever getting you to write your letters otherwise than at one sitting; - whereby you omit, for want of jotting them down when you think of them, many little things that would interest me greatly. ---- I have been reading you last three letters all over again; and they remind me of so many things to make us happy on my return that I <u>now</u> think <u>no</u> inducement could get me to come here and settle. If I had no family it would be quite another matter; as I could easily make myself comfortable, and it don't matter what becomes of old bachelors – they are generally of " no account, no how". (Tell George to put <u>that</u> in <u>his</u> pipe.) As to the office, if it is not yet given up, keep it; - I shall soon want it again in all probability. And if I do not return in time to do so myself, I wish Father to re-engage it for a year at least, and for five years if he can get it upon the same terms as I have heretofore had it. I don't know why it is, but I am so strongly impressed with the opinion that we shall be so happy at Washington that it seems to me that I cannot wait another week here. Night.

This afternoon the Secretary of the Grand Duchess came to me from her, and what do you think he brought me? Now guess all around. Seven hundred silver rubles, and a most magnificent diamond ring, worth – God knows how much – but certainly a great deal of money. You may prepare yourself for a sight worth seeing when <u>that</u> is to be seen. This sketch may serve to give you some idea of the present.

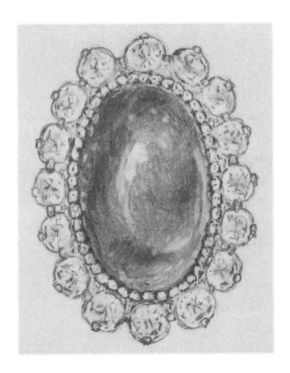

In the centre is a magnificent dark wine red stone which I think is carbuncle. Around this is a border of about 50 diamonds and outside this border is a row of 16 superb ones – brilliants of the first water – any one of which would make a very beautiful ring indeed. God grant I may not lose it before I get home for I prize it more on your account than my own; and when I do wear it I shall wear it as a greater honor than if it had been a coronet gained by court intrigue. Good night.

Above: The "Magnificent Ring" given to Dr. Edward Maynard March 10, 1846 from Her Imperial Highness Grand Duchess Helen as a thank you present for Dr. Maynard's Professional services to the Imperial Family as "Dentist to the Imperial Court". The ring consists of a large red Garnet surrounded by fifty small diamonds, surrounded by sixteen large diamonds as described in Dr. Maynard's letter to his wife.

Monday morning, March 11, 1846. – The Secretary also informed me, yesterday, that the Tcezarevna would not be able to have her teeth operated upon for two or three months and therefore I was not to wait for her. (I suspect she is expecting an addition to the Imperial Family). This of course cuts off all my hopes of getting my gun before the Grand Duke Alexander; so I have now only to get away as soon as possible; - consoled, so far as regards the object I had in coming here, by having unexpectedly received such a distinguished honor as to be called to practice for the Imperial Family and having made, as I am confident, a good impression in favor of the skill of our countrymen in my profession.

Wednesday morning, March 13, 1846. – Have been very busy indeed at my room, operating, since last writing. At it again today. Last night I went to the Michael Palace and sent my thanks Etc., etc., etc., etc. through Mademoiselle Troubat to Her Imperial Highness the Grand Duchess Helen for the very handsome manner in which it had pleased Her Highness to manifest her satisfaction with my services etc., etc., etc., etc. had some more conversations about my coming back – even if I came only for a few months, when I might be sent for etc., etc., etc. Mademoiselle says that there are many ladies of the Court who wish me to operate for them and that if it were known that I should return everybody who could would wait for me rather than employ any other Dentist. She told me again how highly delighted the Grand Duchess was with my operations etc., etc., etc. Tomorrow I am to operate for the Countess Cheremetef (Sher-e-me-tef) (at my room) having already operated for her sister, who comes again today.

I am not sure that I shall start for Berlin on Saturday next. Mr. J. S. Ropes who goes then will try today to make some arrangement for getting my models to Berlin with us without their being subject to custom house examination at the frontiers. If he succeeds, I go; if not, I shall soon know, - in an hour or so; and shall have to stay till some other way comes into play. It would be folly for me to go without my models as I can do nothing without them. If I can't take them now I'd better stay where I can, <u>at least</u>, pay expenses until some means of conveyance offers that will permit me to take them. The Grand Duchess said, (before I agreed to remain after Colonel Todd's departure) that my baggage should be sent to Berlin – I having explained to her that going with Colonel Todd would give me the advantage to taking it where I could not take it by post or diligence. Nothing is said about it <u>now</u>, however, and whether the subject is forgotten or not I do not like to speak of it after the very beautiful present I have received, and shall not do so if I can avoid it without great loss. Night. – Can't go by post- don't take at <u>any</u> <u>price</u> half as much weight of baggage as I have. Busy all day. Countess don't come tomorrow – "indisposed" – somebody else's daughter applied while I was out this evening and she comes in the place of the Countess.

There is a very rich church here, called the St. Alexander Nevsky Church. It is said to stand upon the spot where a battle was fought between the Swedes and the Russians, the latter gaining the victory under the direction of St. Alexander Nevsky, who came down the river Neva on a millstone and landed at that spot; where after the fight, a chapel was built, which from time to time has been enlarged and enriched until the property of the concern is immense. This is the church which contains the great quantity of silver of which I wrote you. Every Department or public establishment even the Government Schools and the post office – each has a chapel or church. No musical instruments used in the Russian church; all vocal music.

Good night my dear Ellen. May your dreams be sweet.

Friday March 15, 1846. – Yesterday I did nothing. Today been operating for two daughters of Baron Seddler – one of them a Maid of Honor to the Grand Duchess Catherine. I am now on the sharp lookout for a conveyance for self and luggage to Berlin, but have little prospect of success without calling upon the Grand Duchess Helen for the fulfillment of her promise.

Mr. Harrison who has just left my room, thinks the offer made by the Imperial Family is a brilliant one and would give me great éclat here – and so insure me a very profitable practice. Major Whistler thinks it would not be worth my while to come here merely for 5 years – nor for any definite number of years – but that if I were to come at all (which he does not think advisable) it should be to stay as long as should be necessary for making a fortune – even if it should be 20 or 25 years – a thing not to be thought of while the Continent of America is above water. No, my dear Ellen, I would rather have a small competence at Cooperstown, or Springfield, Massachusetts than have riches here. Ah Ellen! What a life we could live on a thousand a year at Springfield! How many, many times I have thought of the blissful week we spent at Alden's! Such beautiful natural scenery – such an orderly and moral people and so generally well informed – such good society – such beautiful residences and so well ornamented with trees and shrubbery and so well kept! – and then the very great advantages of short and rapid communications with Boston and New York and Albany – why the place is s perfect paradise in every respect – especially now that cold weather is no bug-bear. When we get the thousand a year – etc., etc.

I wish Father to tell Major Smith that I have failed in getting my gun before the Grand Duke Alexander which was the great inducement I had in remaining longer than Colonel Todd did – and that I shall get away just as quick as I can and do all I can to effect sales elsewhere. This will do just as well as writing him a letter for which I should have to pay an enormous postage – as I do upon all letters I send now. By the way, I expected two or three letters from Mayor Smith when yours came a few days ago – but not a word have I received from him since September!

Saturday night, March 16, 1846. - Operated today for Mrs. W. H. Ropes. Tonight I received a little token of good will from Miss Cheremetef for whom I operated t'other day – a bottle of homemade Mead – a pleasant sort of sweet beverage. Also a large pear, which I was to divide with the lady who brought it – she having been the interpreter at the visits of Miss Cheremetef. The Countess Cheremetef is her sister but is a Countess by marriage with a cousin who is a Count and bears the same family name. This will explain to you why the sister is not also a Countess according to what I wrote about all the children of Counts being Counts or Countesses etc., etc. This Countess Cheremetef failed to come at the expected time appointed – day before yesterday – and now sends to know if I will go to her to operate – to which I reply - no – can't go out except to operate for the Imperial Family who always expect it. So she will come to me probably. Her brother also wants me to operate upon his front teeth – to which I have assented provided he comes before I go – but I tell them all I shall go by the first opportunity of taking my luggage if it be even within 24 hours notice. Good night.

Monday night, March 18, 1846. – This morning I received a message from the Michael Palace requesting me to go there <u>if</u> I had made arrangements to leave town tomorrow – as was supposed at the Palace. I wrote, in reply, that as I might <u>possibly</u> have an opportunity of going tomorrow I would attend at the Palace at the hour appointed – 2 o'clock. Went. Nothing very particular the matter but wanted to see me to see some teeth upon which I had operated for want of time to treat them as I thought they <u>should</u> be treated. Grand Duchess Helen had been suffering some from a tooth, the removal of which I had advised – and some other little matters were talked about concerning some other teeth – Had nothing to do; but had an excellent opportunity, and embraced it, of saying what difficulties I met with getting my luggage to Berlin. Grand Duchess Helen graciously condescended to talk over the matter in quit a sensible manner and thinks there will be no difficulty in sending the box of models by some official conveyance – as, for instance, the property of the Government – to be delivered to me at Berlin. This was not exactly expressed in such words, but such was my understanding of what was said by the Grand Duchess who wished me to talk with her secretary (de Hassing) about the manner in which it was to be effected.

So much to bring up the history of this evening when, on my return from the Palace I found a letter from Brother George dated February 25 giving me the distressing news of your illness. Although the letter states that you are better, still such illness is so changeable that scarcely any calculation can be made based upon anything short of absolute and total recovery from it. Thank God, you have the best attendance and need not suffer from want of any comforts which can be bought for you. This is a source of great consolation to me. George gives me a very excellent account of our dear little boys – Heaven bless them! How I long to embrace them again! As you wrote in one of your last letters that you intended to visit the north for the warm season I suppose I shall find you at Cooperstown with Sister Mary. Try to be as comfortable as you can and do not have any uneasiness on my account if you can avoid it.

Yesterday I received for you a very pretty piece of needlework; being a white satin pocket or bag or whatever it may be called. As it lies on the table it looks like a thin <u>cushion</u>, about 10 inches long by 6 wide; - at each corner a pretty tassel; the top wrought, (in chain stitch) into a pretty border enclosing the word "Ellen". This was the work o f Miss Finley, an English governess, cousin of the Bensons. She is dependent entirely upon her own exertions for her support and unable to pay for having her teeth upon. I have operated considerably upon her teeth at such times as were convenient and made her a present of the service. She wishes to testify her gratitude and so she sends you this token of it. Some time ago she wrought and gave me a purse – by the way – not <u>that</u> <u>purse</u> of which I wrote you – nor is she the same person – nor the same sort of person. The <u>other</u> one went to Moscow a month ago to be married to a Frenchman <u>she said</u>, but few believe it. I'll have a long story to tell you about a nice fix that a certain Chevalier <u>didn't</u> get me into on her account. Tried to scare <u>me</u> and got most capitally frightened <u>himself</u>.

I have read the correspondence between our Secretaries M.M. Calhoun and Buchanan and Mr. Packneham and, although I think we have by far the <u>best</u>, if not the <u>only</u>, title to the Oregon, still I think there are some very skillful cuts given by the English minister. Our Charge here Mr. John Randolph Clay lent me the document containing the correspondence.

I intend to bring home some of the letters you send me just to show you how they look when I get them. You won't know 'em. Will you believe me when I tell you that an Englishman in a respectable official position under the British Government – a man looked upon as a gentleman – asked me the other day if "that Oregon territory was a continuation of the American Continent?" - fact. It is really amazing to see how little of <u>us</u> and <u>ours</u> is known by Englishmen and how what little they <u>do</u> know is measured and shaped and colored by English pride, English prejudice and English bias. They are compelled to do us justice occasionally however. They have learned some things about us that are not easily forgotten and will <u>never</u> be forgiven. Good night.

Tuesday night, March 19, 1846. – Today I saw and purchased a small bust (in plaster) of the Grand Duchess Helen; - taken several years ago, but still very much like her. So you will be able to form a pretty correct idea of her. If I could afford it I would have a drosky and set of harness sent out to us this spring; but there are so many things that are of more use to us to be had for the same money that I defer the purchase. Mr. Ropes will buy and send me anything of that kind I may want hereafter, and will, he says, just as soon have me pay for them at home after they are sent as to pay beforehand. Those droskies are, I think, the most convenient things to driver about town in, and the easiest to ride in, of any carriage I ever saw. You step into them as easily as into a house door one step high; if you fall out you don't go far enough to break any bones; - not a particle of mud reaches you; and the carriage is hung so low that it never turns over. I saw several new ones today, that were perfect beauties – some with calash tops to be raised or let down and which could be taken off and put on easily (as the weather might necessitate). Willoughby would be delighted with the Russian harness, or rather with the peculiar principle upon which it is made. I explained it in my first letter from this place. I am told it is a rare sight to see a horse's breast galled by his collar in Russia. There are some things about the harness that are adapted to this people and this country and might be altered with great advantage for ours; and then for <u>one</u> <u>horse</u> I think it would be very far superior to the harness used generally in America. This can't be very interesting to you, my dear girl, but it may not be altogether nonsense for Willoughby and John. Tell them I have studied this matter and have made sketches of every part of the "gearing" – and ditto as regards the droskies.

I fear I shall have to send this for the steamer of the 19th April before I know when I am going to leave St. Petersburg. There is great difficulty in getting to Berlin during the close of navigation without great expense unless you take a place in a mail-post or diligence 2 or 3 weeks in advance and even then you can take but very little luggage with you. My beautiful trunk I find not fitted for European traveling; - too heavy by far; and I think of getting a lighter one here and having the other sent home (with some things I don't need with me) by ship – as I sent the slippers; - which slippers I am glad to learn , seem to please you. Bed time – pleasant dreams to us both, <u>of</u> <u>each</u> <u>other</u>.

Thursday night, March 21, 1846. – Tomorrow I am to take my box of models to the Michael Palace; from whence it will be sent, under the Imperial Seal, to the Russian Charge d'Affaires at Berlin, who will deliver it to my order unopened.

Dined today in company with most of our countrymen here at the table of a Mr. Gellibrand brother-in-law of Mr. Ropes. Mr. Gellibrand is an Englishman and a merchant I believe like Mr. Ropes. Spent a very pleasant evening; and had four applications for my services. Good night my dear Ellen.

Friday P.M., March 22, 1846. – This morning I sealed up my model case and had it taken to the Michael Palace, where I was told by Mr. De Hassing and Mademoiselle Troubat that it would go safe to Berlin – starting by the post of <u>next</u> Monday.   Fearing that <u>something</u> might happen to the models I took the precaution of taking off the locks of all the arms except that of the pistol which arm I took out all together, and put it with the locks, in my port-manteau (trunk) and shall put them in the sealed <u>despatch</u> bag which I am to take from our Legation here to Berlin – Mr. Clay having kindly offered to get me a Courier's passport. Today I have turned nearly all of my funds into a letter of credit – that being the best I could do – although <u>that</u> cost a heavy percentage. I have had to buy some gold foil of Russian manufacture for use; and I found it so good that I have engaged about 50 rubles worth more. I think there must be some peculiar excellence in the metal independently of the working it.

The Countess Cheremetef is still indisposed. Her husband is the owner of between 100,000 and 120,000 serfs or peasants – <u>slaves</u> in fact; but slavery here is not like our slavery. I must tell you about it on my return; but will just mention now that the proprietor who attends to his estate divides his land into two equal portions; his slaves cultivate one portion for themselves and one portion for their master – working 3 days each week for him and 3 for themselves. Those who do not choose this plan receive so much from the slaves and they may cultivate the land or let it out – just as they please. The serfs are considered as part of the estate upon which they reside and cannot be sold without it. Every second, or third, or so year, the proprietor must furnish the Emperor with a certain proportion of men for his army. I think the present rate is seven men in one thousand; and then there are numerous taxes for other purposes of Government. These items of information I get from our fellow boarder Count Bouterlim, who is himself a proprietor and is very communicative.

Sunday night, March 25, 1846. – The English Courier arrived this morning and I sent immediately to engage a conveyance with him to Berlin; but he sent word that a friend of his would accompany him back, and therefore he could not take me. These Couriers are in the habit of taking passengers in this way and they make money by it; - the conveyance being rapid, safe and without delay or trouble, is eagerly sought for during the close of navigation. The next English Courier (no others take passengers I believe) goes in about three weeks – so I shall go tomorrow and secure the earliest place I can by the mail-post and get along with my one language as well as I can. (One thing I intend to have my children do, and that is, if they never learn anything else they shall learn the French language). I hope now to start in about a week; and I expect to be pretty busy professionally until I go, as there are seven persons who have expressed a wish to have me operate for them before I go. Everybody tells me I ought not to go away at all – or if I do, that I should come back again – now that they have seen my operations they say they shall never have sufficient confidence in anybody else here to employ upon their teeth. Only think of a City as large as or larger than New York without one Dentist who has the confidence of its inhabitants. What an opening for a skillful man who could speak French, German and Russian! This between ourselves. – I don't want any quacks to come here from our country and injure the good name American Dentists now have here. Good night; sweet dreams.

Monday night, March 26, 1846. - I am so provoked that I hardly dare trust myself to write. I learned this morning that the places by the Mail-post are all taken up to the 23rd of April (old style) - nearly a month! – and now it is a question whether I can even go with the next Courier – three week hence. God knows what I shall do – I can't pay four or six hundred dollars for a private conveyance. I must wait as patiently as possible and hope for some lucky opportunity to take some vacated place by post or go with somebody who wants a traveling companion. With <u>us</u> there would be stage coaches every day in abundance; here one must take his place a month in advance.

I must close my letter tonight for tomorrow's mail. You know all about my situation now and must exercise your good nature toward me by pardoning my continued absence. If you knew my anxiety to get away from this country you would do so cheerfully.

I have said very little about our dear children; - do the best you can for them and tell them papa will come home Justas soon as he can finish his business on this side of the Atlantic. Give them an extra kiss each from me; and tell them I love them more than ever. I thought to send you some funds in this letter, but you gave so good account of home that I supposed the $500. Which you must have received <u>after</u> writing the last letter would insure you from want until I returned. Of I am delayed longer than I expect I shall send you funds so that you will not suffer. My love to all.

Forever your, Edward

Chapter 16 (Twelfth Letter)
On To Berlin, Prussia

My Dear Ellen,

I arrived here at 2 o'clock this morning very much fatigued by the journey but with an excellent appetite. In order to keep up a running account of my doings I must go back to the time of closing my last letter; at which time I was on the sharp look-out for a conveyance to this place. A day or two after closing that letter I concluded an arrangement with a Mr. Miller who joined me in expense of a second hand vehicle and all other expenses – all half and half. We fixed upon Tuesday a week ago yesterday to start, and did so; and, with the exception of one night that we stopped because the roads and ferries thereabouts were in bad order, we came night and day. Mr. Miller slept that one night in a house but I slept every night in the carriage; shall tell you all about the trip when I get home.

On the day (Monday) before we started the Grand Duchess Helen sent to know when I was going away and that if I was not going for a day or two, she wished me to come to the Michael Palace at 10 on Tuesday (the next day) with my instruments etc. I went Monday evening and informed Her Imperial Highness that I was to start the next morning; and I was then informed that she wanted one other tooth plugged and she urged so hard to have me stay that I promised to use my exertions to induce Mr. Miller to wait until 12 o'clock to enable me to plug a tooth. On my way home I called to bid the Whistlers good bye after seeing Mr. Miller and when I reached home I found the Grand Duchesses secretary waiting to learn my answer – had been waiting two or three hours and had been even directed that, if Mr. Miller's haste was the only reason for my not waiting to operate for her, then he was to go himself and give her compliments to him and ask him to wait as a favor etc., etc. This was not necessary however; as I told the Secretary that I had got Mr. Miller's consent and that I would be at the Palace by half past 8 or 9 at farthest. So at 9 a.m., I was at the Palace and very soon was met by a very pleasant smile and manner which told me better than words how glad the wearer was to avail herself of my services again. I found the tooth to be plugged a <u>lower</u> <u>wisdom</u> tooth plugged in three places. Already and decaying around all the plugs – 2 in the top and one in the side. I cut all three into one cavity and then there was not much but cavity left – however, in 4 hours I finished the operation and received her highest praise of the skill exercised and her thanks – and 20 ducats in gold, equal to 60 silver rubles. This last was brought me by Mademoiselle Troubat who told me that she was directed to say to me that Her Imperial Highness would insure me for what operations she would require in her own family 5,000 <u>banco</u> rubles (about a thousand dollars) if I would come back and stay a month or two as late as October or November next, (by which time she will have returned from her summer traveling) and that probably the Empress, The Cesarovitch and the Cesarevna would each be disposed to add to the offer. I gave no decided answer but promised to write from Paris or London to state whether I could make my arrangements to come back at all and to say when my farther communications may be addressed to me from the Grand Duchess. So you see there seems to be an increase rather than a falling off in the favor in which I am held by the Imperial Family. Again my friends urge me to go there and settle – that what I have already done there, and the fact that I was induced to return to operate for the Imperial Family etc., etc., would be sufficient to give me a great practice at once. But I dare say you have heard quit enough now about Imperial Highnesses and Grand Duchesses – so we'll drop that matter and take a jump to Berlin. Mr. Clay (our Charge d'Affaires) gave me some despatches and procured me a Courier's passport so that I came without any delay or trouble; but I found the journey very expensive. However, I could do no better. This morning I called upon Mr. Fay our Secretary of Legation here. He seems, and also Mrs. Fay and a fine little 6 year old daughter, all very good people. Mr. Fay dined with me this afternoon and tells me that there is not a Dentist in Prussia who deserves the name and that no doubt the Royal Family here would be glad to employ me if they knew how I was regarded at St. Petersburg. Good night – I must go and take a bath – good night.

Wednesday P.M., April 22, 1846. – I called upon Mr. Wheaton our Minister here today and the result of our conference of 5 minutes is that I shall make no attempt to exhibit my gun here until it has been adopted in France – so that after a little rest from my journey I shall "put out" for Paris. I shall probably go by the way of Brussels but I have had no time yet to make any enquiries or arrangements about the trip.

I have been walking about nearly all the morning and have seen a great deal to admire in architecture, painting and sculpture – three arts highly cultivated here I should think. This is, you must know, one of the great Cities – having some 400,000 inhabitants – about the size of New York or St. Petersburg.

I have left my Springfield trunk at St. Petersburg and jammed it full of things to be shipped to Boston and thence sent to Washington. I am not sure that it will arrive safely; but if it does find its way home you will please send for Mr. Schneider to come and pick the lock if he can, and if not, to get the trunk open "anyhow". You will find in it a little packet directed to Mrs. Hoover, from Mr. Eastwick. This you will please have delivered safely by Father or Brother George. The rest of t he contents of the trunk you will know how to take care of better than I can tell you. I put a good deal of tobacco among the woolen and fur clothes to preserve them from the ravages of the moth. The fur morning gown you will you had better take to pieces, as there are two thicknesses of fur; and it will be necessary to take great care of it to prevent its destruction. I have sent in the trunk a plaster bust of the Grand Duchess Helen which you will please take great care of – allowing nobody to handle it. A good place for it will be on the mantle shelf in the parlor. Should it get dirty it can be washed the same as marble – the plaster being prepared for that process. Mr. Miller has gone on to England – I have given him half of the highest offer we have yet received for our carriage. Should I sell it for more I can account with him hereafter? Like most travelling companions that I have had since I left home, I was glad when we parted. He is a good fellow enough in all except an apparently unconquerable disposition to take advantage of people in inferior stations – hackmen – postillions, etc., etc. He seems to regard them as rogues, thieves, etc. – and evidently prides himself upon cheating them. What I should have done without someone to speak Russian and German on the route I don't know; and, notwithstanding that I was glad to have him leave me, still I feel under obligations for his activity and care in attending to all arrangements for the journey.

Thursday, April 23, 1846. – My case of models has not yet arrived and as there are some letters in the box to be delivered here I must wait for it. Moreover, if I do not take the box with me it will be 30 days on its way to Paris!!!! – think of that once and compare it with the facilities we have in <u>glorious</u> <u>America</u> for sending packages. If I take it with me I am told that it will cost me some 20 dollars for its freight; - if I send it, only about 5 dollars – but I would not leave it 30 days for 50 dollars. I have more than half a mind to cut my models in two or so to get them into my trunk and so send the box to the devil – for it has cost me more annoyance than half a dozen trunks would, on account of its shape. The only objection to this plan is, that if they were to be tried they will not be proper guns for trails of comparison with other guns – as they will be too short to be loaded with facility. It is probable that a small cask will be sent with my trunk, from St. Petersburg. It contains some anatomical preparations in brine. Should it arrive I wish Father to take out the bung, if there is one, and if not to bore a hole in the cask, and if it is not full of brine, to fill it; the brine to be as strong as that used for salting pork, - and to keep the cask, (stopped tight) in the cellar until I return.

I have seen a great many pretty things here that I wished to take home but I am told everything in the way of casts in plaster, papier mache, etc., etc, can be better procured in Paris. They are very cheap here, and the temptation to spend a few <u>thalers</u> (ta-lors) is very great and would be much greater if I had any way of taking the purchase with me. The <u>thaler</u> is about the same as the silver ruble – 75 cents, or so. I feel very much provoked to learn that my box has not arrived as I had been led to believe that I should find it here on my arrival – but I am learning one important lesson for a traveler in Europe – not to fret at delays – by and by I shall perhaps be contented with such things but as yet they are not very pleasant. Night. – The box has arrived and I have made arrangements to have it sent by post to Paris, to the Russian Embassy there, - where it is to be in 14 days from the day of its starting, which will be probably on Saturday. I am making arrangements to start for Paris on Saturday or Sunday morning and hope to arrive there in about

7 or 8 days. I expected to find one or two letters here from you and at least one from Major Smith, but found none. So I probably made a wrong calculation of time and I suppose there are now 3 or 4 from you in London. I shall write to have them forwarded to Paris immediately so that I may get them on my arrival there. I may be detained a day or two in Brussels and so not reach Paris before the 5th of May; and I can scarcely think of knowing what I am to do there in less than 5 or 10 days more. Should I meet with no encouragement I shall go to London – pay up my postage bills etc., and see if I can do anything there; and if I fail altogether, <u>as</u> <u>I</u> <u>expect</u>, then I shall be ready to sail by the Steamer of the 4th of June and hope to see you before <u>the</u> year is passed, which it will be on the 3rd of July – I think that was the day I left you at East Springfield. I anticipate great happiness when we do meet – it will be like a re-marriage, we have been so long without – ahem! Without seeing each other. "We shall see what we shall see" – and feel it too. Good night.

Friday P.M. April 24, 1846. – Today I walked out with Mr. Fay to Charlotenburg – four miles – (<u>one</u> <u>German</u> mile). At Charlotenburg I saw a mausoleum of the present King of Prussia's Father and Mother; - a beautiful temple containing the vault in which are placed the bodies, and above are two statues of great beauty of execution representing the King and Queen lying on their backs and apparently in a pleasant slumber. The statue of the Queen is by a man who was once her servant, and a more beautiful thing of its kind I think I never saw. Here is a rough idea of the way in which the statues are placed – on a sort of bed or mattress (represented in marble of course) and this again on a sarcophagus – all white marble.

Our walk was nearly all the way through a level piece of ground covered with a pretty thick forest, intersected in all directions with beautiful walks and drives and ornamented with lakes, statues, etc.,etc. There must be hundreds of arms in it I should think; is kept in good order, and is if inestimable value to the people as a place of recreation, exercise, etc.

Your likeness has been seen by a great many persons and has procured you compliments enough to satisfy any reasonable woman for a while; - and, as a Daguerreotype, is pronounced by all as the most beautiful they ever saw, I have seen none so well colored in Europe yet, and not one with a pleasant expression of the face.

I shall probably be able to receive one letter from you if it is sent <u>soon</u> after you receive this, to London, care of the American Minister, same as I told you before. And when you <u>know</u> <u>certainly</u> about the time I am to return I wish you to write to me at Boston, about three days before my arrival, "care of Tremont House:,- and on one corner write "Expected by next steamer from Europe". I must close this now to insure its going by next steamer. Give my love to all the family – Father, Mother, Brothers and Sisters. Eddy, George and John are with their Mother in my mind constantly. I hope to have the happiness of embracing you all soon and of endeavoring to make you all happy as far as I can. My best kisses to you and our dear boys – God bless you all.

Forever yours,

Edward.

Chapter 17
(Thirteenth Letter)
On To Brussels

Cologne, April 30, 1846. (Thursday)

My Dear Ellen,

My last letter to you was from Berlin, which place I left on Sunday morning last in company with an Englishman, Mr. Austin, whom I had known in St. Petersburg. He has been of great service to me from his speaking German. We arrived here night before last; and I am sure you will justify me for spending two days (yesterday and today) in going by steamboat up the Rhine to Mayence (My-onts) and back again – this being the part of the Rhine so famous in history and so much run after by sight-seers. I shall postpone all descriptions of its peculiarities until I return when I hope to bring some illustrations to assist me. I tried to make some sketches but the constant shifting of my position from the movement of the steamboat prevented my doing so.

Having no Patent for Prussia I did not feel justified in showing my invention to the Minister of War at Berlin. Tomorrow night I shall probably be in Brussels; and I must remain there a day or two at least to attend our matters – General Tyson having opened them there.

From Berlin to Hanover I came by railroad; - thence to this place by diligence; - and hence to Brussels I go by railroad. I dare say you have been thinking whether I have bought any real genuine eau de Cologne – and I will satisfy you by saying that having no room in my port-manteau I could only get a very small bottle; this I did get at the veritable Johan Marie Farina's, as I was told. So if I don't lose it you will be able to judge of its quality. The people here call this place Kolne – the German pronunciation of which is keln, or something very much like it. I have visited here the celebrated Cathedral which when finished will be as immense building – the towers being, or rather to be some 500 feet high. But as only part of the body of the church, 50 feet in height of one tower, and a little more than the foundation of the other has yet been built; it is difficult to say when the whole will be completed – for the building was commenced more than six hundred years ago! The parts completed and not yet decayed from age etc., are extremely fine. I have also seen today the celebrated picture here by Ruebens – the crucifixion of St. Peter. It is the altar piece of the Church of St. Peter and is perfect, I think, beyond all power of language to describe. I have had time only to sketch a few beautiful gothic windows which possessed beauties which were new to me - and my sketches merely a few lines on the backs of hotel bills – fly leaves if letters etc. , but they serve to impress the subjects more deeply upon my memory. Good night – This "good night" I have the pleasure of writing occasionally;

but I have every night, with <u>but</u> <u>one</u> exception given you <u>boys and all</u> your kiss of good night, since I left America. That one night I did not kiss you but thought a great deal of you and the family, and those thoughts probably kept me from a serious quarrel with a blustering Englishman who was then under the influence of wine or something stronger. This was months ago at St. Petersburg. I'll tell you all about it when I get home. Good night and the most delightful dreams to you.

Friday night, May 1, 1846. - <u>Bruxelles</u> (as they spell it here) – Arrived here at 5 P.M.; too late to call upon Mr. Clemson our Charge here, to whom General Tyson stated our object with guns. Tomorrow morning I shall go to Mr. Clemson's residence to deliver two very complimentary letters – one from General Tyson and one from Mr. Markoe of Washington. On my way here I passed through several important towns – Aix la Chapelle – Liege (le-azhe) –Vervay – Malines (mah-laen) etc., etc. and saw some most interesting scenery. My companion left me at Malines; - he branching off or Ostend, on his way to England. What I saw of <u>this</u> town on entering it has given me a very favorable opinion of its architecture; and from the fact that it is a great resort for people who have moderate fortunes to support them by their interest thereon, I think it must not be a very expensive place to live in. Staying at a hotel, however, is very expensive all over Europe, I think, I do not blame the hotel keepers – for Europeans require as much waiting upon as babies – and Englishmen particularly are as difficult to please. They are constantly cussing the landlord or the servants for things that occur entirely through their own carelessness, or stupidity. I speak of them <u>as a class</u> as they have appeared to me.

I did not tell you that I received <u>at</u> <u>Berlin</u> a letter which had been forwarded so many times that it was covered with addresses and erasures and post marks. It was from Father dated in February and announcing to me the death of my brother John. It seems Father had but recently heard of John's death, although it occurred some 6 or 10 months before the letter was written. He just before the time of his death removed to <u>Iowa</u> where he died. Father had heard no particulars. I have seen so little of him for the last 20 years that it does not seem to me like what I think it would if I had seen more of him.

I have just wrung the bell for my coffee to be brought, and if you were here in this little room to share that and some other things with me I should forget all about the great enterprise upon which I came to Europe, - to <u>fail</u>. Well! Never mind – if I fail with this invention I shall not try another in the same way. I shall have the kind of consolation that comforted the Paddy when he was about to be shot – "it <u>can't happen again</u>."   I think I wrote that I was travelling as a Courier

of our Government with Despatches.   A despatch bag is about a foot wide and eighteen inches long and is sealed with the seal of the Legation where the bag is filled, and is sacred at all Custom-houses. This is the custom with all civilized nations. Now it so happens that other things besides government papers get into such bags and go along safely. And it so happens with mine. Uncle Sam would laugh a little to see what innocent frauds are sometimes covered by his seal as well as by the seal of other nations in this way. I was saved the annoyance of an examination of my baggage three times on my way here, in virtue of my being a Courier. Here's the coffee – enough for two cups, so I'll drink one for you.
Your very good health Madam. Good night.

Saturday night, May 2, 1846. - Called upon Mr. Clemson and found him very civil and ready to do anything in his power for me. He went with me to the proper office to procure our Patent, I supposing that it was only necessary for me to apply for it at once; - when lo! The Patent had not been issued – not a single cent having been paid by General Tyson for it! - Indeed the office informed us that in strict conformity to the law the first fee of 50 francs (about $10.) should have been paid many months ago. However, we arranged to get the Patent next Monday by paying that sum then. The whole fee is some 630 francs; but the balance need not be paid for about a year to come, I understand.

Mr. Clemson thinks it probable that something may be done here in the way of having sporting guns made upon my plan; and as, if made in large quantities for the American trade, they would form an important article of the commerce of this Country and so be a matter of great interest to the Government, he called tonight upon the Minister of Foreign Affairs and talked with him about it; and tomorrow morning we both visit him to talk farther and show the invention.

Mrs. Clemson is the daughter of John C. Calhoun; and I find her not only very talented and clever, but a true American: and Mr. Clemson quite the same. On Tuesday he is to go with me to Liege, the great gun-manufacturing town (some 3 or 4 hours from hence) to see some persons there about the matter. As for doing anything with the Government in the way of military guns – the thing is out of the question – the King himself could not have it introduced without dozens of commissions, trails, boards, etc.,etc.,etc. and then an act of law passed by the Chambers, and appropriations for payment, etc.

As I am likely to remain four or five days here at least I shall write to Paris to have your letters sent here, and I hope to read them within three days.

Sunday P.M. May 3, 1846. – Mr. Clemson took me today to the Minister of Foreign Affairs (as arranged last night). He was so much pleased and interested by the gun that he sent for the Minister of War who was also highly pleased with it and they were anxious that the King should see it and one or both of them will speak to His Majesty of the matter and he will probably send to Mr. Clemson to come to him and bring me with him. Mr. Clemson seems to know a thing or two about the management, and says he has no doubt that he can put me in the right way of doing something handsome here with the invention; but, that it will require time; - it being a matter that cannot be hurried; and that someone who understands the gun perfectly should be here to exhibit and explain it and answer all objections, enquiries, etc., etc. All which is very reasonable and I shall stay a week or so and see what the prospect may be then; and if it is not good I shall soon be on my way home

I shall probably enclose you some funds (out of my earnings at St. Petersburg) in this letter. If I make anything here I intend to purchase you a supply of house linen of Belgian manufacture. Mrs. Clemson tells me it is a great deal cheaper than Irish linen, a great deal better, a great deal handsomer, and will last a great deal longer. So I think it must be quite an object to buy it. And if I don't make anything here, still I must get you at least some Belgian linen.

I have not heard from either Major Smith or Tyson, they do not write me a single word, although I have written to Smith several times asking to know how our affairs were doing at home. They leave me to do all the work and pay all the expenses since Tyson returned home. I cannot afford to give away any larger share of the interest to induce others to do what it was their duty to do.

There are some very elegant buildings and streets here; and the tower, or steeple as we should call it, of one gothic building here, the "Hotel de Ville" is said to be the finest specimen of a gothic tower in existence. I have a set of views of buildings here, in book form, which I shall bring home. Good night.

Tuesday night, May 5, 1846. – Tomorrow at 4 P.M. I am to be presented to the King, by Mr. Clemson, to exhibit my invention to His Majesty. 'We shall see what we shall see". I dreamed twice about you last night. O that I could be presented to you tomorrow instead of to Leopold – I'd tell His Majesty I couldn't come 'fore next day – certain – maybe not for a week.

Yesterday I was strolling about the streets and thought I perceived something very like chimneys on the other side of the wall; and on stepping through a gate, judge of my surprise on finding that they were really of houses three and four stories high.

All over the city the sidewalks are, at every few steps covered with puddles or crossed with streams of urine – and in a great many places there are funnels along the sidewalks to make water in – perfectly public – and people seem to think it no impropriety.   Thank God! – We are not quite at that degree of civilization yet. Good night.

Thursday night, May 7, 1846. – Yesterday by appointment made with Mr. Clemson he took me to the King's Palace to show my gun – but on account of some strange and as yet unaccounted for mistake His Majesty was out taking a ride.   But as the time had been set for with Mr. Clemson and the interview had been sought on the King's part it was thought best to return in an hour – so we went again – not yet returned – so there the matter stands – to be explained on the part of the King by some polite notes from the Minister of Foreign Affairs to Mr. Clemson.

Tomorrow morning Mr. Clemson and I go to Liege to see some persons there whose opinion of the gun will have considerable weight; and to see the great manufactories of sporting guns, etc., etc.

Last night a Colonel Eenens was sent by the Inspector General of Artillery to see the gun; - and he reported so favorably that the Inspector General himself came today to see it and he seemed to think it would answer for Military purposes. Several propositions have been hinted at on the part of the Government – one to arm a regiment with guns with my improvement and let them try it. – Another to have 10 or 12 guns with the improvement put in the hands of Soldiers and fired a great number of times etc., etc., the Government stipulating to give a certain sum for the invention if they adopt it, etc., etc.

I objected to the first because it would make the thing public too soon for my purposes – my Patents being not all secured. The second was more favorable, but was declined for the present for want of time on my part to attend to any but the sporting guns just now – that being of vastly greater importance to me. I say for them to consider the value and importance of the invention as a <u>settled</u> <u>thing</u>, and therefore I don't choose to spend any time in going over the ground of trail again; - that there is s market for an immense number of sporting guns in America if they have my improvement and that they will pay such a profit as to be of greater consequence than military guns. But that if the Government wishes to buy the right for the military guns or the whole right I shall be glad to hear any propositions for that purpose. I am quite convinced that nothing is to be done in Europe by asking Governments to do; - better make them come to you. Good night.

Monday, May 11, 1846. – Last Friday Mr. Clemson and I went to Liege and returned yesterday; having accomplished the object of our visit which was to see and exhibit to one or two Officers my gun and to see what sort of guns I could get made and what they would cost etc. The Officers Colonel Fredericks and Timmerman, and two other others, Professors in some Government institutions I believe, were highly pleased and with the exception of Timmerman were in favor of having the Government adopt the gun at once. Timmerman thought the experience of one campaign should be had before its <u>general</u> adoption, but could see no fault in it; nor anything that he thought would be found objectionable in service. They seem to think so highly of it as did the Inspector General who even complimented me highly for being the author of so credible an invention. Mr. Timmerman showed us through several, and offered to through all, the workshops of the Government in which muskets are made. He enquired about our lathes for turning gunstocks – a thing unknown here. I gave him a sketch from which, with my explanation, he understood the lathe and will probably have one made. I had previously enquired whether I could procure one of their musket locks (which differ greatly from ours) and he now presented me with one and enquired whether there was anything else I would like to have; and expressed a desire to obtain farther information about our machinery for gun making, which I replied I would give cheerfully; and gave him the address of Mr. Ames who I told him would make him copies of anything we used at home for that purpose; and that if his Government would send a man to examine our works they would be shown most fully and cheerfully.

As to the Sporting guns – both Mr. Clemson and myself, although we had heard a great deal about cheapness of such things at Liege, were very greatly surprised – really astonished to find what we <u>did</u> find: viz: - the most beautiful guns I ever saw – far more beautiful, and quite as well made in <u>every</u> part as guns I saw <u>in London for 50 guineas</u> are made and sold at Liege for 50 or 60 dollars!

I had no idea that such perfect gems of beauty were ever made in the shape of guns. After fully talking over my matters with Mr. Clemson, it is perfectly evident that nothing can be done without having one or more sporting guns to show and then to enlist some <u>Capitalist</u> to purchase the Patents. And as this is in fact the only place in the world to have the guns made I must have one or two made while I am here; - so I have taken lodgings near our Legation at a cheap rate – 8 francs a week for the rooms and attendance, and 3 ½ a week for breakfast – until I get the guns made. I have just got into my rooms this morning – not elegant of course at their cost – but they'll <u>do</u>.

I expected to find some letters from you on my return from Liege but was disappointed. Perhaps they'll come today. Mr. and Mrs. Clemson are very kind and tell me to come there at any time. Tomorrow I am to operate for Mrs. Clemson – being the only return I am able to make for their hospitality and trouble. Night.

Tuesday May 12, 1846. – Have been arranging the lock for the fowling piece, and have succeeded very much to my satisfaction. Went to a restaurant for my dinner; - bread, beef steak and potatoes – 80 sous. 100 sous are 1 franc; - so my dinner was not very expensive one. You must have observed that I write very little about our dear, <u>dear</u> children. I cannot do it. Even the crying of a child in the street has such an effect on me that I am ready to cry myself. O Ellen! How much I have grieved and repented for having spoken harshly or too sharply, to Eddy particularly, when disturbed or annoyed by their noise. I did not know or think that the time would come when I should have been deprived of the society of my wife and children so long that even the merest trifles concerning them are thought over and reflected upon and weighed and considered in every conceivable way. The more I think of the blessing I have in such a family the more deeply do I love you, the more fervently pray for your happiness, and the more anxious am I to return home. God grant the next letter I get from you will assure me of your return to health and its enjoyment by you all. Good night. Sweet dreams to you.

Wednesday night, May 13, 1846. – Yesterday I plugged three cavities for Mrs. Clemson and am to remove tartar for her tomorrow. She was dreadfully afraid of being hurt, having been in rough hands before, but soon felt easy after I had commenced; and after I finished she and Mr. Clemson were both highly pleased; and when I left the house told me to come and go whenever I pleased and make myself at home when there. This was very kind and I think they were sincere. Since my return from Liege I have been arranging the lock for sporting guns and Mr. Clemson thinks I have done it <u>well</u>.   I am now making models in wood for the workmen to make the new gun by – or rather to assist him in comprehending the drawings.

Your letters do not come from London; and I am beginning to suspect there were none there to come, you having expected me to sail on the 4th of last month from Liverpool. If so I shall probably not hear from you again until I arrive at Boston.

The King sent through his Minister of Foreign Affairs an explanation to Mr. Clemson respecting the visit to the Palace 'tother day. The blame was placed upon somebody about the Palace but what the cause of the mistake was I don't know and it's no matter.

Here I have spoken another, <u>to me</u>, new language – the Flemish; - but French is the language here in general use. Queer old place this; and Liege ditto, but very picturesque and altogether such a place as I should like to spend a few weeks.

I have coffee, or something intended to be like it, every morning, but it is so villainously bad that I am never disposed to drink an extra cup for you. Ah! 'There's no place like home' for <u>that</u> drink; as for <u>tea</u> – to <u>be</u> tea it should never cross the ocean. Such tea as I drank in Russia has never been tasted in America – it being brought over land from China in <u>skins</u>. Russia and China are adjoining Empires as you need only be reminded.

To go by the next steamer this letter must be sent off on Friday or Saturday of this week. As I have said before, our matters at home must be left entirely to your judgment – I know so little about them that I have no advice to give. Fortunately for me, I have a wife who knows the value of money and had too much prudence to spend it unnecessarily. I trust everything to you, my dear girl – confident that I shall not have a single occasion to wish you had acted differently. How few there are who can say as much for their wives! – and alas for men! – How few <u>wives</u> can say so of their <u>husbands</u>! Good night and sweet dreams.

Thursday night, May 14, 1846. – Have been busy nearly all day operating for Mrs. Clemson. In the mean time my gun business is progressing as rapidly as it can at the beginning. Mr. Clemson tells me to be <u>certain</u> of going by the Steamer of the 19th. This letter should be sent off by tomorrow's mail – too soon for me to procure you a bill of Exchange for a small sum, as I had intended; but perhaps it will be as well not to send it until I hear from you, as I can send it with such instructions as you may need if you should be at Cooperstown.

Remember me to all friends who enquire for me and most affectionately to all our brothers and sisters and to Father and Mother. I hope they are all in good health and happy. I shall have some long yarns to spin for them by and by. My dear Eddy and George and John must have their extra kiss. I shall have a great many stories to tell them about the queer people and things I see in Europe. Ten thousand kisses for you my dear Ellen. May I live to see you again, and to show you how much more worthy of you I wish to be than I have ever been. I trust this is to be the last time we shall ever be separated for even a month in this life. Do not blame me for staying here longer than I intended when I wrote last. My prospects with the gun were never so good as just now and it would be unjust both to myself and to Smith and Tyson to leave the matter as it now stands. I am daily expecting to hear from a man who will probably take the affair in hand and for a share of the proceeds, make something of it. This is my only way –I must give away a good share or get nothing – for I can do nothing alone. If I do nothing here I shall in all probability abandon the hope of doing anything in Europe, and go home and see what has been and can be done in America. I feel the less regret at staying here on account of the season, inasmuch as if I were in America I should probably not be at work but spending the hot weather at Cooperstown. (Now this last sentence don't sound very well – it seems to say that I would rather be here than with you – whereas I meant only that I should not be earning anything at this time of the year at home, and so could spare the time better. But I am sure I needed not to have made this explanation.)

If you are at Cooperstown have John make some enquiries about such a place as would suit us to buy or get in exchange for our Washington property, which ought to buy us a very handsome farm with a good house and other improvements. O! How I long for a home! You would have no uneasiness about my staying one day longer than I felt justified in staying if you could only know my anxiety to see the blessed shores of Uncle Sam once more. Good bye, My Dear Ellen, Keep up your spirits and get as fat as you can by driving away all anxiety on my account. I'll come just as soon as I can. Good night and sweet dreams to you.

From your Edward

Chapter 18 (Fourteenth Letter)
Building a Gun from Scratch

My Dear Ellen,

      My last letter was mailed on Friday – day before yesterday. On Thursday afternoon Mrs. Clemson was at the house of the English Ambassador Sir Hamilton Seymour and was giving as an excuse for something the fact that she had been in the hands of a Dentist – upon which Lady Seymour remarked that she was just about to write a note to her Dentist here, an Englishman, Mr. Alex, to make an appointment with him. This led to the introduction of my name, reputation, skill, etc., etc. and the result was that Lady Seymour was very anxious to have me operate for her. Mrs. Clemson told her I was in Europe upon other business, and that she could not say that I would operate for her, Lady Seymour, but that she would mention the thing to me and inform her Ladyship of my decision. The Clemsons advised me by all means to operate for her as it would be an excellent opportunity of establishing a name here, and the fact of being employed by the very highest rank here, next to Royalty itself would be of great use to me if I should ever wish to practice here. So, having Saturday to myself I consented, as a favor to Mrs. Clemson to operate for her friend Lady Seymour and accordingly I operated upon her teeth from 11 till half past 5 yesterday – so much to her satisfaction that I am to go again this (Sunday) morning at half past 10 and continue – and she is anxious I should operate for her children – and said if I should get any more time, even an hour or two, that she would sit at any time; both Lady Seymour and Sir Hamilton congratulating themselves and feeling very happy that they should be so fortunate as to avail themselves of my services. And Lady Seymour begged that if I <u>should</u> return to St. Petersburg in the autumn, I would come via this city and stop long enough to operate for her family – intimating that she and Sir Hamilton would be happy to render any service in their power etc., etc.

So you see I have established another practice – for another family in 'high life', friends of the Seymour's, have <u>already</u> expressed a great desire to have me operate for the <u>whole</u> family; and you know how that thing spreads when it starts from a high source – as is the case in this instance. Now, as Lady Seymour from rank, takes precedence of <u>all</u> other Ladies at the Royal Table, save the Queen herself, by whose side she sits – and as Lady Seymour and Her Majesty are upon the very best of terms, and both fond of talking – and as Lady Seymour really feels that Mrs.. Clemson has conferred a great favor upon her by prevailing upon me to operate for her, the probability is that she will so represent me to Her Majesty that, if anything is needed of a Dentist at the Palace I shall be sent for. This Mr. Alex is considered the <u>best</u> operator here. There is another, Mr. Talma, who is the competitor for the first honors – but, to speak in the elegant language of the Port, "their noses are both out of joint" just now.

Sunday night, May 16th, - Operated from 11 till half past 5 again with <u>increased</u> satisfaction to Lady Seymour who is so anxious that I should do all that her teeth or her children's require that she offer to put off everything else if I will only come to operate for her even if I can only stay an hour at a time and come whenever I can spare an hour or two.

This is one of the greatest compliments, and can only be understood by knowing what things <u>such</u> people must do for their station, etiquette, etc., etc. I have been daily expecting to hear from a man in England about my affairs and until I do so I may occupy myself to pay expenses. My models and patterns and drawings are all made and ready for the workman so soon as one can be found who can <u>understand</u> English. So much for my damned ignorance of French. I dream of you and the children very often and generally very agreeable dreams. Good night to you, Ellen.

Tuesday morning, May 18, 1846. – Operated a little yesterday for Mr. Clemson and then he went with me to various places to find a workman who could understand English to make my lock but we could not find one. We heard of one optical instruments maker who spent a year in England, and we are now hunting him up with hope that he may answer my purpose. Our trip to Liege 'tother day was reported in one of the papers here – so much is made of every movement of a Foreign Minister that my name was given – probably under the impression that, being with Mr. Clemson I must be <u>somebody</u> and therefore worth naming. The Chevalier Iobard, Director of the Museum of Industry here, was with us and his name was in the report also. He is a remarkable man – Mr. Clemson calls him a 'living encyclopedia' – so various and general is his information. He writes a great deal upon scientific topics and is a great admirer and friend of Mr. Clemson whose knowledge of the sciences is much more profound. The Chevalier is very civil to me – admires my gun – tells me he has invented <u>6</u> himself – none of which, by the way are in use, and has presented me with 4 of his pamphlets to read.

On my way to Liege, I sat beside a Catholic priest who spoke English and seemed very intelligent. He told me that unlike other countries, Belgium was free from all discord in the Church – the utmost harmony prevailing; but he could not say much for the education and advancement of the lower classes. He said they were indifferent about learning; - but he did <u>not</u> say, and I did not like to tell him so, - that the lower classes <u>never</u> <u>would</u> advance until they threw off the trammels of Romanism. This is, proverbially, the most priest-ridden country upon earth; and the consequences are such as might be expected – an ignorant, superstitious democracy – a proud, polished and corrupt aristocracy, and an impudent priesthood. I am informed that there is scarcely a town in Belgium that contains as many souls as it did many years ago – and that very few of them show any signs of prosperity. How different all this from <u>our</u> happy, free and prosperous nation!

Thursday night, May 20, 1846. - Have found the workman and I think he will <u>do</u>; - is to commence tomorrow or next day. Tomorrow morning I go to operate for Lady Seymour. I understand that the <u>great</u> Brewster gets 20 francs for plugging an ordinary cavity. I get <u>only</u> <u>40</u>. Mrs. Clemson says she could get me 20 weeks work here if I chose to practice. Say nothing about my charges except at home – at least only say that they are higher than those of anybody else in Europe – don't say exactly what they are.

Last evening Mr. Clemson and I walked around the city, four or five miles I think it must be around – and the most delightful boulevard, with several rows of trees nearly all the way. This is you know accounted one of the most delightful Cities in Europe for a residence. I should like the town better if it were not for the fact that the sidewalks (where there are any) seem to be intended, not to walk on, but to make water on. I think the people here must live by <u>drinking</u> – not by eating – and they seem to delight in showing it. You would be amused to see how I live here. Can't say I like it altogether – but the way is interesting and funny from its ups and downs. My expenses are very little; - when I dine <u>grandly</u> it is at the table of a Minister; - when I dine alone and have to <u>pay</u> for my dinner, one or one and a half francs pays the whole bill. I don't expect to <u>live</u> <u>well</u> or <u>feel</u> <u>well</u> until I get <u>home</u>. I can scarcely believe that there were no letters from you in London when I wrote for them. Mr. Clemson has written in one of his letters to our Legation in London to have my letters sent here if there be any for me there. I wish you would write me immediately on receiving this – to me in London, care of the American Minister. The steamers ply so often now that I shall get the letter before I can possibly be ready to sail from Liverpool. I cannot hope to have my guns finished here under 3 weeks from the commencement and then I must spend some time here <u>probably</u> but I hope not more than a week to close my matters in <u>some</u> shape; - either to sell or leave authority with someone to sell for me. One thing is very certain – if I do not succeed here I shall not try anywhere else, for this is on every account the very best country to have the guns made in. Good night. Sweet dreams.

Friday morning, May 21, 1846. – Having nothing else to do yesterday I operated for Lady Seymour – spent nearly all day in plugging four cavities. This morning I go again to operate for her and, if I have time, for her children also. Lady Seymour paid me another compliment yesterday by telling me that I was her best friend – having referenced to my services upon her teeth – she being, as I am, of opinion that but for those services she would, <u>in a few months</u>, have lost 5 or 6 teeth.

Friday night. – Plugged eight cavities today and feel as if I had done a pretty hard day's work. Have now finished with Lady Seymour, but she is so anxious about her little daughter's teeth and urges me so hard to operate upon them that I have left my instruments at her house and have promised to comply with her wishes if I can get time to do so. Their home is almost a Palace – so large. Good night.

Saturday night, May 22, 1846. - And yet no letters from you. Good night.

Monday night, May 24, 1846. – Went to Sir Hamilton's again today and operated for one of the daughters. Finished with the family. Paid me eleven hundred and sixty francs. Rather better than nothing. Yesterday I took a long walk into the country and on my return took a short one with Mr. and Mrs. Clemson and their 2 children on the boulevards. All around the City there are at certain places, gates by which, and which only; persons pass into, and out of, town. At these gates are stationed persons – a sort of custom-house-officers – to examine goods, provisions, etc. entering town; - upon certain kinds of which a duty is paid to the town. Hence living outside the barrier is cheaper than living inside. The man from whom I have been expecting to hear has not been in England since he was written about my affairs. He is now in Paris. A letter has gone to him <u>today</u> – will reach him tomorrow; and within 24 or 48 hours afterward he will either come here or write. I do not know that any time has been lost here unnecessarily – The sporting guns could not have been got under way sooner without being unsatisfactorily made; and if anything like impatience or great anxiety is shown about disposing of the Patents, <u>distrust</u> will be engendered and sales prevented. The thing must have <u>time</u> – and then it must have a certain <u>management</u> by some such man as this now in Paris – one who knows a great deal about the people – <u>speaks their language</u> – <u>is a business man</u> – <u>knows the world</u>, etc. – a list of very essential qualifications, in which, I regret to say, your beautiful husband is very essentially deficient. Somebody said it was one part to invent a thing a nine parts to make money out of it. Very few inventors have the nine parts. Perhaps they wouldn't <u>invent</u> if they had 'em. Good night.

Tuesday night. May 25, 1846. – This morning while I was at Mr. Clemson's there came a passport to get a <u>visa</u> for two brothers of the name Stone. On enquiry I found they were sons of W.J.S. the engraver at Washington. I called upon them after dinner and they walked home with me. They are, like all our countrymen I have seen abroad, more fond of their own country than ever. I have been nearly all day with the same man who is making my lock. He is going on pretty well, considering that he has nothing to work with. By the way, the Stones tell me this trip to Europe has been as good as 20 years added to my life – never saw me looking so well – so fat – so hearty – so etc., etc., etc., etc. Good night.

Thursday morning, May 27, 1846. – At work on the lock all day yesterday. With the aid of Mrs. Clemson who selected and advised etc., I have purchased a supply of linen socks. They are not very nice but they seem to be good and cheaper than at Washington. Still no letters from home. I must mail this tomorrow or next day.

Afternoon. –Mr. Clemson went with me this morning to the banker here whose name is in the letter of credit –but, although I could get money if I wanted it, I could get nothing like a bill of exchange or anything else which would enable you to get money for it, except by a most provokingly roundabout way – for instance – he could sell me a bill on London, which I could send to somebody in New York who could sell it again and send you the proceeds; - which would cost several commissions, charges, etc., etc., and if it ever reached you at all it would probably not be within a month or two – perhaps not until after I get home. So I thought it better not to send from here at all. From what you wrote me when you expected me in April I am induced to think that the money I sent since you wrote the letter – namely $500. – will keep you from want until I return; but if you are in want, or are likely to be, ask Willoughby for what you want and I will pay him with interest when I return; or you can pay him from funds that I shall send if I don't return soon – as I can get Mr. Clemson to procure a bill in Paris by writing for it. Again I must ask you to keep up your spirits – rely upon my great anxiety to see you all again as an inducement to me to go home as soon as I can possibly do so in justice to you all as well as to myself and to Smith and Tyson.

I have reason to hope that by waiting a little I may insure a competence for our days, and to educate our children as well as support our Parents without the necessity for my working so industriously as I have done these 10 or 12 years past. You would not I am sure, Ellen, charge me with neglecting either you or our children if you knew how much I think of home and its endearments; and how anxious I am to place our families in a better sphere of life so far as their cares for old age are concerned. If I do not succeed in bettering their fortunes I shall at least have the satisfaction of having used my best endeavors to do so; - renewed health and with the considerable advantage of having obtained a European reputation. Whatever advantage I have obtained, or may obtain, honorable or pecuniary, are more than due from me to you for all your goodness and patience with me and the boys; and I shall bring them to you as but a small return for all the benefits I have derived with my gun now that I have little or no time to look for things worth writing a description of; though there are plenty of them here – indeed all Flanders is full of objects and customs worthy of description and comment. Good night.

Friday night, May 28, 1846. – The gun is getting on very well. I have been at work on it myself today – doing some parts which I did not like to trust to one who might not understand me very well. If this gun looks as well itself as its likeness on paper does it can scarcely fail pleasing.

As I say every time about matters at home – do what you think proper and just. I trust entirely and with utmost confidence to you judgment and good sense. I have given up the hope of getting any letter from you until your answer to my last or to this arrives. Do not fail to write me immediately and give me a long letter if you have to get ten women to help take care of the children while you write. Give Eddy and George and John their extra kiss from Papa – who kisses them a regularly as he goes to bed – as well as their dear Mother. Remember me most affectionately to Father and Mother and Sisters and Brothers. I hope to see you all again soon and such a glorious time we'll have of it don't come often.

That ring is safe and I intend to keep it so until I have the pleasure of putting it onto your thumb – it's rather too large for any finger you've got – but it makes a capital tie for a handkerchief. Good bye.   Forever your Edward.

P.P. Direct your letter thus, you will have to pay the postage to England:

"Dr. Edward Maynard
At the U.S. Legation
        Brussels
        Belgium.
Care of the U.S. Legation in London"

Chapter 19
(Fifteenth Letter)
European Delays

Mr. Ellen S. Maynard
Cooperstown, N.Y. United States of America

Brussels, 1ˢᵗ June 1846.   **Page 1**

My Dear Ellen,

      My letter mailed, or rather sent per courier, day before yesterday, will lead you to expect that I may do something very soon with the gun. When that letter was written I had good grounds for hope that I should accomplish my object in coming to Europe through the person of whom I wrote, - who was just the sort of person to <u>manage</u> the matter properly. On Sunday (yesterday) I learned that he was so much occupied with another matter (out of which he is realizing a fortune) that he is unwilling to divert his attention from <u>it</u> to attend to mine. So that hope has gone; - now for another man – if another such can be found. In the meantime I am pushing the sporting gun as hard as I can and have the work well made; - working a great deal on it myself. The worst part to do is already done satisfactorily and I feel better and better pleased with it as I see it growing under my hands. Good night.

Sunday 7ᵗʰ June 1846. – All this week past since writing the last page I have had the <u>blues</u> and so didn't feel like writing. Things don't look so promising ahead as they did when I wrote last. The locks too don't get along so fast as I expected, - on account of having to <u>make</u> <u>tools</u> to make the locks <u>with</u>, etc., etc., etc.

However there will be an end to the matter <u>sometime</u> – that is some little consolation; and whichever way it ends – for profit or loss; - it is the last invention of such importance I shall ever be disposed to undertake to introduce. <u>No compensation that could be named</u> would induce me to undergo the loss of the comforts and pleasures of home for so long a time again.

Yesterday Mr. Clemson took me in the carriage with his family for a drive some four or five miles. The Clemson's continue their kindness to me; and I sometimes have long talks with Mr. Clemson, very much to my edification, upon taxes, tariffs, treaties etc., etc., etc. You are surprised, perhaps, that I don't say anything about one <u>War with Mexico</u>. I am <u>disposed</u> to look at it as a war produced by those who desire a continuance of high duties; and it will be likely to continue as long as <u>they</u> please. Very naturally you will suppose that I have received this notion from Mr. Clemson – and I must confess that I have – not because it is <u>his</u> belief – but such is the conclusion to which I arrived after talking with him upon the subject. He put the tariff question in a light entirely new to me; and by very simply and convincing chain of reasoning showed that our twenty millions were taxed to enrich some hundred and fifty. This will startle you perhaps as it did me. I must have a good long talk with Father Owen when I get home upon this subject and perhaps he will upset the arguments of Mr. Clemson.

You know I am no proficient in the science of political economy; - in fact I am just the person to be easily convinced for either side provided I don't hear the other. During our ride yesterday we visited the tomb of the great singer Malibrau; the most exquisitely beautiful idea for a tomb that I ever saw. Imagine first a neat structure, like a little chapel; some eight feet square with bronze doors on one side and a sky light through a dome. You enter – and before you is seen rising from her tomb Malibrau – represented in white marble – a perfect likeness, 'tis said – in her shroud. She seems to be just leaving the earth; - and such is the skill of the sculptor that the statue really seems not to have any weight – it looks as if it would rise from its very lightness. I wish you could see it – I wish you could see all the beautiful, interesting, new, or grand things that I have seen in Europe. I shall not attempt to describe to you my anxiety about home. I must not write about it. Good night.

Monday night, June 8, 1846. – Nothing new – Work goes better. Good night.

Tuesday night, June 9, 1846. – Ditto – ditto – Good night.

Wednesday night, June 10, 1846. - Ditto. Did hope to see a pair of locks for a sporting gun finished this week; but I fear I shall be disappointed. Today, (as I do nearly every day) I worked on them myself, and find it necessary for me to be at the shop as much as two or three hours at least every day to prevent mistakes. Next week I expect to go to Liege to have the locks applied to the gun.

Night before last I had such a dream that I awoke and could not sleep again. I dreamed I was telling you some amusing story up stairs when I hear a child crying. After great difficulty I tore open a window and looked down and there stood little George crying as if his heart would break for fear of a great dog that was near him. Several persons were standing about paying no attention to his distress and when I called to him "Georgy – papa come to Georgy" he put up his little hands towards me and gave me such a supplicating look to do so- O Ellen – I shall never forget it. And I cried too – I couldn't help it – not because it <u>was</u> so, but because there were so many such things in a child's experience that he must naturally meet with some. It seems to me that the longer I am from you all the more sensitive I am about everything that may mar your comfort or happiness. Thank God! There will be some sort of an end to this gun matter soon and then Heaven please I will soon embrace you all again, and be happy. Good night.

Saturday morning, June 13, 1846. – I learned from Mr. Clemson this morning that to go by the next steamer this letter must be sent off this morning. So I must close it at once. He also tells me that he has made an appointment to show my invention to the Austrian Ambassador at 12 today as his (Clemson's) house where I am to be with the locks etc.   Whatever I write you about the gun and about what I do with it I wish you to <u>keep to yourself</u>; as it may be important to our interest as affecting sales etc., etc., etc.

Kiss our dear little boys for me again and tell them how much their papa loves them and that he never sees children without thinking of his own. There is every prospect of my being ready to start for home about the time of receiving your answer to my last. Write again, <u>and keep writing</u>, until I state <u>positively</u> that I shall sail on a certain day. Direct as I wrote last, to me at the U.S. Legation here, care of the American Legation London. Your letters will then be sent to London by mail and from there to Mr. Clemson by the man who brings <u>his</u> letters.

Do not suspect for an instant that I shall stay one day longer from home than justified to all concerned will warrant. It is impossible that you can be more anxious to see me than I am to see you and the children. Imagine that <u>you</u> have not seen them for a year and you will have some idea of <u>my</u> anxiety to see them. I was shown a note this morning from a Lady, (friend of the Lady Seymour for whom I operated) to Mrs. Clemson begging her to intercede for her with the great American Dentist to induce him to give her a day of his time; - to which they said great etc., etc., graciously condescended to reply that perhaps he would grant the prayer sometime next week, but could not designate any day etc., etc. The fact is I do not like to take my attention from the gun for even one day until it is farther advanced or finished – something is sure to go wrong if I do and then there is delay and bad work etc., etc., etc.

Remember me affectionately to the family; and try to be as happy all of you as you can; and if I get rich I'll make you happier; and if I don't I'll g back into the old harness and do what I can for us then. Anyhow with the blessing of health we shall prosper and by a life of industry and honesty we shall be better off than one in ten thousand here or anywhere else.

Again a thousand kisses to you my dear Ellen: we shall soon meet again and then we can enjoy them.

Forever your Edward.

Chapter 20
(Sixteenth Letter)
A Tragedy at Home

Mrs. Ellen S. Maynard
Washington City D.C. United States of America

Brussels, 18 June 1846

My Dear Ellen,

Overwhelmed as I am with grief by the contents of Brother George's letter, I commence this letter to you, not with the vain hope of consoling you; - feeling as I do I can imagine nothing so great as to console a parent for such a loss. O my dear Ellen! - had you seen how fondly I kissed the seal of you re letter, assured by its color that my fears dad no cause – and then to find such painful intelligence! God help us, my dear wife, to bear this great affliction – it is our first of its kind – may it be the last we shall see, if such may be the will of heaven. My dear, Eddy! How you must have suffered! And your Father not near to say a kind word to you, to kiss you, to watch with you, to fold you in his arms, and perhaps to allay your pangs; and, O my God! The thought that any possibility I might have saved you! My poor boy! So good – so innocent – so cheerful, so intelligent for your years – the favorite of all who saw you – the pride of all your relatives – the fondest hope of your parents! O God! In this your hour of trail, if the prayers of the honest of heart are any avail, help us bear this calamity! – And if, as we are taught to believe, the end of life with such children but the beginning of their happiness, make us feel that is so. * (See below note)

My dear wife – you whose soul was devoted to our first child – what ought I say – what <u>can</u> I say to you? I need say nothing to tell you my sorrow – but can I say anything to lessen the sorrow you feel? Can any words, any expressions of affection, of unabated love for you and our children – now dearer than ever to me – can these or anything that a devoted girl, to believe that "all is for the best", - however difficult it may be; - and try to console dear Mother, whose loss is scarcely less than ours – she was so perfectly a mother to or poor boy, and he so fond of her! I am sure that all that could have been done by you for him was done; and I shall never be able to discharge my obligations to Brother George for the service he has rendered the family since my absence.

* Little Edward Maynard, eldest son of Edward and Ellen Maynard died April 27, 1846 age 6 years 5 months and is buried in Congressional Cemetery at Washington D.C. This being the case, it appears letters took about 7 weeks to get from Washington to Brussels in 1846.

Heaven only knows when I shall return. If my presence could be serviceable, or more so than a letter, I should feel justified in quitting this enterprise at once. But, however impatient we may be to see each other after such a long separation and such an overwhelming affliction, it is proper that we reflect upon the consequences of my going home now. I cannot say that I <u>believe</u> anything worth a month's absence will come out of my business here.

But the matter has been opened in such a way to the great banker Rothschild and others, and is now in such a shape, that to leave it would be to forfeit all chances of success and therefore all reward for coming to Europe and for a year's absence from business – to count nothing for the absence of home and friends. It is some consolation to me to learn from George that these reasons for my prolonging my stay have been satisfactory to you; and you will be sure that I am strongly impressed with their importance if I allow them to detain me any longer. These reasons and all I mention of business is very painful to me, and I only write this part of my letter to show you why I do not at once start for home – to be, perhaps, some cause of consolation to the family.

I have said nothing of your own illness or that of dear little George – I scarcely feel that I may rejoice at recovery of you both, through the fear that, ere this, another affliction has visited us.

Sunday June 21, 1846. – I have been trying my dear Ellen since writing the preceding part of this letter to reconcile myself to this heartrending affliction; - and the Clemson's have exerted themselves very kindly to keep my mind from it. While I am with them and talking of other things I succeed in partially mastering the manifestation of my grief – but if this subject is touched or if I am alone – O my dear Ellen! – Can I ever cease to think of our poor Eddy? Our dear, pure hearted boy! – I must not indulge in this grief – I know it – I feel it renders me unfit for all business – but I must write my dear wife, - and I cannot write anything else – for me there is nothing else to write – I have said all that is necessary about business; you will feel sure, I know, that I feel justified in not going home at once. Perhaps before closing this letter something like progress will be made in my business. It is impossible to hasten it.

I can no more write cheerfully – my buoyancy of spirit is all gone. Life itself, were it not for those dear persons depending upon me, would seem scarcely worth striving for. My dear, dear wife, - how shall we meet after this loss! With feelings how different from those we anticipated! O God! To think that perhaps we shall none of us meet again! What will become of you all if I should be taken away without having provided for your maintenance? - When I think of this I scarcely feel justified in leaving home and incurring the risks of such a route as I have taken. Unwise as I may have been I thought I was acting for the best for us all. God grant it may yet prove so!

Friday June 26, 1846. – You will perceive by the dates that I do not write often. I cannot write without recurring to our great affliction; and my conviction is that I ought not to dwell upon the subject when I can avoid it. Mr. Clemson tells me to go out and try to occupy my mind with something else – anything that I can – and not to stay in the house – that I shall be sick if I do not take his advice etc. I have taken it and do try all I can to find reasons for not grieving; but I need not tell you how unsatisfactory most of the reasons are to my feelings.

I must finish this letter tonight so that Mr. Clemson may enclose it with my despatches for Washington. My models will be here in a few days; and by the time of their arrival I hope to know whether some steps that I have taken with persons of high and influential positions will be likely to bring about a sale of the invention. I will not tire you with a useless statement of what those steps are but will explain all to you when I have thanked God for having returned me safely to your arms. I cannot say when I shall return; perhaps by Steamer of the 19th July, which will be the next after the one that takes this letter. I have written to Smith and Tyson to send me a full power of attorney to dispose of all interest they have in my invention. Their answer will probably be received by the Steamer which sails from Boston on the 1st of July. If I wait for it I shall not be able to sail on the19th; but if I can get ready perhaps I can make some other arrangement and not have to wait. But, as I wrote last, do not fail to write, for I may be detained much longer; although I cannot believe that I shall be. George tells me that Mr. Johnson is willing to let the office remain as I left it etc. I wish George would thank him for his kindness and tell him I shall not forget it. And I would like to have him thank the Physicians and all others who were attentive and kind to my poor boy and to the family during your time of great distress. Do try, my dear Ellen, to bear your loss with resignation. Heaven knows how unfit I am to give you counsel in a matter affecting my own feelings so deeply. I will not try to console you my dear girl otherwise by trying to add to the affection I have borne for you, all that I have felt for our lost one. If it be true that "of such is the kingdom of Heaven" then indeed is "our loss his great gain". He has left a world where little good and great evil exists; and left it before his heart had been seared by finding how very little good it is in the power of one man to do. It is consoling to know that no pains or expenses had been spared upon him to make him healthy, happy and useful. If we had done our duty we have done all. We have still, I trust, great blessings in our other children – may God see fit to preserve them for usefulness and happiness for themselves and others.

Try to be cheerful Ellen, and do not distress little George and John by permitting them to witness your sorrow. They are old enough to receive lasting impressions and George has I know a most susceptible heart. Do not let him be unhappy. My dear wife I must now bid you good night with the hope of bringing my next letter to you.

Forever your Edward.

P.S. My affectionate regards to our friends. Tell little George and John I will bring them something.

Chapter 21
(Seventeenth Letter)
The King of Belgium Examines the Lock

<u>Legation of the United States Brussels</u>
Mrs. Ellen S. Maynard
Cooperstown, N.Y. United States of America

Brussels, Monday June 29, 1846. **Page 1**

My Dear Ellen,

My last letter to you was in answer to the one having such melancholy news, from Brother George. It was closed on Friday last and sent off the next day too soon for me to say that the King had sent for Mr. Clemson to go to him and bring me and the invention that it might be exhibited to His Majesty. The time appointed by the King was 5 P.M., Sunday – at which time we were at the Palace and after a few moments delay were ushered into "the presence" – of a very plain, not at all remarkable looking man in a military uniform and bearing some half a dozen decorations on his left breast. As His Majesty speaks English well the conversation was free as etiquette will permit between kings and common people. He examined with much apparent interest the various locks and the primer and snapped the pistol twice to see the effect etc., and expressed great admiration and his good opinion of the invention – specifying several of its advantages with a degree of earnestness and in a manner that showed a practical knowledge of the subject. You may not be aware that he was in the military service for some timer; and it is said that Napoleon (under whom he served) regarded him as a most extraordinary Officer – even speaking of him as one of the remarkable men of his time. Before and after I was presented I had an opportunity of exhibiting the invention to two Officers who were in an antechamber - both of whom being known to Mr. Clemson. I was introduced too. One of them a Colonel Borreman (of Artillery) is said to be one of the most scientific and distinguished officers of this Country. I have no doubt he was placed there to see the locks, and I am glad to say that he was highly delighted with them.

I believe the whole Government must be in my favor now – the King, the Minister of Foreign Affairs, the Minister of War, the Inspector General and several others of the best officers for such examinations have now expressed their opinions in favor of the invention. Whether the Government will propose anything farther remains to be seen. I have gone as far with a pair of <u>back-action</u> locks for a sporting gun as I can before my visit to Liege to have them applied to a gun. I am now making – partly as an occupation for my mind – a rough model, at little expense, of the invention as applied to the forward-action lock. Tomorrow being the day to expect the steamer at Liverpool from Boston I shall look for another letter from home on Thursday or Friday. For the first time, I feel a degree of dread at hearing from home, notwithstanding that the interest I feel is even greater than usual. Good night.

Thursday night, July 2, 1846. – But no letter; and no progress in my affairs except with the locks upon which I am working. If I do not get a letter tomorrow I shall not expect one until the arrival of the next steamer. I dreamed last night of arriving at home and meeting you and little George and John and we were all <u>so glad</u> to meet; - but for you and I meeting was not all joy only; - our dear little boy was too present to the mind of each of us for our happiness to be perfect.

I am now expecting to visit Liege on Monday next, and shall probably remain there several days – perhaps a week, to have a gun finished – the locks of which are ready to be applied, though not completed. I get all the political and war news by the papers at the Legation; - and I am pleased to learn that the bluster on both sides of the Atlantic about the Oregon question is likely to give way to a peaceable settlement. And although we lose Van Couver's Island it may be better for us to have its coal brought to us by English Capital; - and besides, it is not impossible that coal will be found, and of as easy access, in Oregon.

As for Mexico – it will be all very well for us to take some few of her Provinces in payment of her debt. European papers speak in terms of praise of General Taylor's despatches and of the conduct of our troops; both of which seem rather to surprise them, - so perfectly have they forgotten that we have twice thrashed what they consider the "most powerful nation". Good night.

Sunday night, July 5, 1846. – And yet no letter. Tomorrow I go to Liege taking with me a young man who has been at work for me and who understands French, Flemish, and some English. I <u>may</u> remain there some two weeks, but hope to return before ten days.

Yesterday being Independence Day I was invited to dine with the Clemson's. I believe there are but two other Americans here – one a Mr. Lee who is not a person to be respected by his countrymen, I'm told, and the other a Mrs. Righter or Riter, wife of a German now in America, who by the way, seems, if accounts be true, to treat her very badly. She has been visiting his friends and has been trying to get home for months. Her husband sends her a check which she gives to his brother to get cashed for her. The brother says she don't need so much money – that she is extravagant etc., and besides – that his brother owes him money – so he keeps a part for himself. In the meantime poor Mrs. Righter's expenses are going on and when she gets the share allowed her by her amiable brother-in-law she finds it will not be sufficient and writes home for more and complains of the treatment etc. – to which the husband replies in such a manner as to how that he thinks his brother has given her as much as she ought to have, or something of that sort. I believe she has made some arrangements to go home this month.

Do not suppose Ellen, that because I say nothing of sending you funds I have forgotten the matter. On the contrary I am very uneasy through the fear that Willoughby may not be able to spare conveniently such money as you may need. The difficulty about sending money from here out of my letter of credit I explained to you. I have to trust entirely to Willoughby for your supplies if you need them, as must be the case. But I hope very soon to put an end to all anxiety on the subject by going home; and going to work again. As God wills. Good night Ellen.

Monday night, July 6, 1846. – Hotel de l'Europe, Liege. – Arrived safely and have had time to walk about a little but not to commence business. Tomorrow morning shall call upon Colonel Frederix with a letter from Mr. Clemson stating my object etc. The young man of whom I wrote is with me. His name is Dumont. He thinks he would like to be a mechanical Dentist and would like to go to America with me to do my plate work. I am in the same room I occupied here at my former visit. Very quiet and clean. Good night.

Tuesday night, July 7, 1846. – Colonel Frederix not being at home I looked in at a shop where I had at my former visit purchased 3 locks very cheap and good and where I had seen some very beautiful guns. I found the man civil, opened to him my object etc., etc. He was <u>ready</u> and apparently anxious to do my work and satisfied me that he thought it for **his** interest to keep the matter as secret as possible. Etc. He talked like a <u>go-ahead</u> man; and, confessing that he had not much education and knew but little else than his trade, he showed me some of the best work upon guns I ever saw and was so very accommodating and candid that I took him to see my pistol and the unfinished locks, with which he was very much pleased. – liked the system – thought it beautiful, simple, good and all that sort of thing and I made arrangement to have him finish and apply the locks to a plain gun to be in the best possible work he can make, for which last he is to have less than fifty dollars. But about the price say nothing as I intend to speculate a little. He put the work in hand at once and in a day or two will have finished the first gun and will have the 2nd under way. Good night.

Wednesday night, July 8, 1846. – I forgot to say that on return to town yesterday afternoon Colonel Frederix called upon me; and today, by appointment, I called upon him and got what I most wanted of him, - the means of getting into some manufactory of barrels for sporting guns. With a letter which he gave me I went to Chand-Fontaine (sho Fontaine) a little village two leagues hence where all the barrel forging is done for all this region of country. There I witnessed the process of making the most beautiful Damascus barrels and got a great deal of information about the manufacture of barrels of all sorts which I wrote down on the spot; and I also procured specimens of the various kinds of <u>twist</u> used to make barrels etc., etc., etc. Altogether quite a satisfactory day's work. My gun maker whose name is Vivario-Plomdeur told me this morning several men were already at work upon my guns. Guns are made here just as watches are made in Switzerland – one man for one part, another for another etc. – some 20 being required for 1 gun; each working at his own house. Good night.

Thursday night, July 9, 1846. – While the man who has the locks is finishing them I am looking about – visiting old churches – curious places etc. I should be with the workman if he were in Liege but he is some miles away – 3 hours walk – in the country. As he can hardly go wrong there may be no necessity for going to him. Today I saw in one of the churches here what is said to be a piece of the table cloth used at the marriage at Cana where Christ changed water into wine. It is preserved with great care together with other relics. I shall be able to show you some beautiful pictures of some of the pulpits in this County. They are carved oak. There is one here, quite new, indeed not quite finished, that is more beautiful than I had supposed carved oak could ever be. Its delicacy, richness, and execution surpass anything I had ever imagined. I am told that no engraving of it has been published. Good night.

Saturday night, July 11, 1846. – Since writing last my work has gone on slowly-so much so that I have told Mr. Vivario that I could not wait to have it done so; and if he could not get on faster I must employ some other man. Today he has done better and will, I think, get the first one done in a few days, but I don't think I shall wait for another as he <u>now</u> says he must have a <u>month</u> to make it; - just double the time he first named. I am constantly in trouble about <u>home</u> – your funds for the family etc. Sometimes I am disposed to give up the gun entirely and go home at once – then I think of my lost time, and perhaps some fair prospect of sale presents itself, and then I think of how much good we could do to our dear parents if we had a few thousand dollars to ensure their comfort for life, and then I think I will try a little longer. And then your not writing me by last steamer – but perhaps you did and the letter is lost – leads me to fear the worst for the health of some of you. I feel too low spirited tonight to write at all; - for notwithstanding what you wrote about my not being uneasy about you – that I left you in the care of Mr. Willoughby etc. – still the idea constantly haunts me that you may be in want of funds for necessaries. I cannot say more than I have said about the difficulty in sending funds from Belgium. But I hope there will be no occasion to do so as I trust I shall be able to arrange matters here so as to go home soon. I feel as if to get home would be better for me than to get rich.

Good night and sweet dreams to you.

Sunday night, July 12, 1846. – This is my last day for writing in this letter as it must be sent off tomorrow. I expect to be in Brussels again with the gun now being made on Saturday or Sunday next. And I have pretty certainly concluded not to have a <u>fine</u> one made in this country. I find such difficulties at every step that if I would save any show of patience I should go home at once. It is not improbable that I shall take the next steamer after the one by which I send this, so as to be home by the 18th or 290th August. But do not calculate on my coming as some favorable turn of fortune may keep me longer.

Remember me to all our friends who enquire after my welfare. Kiss our dear children daily for me, and take many, very many, for yourself. I have nothing to say about home affairs, for the same reasons given before – I don't know how they stand; and I trust them entirely to you. The office I wish to have kept for me if Mr. Johnson will do without the rent until I return to pay it.

Keep up your spirits, my dear Ellen, if you can; and depend upon my coming home at the earliest day you would wish if you knew <u>exactly</u> what <u>encouragements</u> and what <u>discouragements</u> I meet with. I will not try to console you for our loss, my dear Ellen; for I feel that no one can console me. My only relief from sorrow is in my forcing myself to think of something else as much as I possibly can. When I am not overseeing and directing my work, I am either drawing at my room or rambling about town, sketching gothic windows in old churches etc., etc. – anything for occupation of the mind.

My health continues as good as I can expect considering changes of water, modes of living, and being away from <u>home</u>, etc. In the sheet No. 2 I speak of <u>both</u> my guns being underway. Mr. Vivario told me they were; but afterward he told me differently. I have already lost much of the confidence I placed in his honesty – and I shall get my matters out of his hands just as soon as I can with propriety.

Continue to write me as before – your letters will follow me back home if I go before they arrive. They will be perfectly safe and if I should get them in Europe will be of great value in my estimation. I feel very confident that I shall return by the steamer of the 4th or 19th August – I must close – Good night my dear wife and, I hope for a very short time, good bye. -

Forever yours, Edward.

Chapter 22
(Eighteenth Letter)
Lost Models Surface and a French Patent

Mrs. Ellen S. Maynard
Cooperstown   N.Y.
S. Hibernia, United States of America

Brussels, 14 July 1846 – **Page 1**
Tuesday night.

My Dear Ellen,

Partly to see if anything farther has occurred respecting the sale of my Patents and partly to be here when the letters for the Legation are expected I came back this afternoon; leaving Mr. Vivario to <u>stock</u> the gun while I am gone. I expect to return on Thursday morning to Liege. Mr. Clemson tells me that although nothing definite had transpired still the prospect is favorable. I must tell you that he has stated the object I have in view and that some other persons of considerable consequence have upon him representations <u>taken hold</u> of the matter – but, although this may seem and really <u>is</u> all right and proper it is <u>also</u> right and proper that nobody should know <u>any</u> diplomatic person has anything to do with such things. So my dear Ellen please say nothing of this, and I will tell you all those things which it might not be well to write. But do not fear that I shall do injustice, or if I can prevent it, suffer it to be done in any manner in which I am concerned. Policy or no policy, <u>honesty</u> is always <u>best</u>. Mr. Clemson understands this and gives me the best advice he can I am sure; and will see that all is done right if done at all.

 Mr. Vivario says he thinks I can have the gun in 8 or 10 days; I am calculating upon 2 weeks as it seems impossible to induce the workmen to hasten or even work steadily. None of them work on Mondays, and many are unfit to work on Tuesdays. Good night.

Thursday night at Liege, July 16, 1846. – Arrived safely. No letters yet by the steamer; probably not arrived. Met Mr. Graves of Kentucky (ex-member of Congress) at Mr. Clemson's last night, and came by the same train here with him and his wife and 1 or 2 friends; - they going to visit the Rhine. You may remember that they are old acquaintances of mine, we having fed at the same table our winter at <u>Mrs. Connor's</u>.

That pulpit of which I wrote in my last as being so beautiful a piece of work is the work of a celebrated sculptor at Brussels, who has placed in the three principal niches of it, three extremely fine statues. I am informed here that the cost of the whole is to be one hundred and fifty thousand francs – about $30,000 – quite enough to build a handsome church in America – but not such churches as one sees in Europe, in some cities. Mr. Vivario, as I feared, was not as ready as he promised to be with my work on my return.

While I am now writing, the small bells in one of the churches here are playing a sort of <u>overture</u> to the hour to be struck by the big ones. Very curious this. At every hour, for a few minutes before the hour is struck, some small bells play a sort of tune – at the half hour the same or nearly so – at the quarter a little less and at the eighth (7 minutes and a half still less) At the eights and quarters the large bell does not strike – but at the half it strikes the same as at the completion of the hour. For instance, at half past 9, the bell strikes <u>10</u> and at 10 it strikes the same, at half past 10 it strikes <u>11</u> and at 11 – 11; and so all day and all night. Good night.

Friday night, July 17, 1846. – The gun was to have been ready yesterday noon on my arrival from Brussels to have the <u>nipples</u> put in but it is not ready <u>yet</u> – I have now another promise that it shall be ready at 8 tomorrow morning. You are wondering why I don't quit the fellow and employ someone else, but you would not wonder if you knew how things are managed or rather should I say <u>mismanaged</u> here. Very likely I should jump from the pan to the fire by changing.

I begin to anticipate another source of vexation – that of not being able to secure a berth in either of the steamers of August – people are so anxious to get clear of sea voyage in September. If I could be sure of being ready I would write to secure a place at once but I cannot be so now. If I take a sailing packet I shall be better accommodated but may be 35 or even 45 days at sea and so be out during the equinoctial winds. But I shall do the best I can to get home at the earliest possible day. Tomorrow I shall expect a letter from you and one from Smith and Tyson as I see by the paper that the Caledonia has arrived at Liverpool. Good night and sweat dreams.

Saturday night, July 18, 1846. – My work has gone on so very slowly and so badly that I have asked Mr. Vivario how much I must pay him if I take the gun in its present condition. He is to let me know tomorrow morning and I shall probably be in Brussels tomorrow night. I cannot waste money and time in this way any longer. – Instead of doing my work as well and as punctually as he promised he has nearly ruined the locks I took him by rough handling, wrenching and bruising. At the rate he has gone on so far there would be nothing good left of them when he has done.

Good night.

Brussels. Sunday night, July 19, 1846. – Arrived this P.M. Mr. Clemson tells me he sent a letter (received from London) yesterday to Liege and today another package – also received from London. I left directions at Liege to have my letters sent back here and shall probably get them tomorrow. The package is probably from Smith and Tyson.

Tomorrow Mr. and Mrs. Clemson and their two children go to Blankenberge for sea air and sea bathing etc., etc., etc. to be gone a month or two probably; but Mr. Clemson will probably return occasionally for a day or two.. Nothing farther about selling except that the persons engaged seems to be in earnest in trying to sell. Mr. Clemson thinks they may succeed and that nothing can be gained by hurry. He has seen the partially made gun which I have been trying to have made and thinks that if it were <u>good work</u> and completed it would be a beautiful gun, as the model and arrangements are good and pleasing to the eye. In order to have a good model of every part of a sporting gun including the ornamental part, I purchased at Liege the handsomest one I saw, which I can dispose of, if necessary, with considerable profit in America. There is one all engrossing subject upon which I do not write – I am trying to keep my mind from it. Good night my dear Ellen.

Monday night, July 20, 1846. – My letters have not come back from Liege yet, or at any rate have not been brought to me. You will be put out of all the patience by reading my complaints and vexations. I know they are of no use except that they may show you how I am delayed and annoyed. Have been working upon the gun today – not because I expect to make much of it but for occupation until the letters come. As for having a fine gun made here upon my system, I have given up altogether. Should any one wish to see how the lock can be applied to a sporting gun, perhaps the one upon which I have been working will answer to show so much and will assist in making another. Whatever I can do to it to make it better without much expense, it will be well to do, on that account. This state of uncertainty about what others are disposed to do and the vexations of delays and deceptions with the gun added to my intense anxiety about home has affected my health as well as spirits; I should scarcely be known as the same person by one who saw me two months ago. But, as I have said so many times already, there must be an end to the business sometime and I think it will be very soon. Today I have drawn twenty five pounds sterling from my banker – having exhausted nearly all I had before drawn and earned here. I am curious to know what Smith and Tyson say in their letter. What kind of face they can show after such failure to do their part of the business is beyond comprehension. Were the Patents all secured by Tyson according to agreement there would have been no risk in showing the invention and so enlisting capitalist in the enterprise; but to have had my hands tied by risking all chance of getting other Patents was in effect to lesson, immeasurably, the chances of selling even in those possession. If a manufactory of such guns were in operation in Prussia without a Patent, the Patent <u>here </u>would be worth very little; and so of all countries; to make the Patents profitable they should cover all countries where such guns can be mage cheap. Good night and sweet dreams.

Tuesday night, July 21, 1846. – And no letters yet. While I was at the shop hard at work at the gun today several persons called to see me but none of them left their names or stated their business. One, whom I suppose is Mr. Fay, Secretary of U.S. Legation at Berlin, is to call again tomorrow. You may judge of my anxiety to get my affairs settled when I tell you I worked at the guns today rather than go 50 rods to see the King review 15,000 troops. On my way to the shop I saw Soliman Pasha, an Officer from Egypt. He wore a red cloth cap with long black tassel – black round-a-bout – very full black trousers or breeches (couldn't see which) and boots up about his knees. Around his waist, under his round-a-bout, but over his vest, he wore what looked like a sort of gray cashmere shawl Mustache very full and long but no whiskers. Perhaps this sketch will assist in giving you an idea of his costume. He seems to be some 50 years old and is quite stout. He was standing as you see him in a balcony as I passed him and stopped to swell the number of people gazing at him. Good night.

Wednesday night, July 22, 1846. – The packet from Smith and Tyson has at last come to hand but the letter sent before to Liege, one day earlier, has not yet come from Major Smith saying that he had written me a letter of condolence and I am apprehensive that the other letter is from him as I have not received the one he mentioned. They send me a full power of Attorney to act for them. Major Smith speaks of having been frequently with our dear little boy of his attending his funeral and congratulates me upon having so superior a wife inasmuch as you bear your afflictions with such strength of mind and such Christian fortitude. He tell me also that you were at the time of his writing (27th June) in the interior of Ney York and all well so I conclude you are with our friends at Cooperstown; and I am glad that you are for the change of scene which will be well for you. He tells me also that my brother-in-law is at Washington taking care of the house etc.; so I feel certain that it will be well cared for. He congratulates me upon my professional success, honors, etc., etc., etc. He says "I advise you to sell, for if you leave Europe without affecting a sale it may be finally lost." Nothing about what the Government is doing with the locks for the army and navy.

Tyson says "If you get anything like a fair price sell, this is our advice". What he would consider a fair price is more than I know. His letter was evidently written by himself for both to sign but his name only is signed – Smith having written another letter. Tyson says "Have you any funds from previous sales, yet in hand? If so would be much obliged if you would remit by return steamer at least the amount of five thousand dollars, or even a smaller sum, as the expenses incurred have subjected us to a very great inconvenience". He thinks nothing of what I have lost by his failure of fulfillment of the contract. But such is always the way- every one for himself. – Well, well! You and I, my dear Ellen, form the only partnership in which I shall ever do business hereafter. We can consult each other's interests and at least do each other justice. If Smith and Tyson are entitled to anything from the sale of Denmark then they are bound to pay my expenses which have been 2 or 3 times their share of that sale. But enough and more than enough of this – I shall short work with them when I return.

There seems to be a sort of conspiracy to annoy me. I have just received a letter from Mr. Vivario, saying that the gun I had bought of him (and for which I had partly paid, the balance to be paid on receipt of the gun here), he had been compelled to let go to a certain Russian who had, before me, asked to have it. I left it to be put up in a case and sent to me. He now says that he will send me another absolutely the same and engraved better if I say so; but I know he has not another like it, or near so handsome; and I have no faith in his promises to make another. His reason for giving it to the Russian is that the Russian threatens to trade no more with him – he nor his family nor his friends, if he refuses. The Russian heard me praising the gun and was thus induced to buy it he admits. The Russian is not to be blamed considering the country he was educated in; - nor perhaps Vivario either, for the same reason – all Europe is one vast school of deception and fraud – one enormous lie from beginning to end.   Good night Ellen.

Thursday night, July 23, 1846. – <u>The</u> letter from Liege has come to hand and turns out to be the answer to an enquiry I made of the Russian Legation at Paris concerning my box of models. The letter is dated the 17th and informs me that the case of models was sent to me on the day before. As the box has had plenty of time to get here, and as there have been several hundred boxes, packages, etc., lost recently between this place and Paris, the strong probability is that I shall never hear of it again. But I am getting accustomed to this sort of thing, and since hearing of our great loss I look upon all these lesser troubles with a feeling I never experienced until lately. The box was addressed to the U.S. Legation here and that fact may save it if it ever comes to light again. I am now of course led to suppose that you did not write by the last steamer; but although my regret at this is great I derive some comfort from learning from Major Smith that you and the children are with you friends and <u>well</u>. I have been hard at work all day at the gun again and have got into something like shape. I begin to despair of selling the right to Europe, as I hear nothing farther about the matter. Good night.

Friday night, July 24, 1846. – Nothing new – same as yesterday, except that I had a visit from General Count Woyna, the Austrian Minister. Didn't see him but found his card on my table when I came from work. One corner of the card was turned down, so I know he called in person; that being the signification. Good night. May your dreams be more pleasant than mine have been for a long time past. Good night.

Saturday night, July 25, 1846. –Today I have written to Mr. Clemson that I must go home immediately and that I wish to leave my matters with him until I can write to him. Whether he will come to Brussels or I go to Blankenberge will be for him to say, - probably he will come here. Nothing new. Good night.

Sunday night, July 26, 1846. – I learned today that the box of models has at last come to light and I expect to get it tomorrow morning. As I passed a shop window today I saw some pretty buttons for George and John and as they seemed to be cheap I bought enough for each a dress. Perhaps you will think best to use some for yourself as there are two sizes – 2 dozen of each. I have not yet purchased that lace because to get anything really good one must pay a considerable sum. The lace most highly prized here is that made a long, long time ago – the older the more costly – and some- such as is worn by Duchesses and Countesses etc. at balls, parties etc. is so coarse that I doubt if any lady in America would be seen wearing it, unless it were to trim a petticoat. I can see very little beauty in it; but I can see that the labor in making it must make it very expensive. I have seen none such before.

Good night.

Monday night, July 27, 1846. – Not having an order from Mr. Clemson for the case I did not get it today. Nothing new. Not feeling very well; I have only been out today to get my dinner. One hears a great deal in America about <u>cheap</u> <u>living</u> in Europe; but cheap and nasty go together here. I can get a good clean dinner for less money in Washington than in any place in Europe that I have tried. I should be ashamed to live at home as I lived here – but I cannot pay for Hotel dinners. I must live upon as little as I can and fill my belly – as for <u>taste</u> – I put that in my pocket, and try to believe I live well. If I supposed any of my friends here knew how I lived I should expect them to cut my acquaintance at once. If I am fortunate as to get home again perhaps I shall recover my <u>fat</u>. Tomorrow I shall probably see or hear from Mr. Clemson and perhaps shall be able to say something more positive about the time of my returning. I am however <u>determined</u>, <u>anyhow</u>, to go soon; and I may sail from Havre by a packet as the steamers are so crowded. Two of Mr. Stone's sons (the same of whom I wrote you) go home, I believe, by the Havre packet of the 8th August and if I can get off in time I shall try to go in their company. Good night.

Tuesday night, July 28, 1846. – Mr. Clemson came today and I shall make some arrangement to leave my matters with him until I can settle with Smith and Tyson so as to act for myself as I think proper. I shall probably take his advice and go via Liverpool – by a steamer if I can- if not, by a packet. Perhaps I shall have to visit Paris to get the French Patent. I now hope to be off this week; and if so shall perhaps sail about the 20th August. Good night.

Wednesday night, July 29, 1846. – Today I got the models, put the locks (which I kept) on to them, put them in order for exhibition and left them with Mr. Clemson to whom I have given instructions to sell. I have now only to finish a little business with him tomorrow morning and then pack up my things. I find that I must have the French Patent and leave it here. So I must go to Paris and perhaps stay a week to finish business there. I shall take with me only a bag – leaving my trunks here until I return from Paris. I shall then take them – go to London via Antwerp – probably stop one or two days in London to pay postage accounts and get the British Patents to send here and the go to Liverpool and then go home as quick as steam or wind will carry me. I shall continue to write but may not write so as to have my letters hit the next steamer. I hope to sail by the 20th August. I must close this tonight to insure its going by next steamer. Remember me most affectionately to our friends at Cooperstown and elsewhere. Kiss our dear little boys for me again and again. Tell them papa will be home to kiss them in a few days and will be <u>so</u> glad to see them, and will tell them all about the ships, and the ocean, and all the things he has seen; and will bring them some presents. Try my dear Ellen to be as cheerful as you can until I come home and I promise to do all I can to render you happy upon my return. I have not 'tis true succeeded with my enterprise but it has not been my fault – it is only misfortune, and as such a one we can bear very well having other means of living if I retain my health. I expect to go to my office as of old and to be far happier then than I have ever been before. We shall now begin a new life almost, and I anticipate much happiness in it. With a thousand kisses to you my dear girl I remain devotedly and forever yours, Edward.

Chapter 23
(Nineteenth and Last Letter)
Patents for England, Ireland and Scotland Secured, Return to America

Mrs. Ellen S. Maynard
Cooperstown
Otsego County
New York
<u>United States of America</u>

Valanciennes, France July 31, 1846.

My Dear Ellen,

You will see by the top of this letter that I am on my way to Paris. I left Brussels at noon today and arrived here in time to take a walk of two hours to see a little of the town and its extensive fortifications which last are being extended. I can give you no idea of them that will be correct without talking of them; so I will only say that they extend all around the City – probably cover a hundred or more acres, and are of great strength. Tomorrow at noon I continue my journey and shall arrive, accidents excepted, at Paris at night or before. Being Bearer of Despatches I was detained but a very few moments at the French douane (doo-an) (custom house). Dumont is with me. I have found him so useful heretofore that I agreed to pay his expenses to Paris and back if he would go; to which he acceded, as he was anxious to make the trip. He having lived in Paris long enough to know the City pretty well and therefore able to save me a great deal of <u>time</u> and <u>expense</u> as without him I must hire such a valet as I might find at Paris to serve me at <u>his</u> pleasure instead of mine. This place is called Va-lan'-se-an; all the <u>a</u>'s are sounded like <u>a</u> in "all", "ball" etc. accent as you see, on the second syllable. Pinch your nose when you say it and you will pronounce it just right. Good night.

Sunday night, August 2, 1846. – At the Hotel de Nantes, Paris. – Arrived here very safe and very tired last night – too much fatigued to say that I had got here. This morning I called upon the man who transacted the Patent business for Tyson, on account of some formality. And he doubts also if the second installment of 100 francs for the Patent due some time ago, has been paid; - and he also doubts whether the Government will now receive it, or declare the Patent forfeited because the money was not paid. Tomorrow he is to ascertain and on Tuesday is to tell me all about it.

This being a great fete day in France there has been a crowd of people to Versailles (ver-sale') to see the Palace, pictures and statuary in and about it and the grand exhibition of the playing of the fountains of Versailles. These fountains are in the grounds of the Palace and are made to play as they did today only 4 times a year – the expense being 30,000 francs a day. I must wait until I get home to give you an idea of the grand part of the day's exhibition. Near the Palace there were other things for amusement – such as charging, blindfold, with a spear at a mark; - running races on foot – ditto with all except the head in a sack – the sack being longer but not wider than a meal bag; climbing a pole, about the size of t he fore-mast of a schooner – made smooth like a mast and greased. At the top are several prizes for the first one who succeeds – a spoon perhaps for the second – a cotton handkerchief for other etc., etc. The first one has the hardest work and is allowed to carry a couple of little bags of ashes or other powder to rub and throw on to the pole as he goes up.

I have taken a stroll around the court of the Palais-Royal (Pal'-lay royal), so celebrated for its shops of elegant goods, jewelry, etc., etc. Here as in Russia one sees a great many soldiers; and to one not accustomed to see the sight of their red pantaloons is rather ludicrous. The Messieurs Stone are not here. Good night.

Monday night, August 3, 1846. – Called this morning upon Dr. Brewster and was received very well. – Invited to dine with him today – accepted and then went to our Legation and left some letters, pamphlets etc. Strolled about until 5 and then went to dine with Dr. Brewster. After dinner took a drive with him in his carriage out through the Bois de Boulogne (forest of Bologne) and back, and then sat with him until near midnight when he accompanied me to my hotel about 10 minutes ago. We had a great deal of professional conversation and told each other a great deal about our Russian Campaign.

I showed him my ring and he showed me several he had received from the Imperial Family at St. Petersburg. Some of his were more valuable; but he received nothing else but presents – no money, except what he got for operating for others, although he went on purpose to operate for the Imperial Family and stayed some 2 months or thereabouts. He showed me a letter from Parmly yesterday written from Holland. Parmly, after staying here a long time without paying expenses, has been doing very well at the Hague, having been, as he writes, employed by the Royal Family; of which I am glad, - as I believe he is a good operator and of good ideas of professional integrity. – Good night.

Tuesday night, August 4, 1846. – Brewster sent one of his pupils with me today to the famous Jardin de Plants (dzhardan de plahn) which disappointed me greatly. I expected to find the finest collection of animals and in the best order of any in the world – but I assure you that it was not at all to be compared to the exhibition of Jane, Angevine, Titus & Co. which you will recollect.

Dined again with Brewster and drove again as yesterday. On our way back, stopped at the Champs des Elysees (shan-da-liz-a) where the pupil and I got out and went to see a peculiar feature of Parisian life – a ball in a garden – the "ladies" being all, or nearly all, somebody's mistresses (and such as are not such are worse) of which I will <u>tell</u> you more.

Now for <u>business</u>. Mr. Merle tells me that the second installment has not been paid – that it was due before or on the 26th of June. He said he would petition the proper office today to receive the second payment and not declare the Patent void – giving as a reason that the non-payment has been in consequence of ignorance of the patent law – absence of the Patenteer etc. As the Patent was issued in Tyson's name it is necessary for Mr. Merle to communicate with him – get authority to pay the money if the Government will receive it etc. I shall leave with Brewster 100 francs for Mr. Merle if it can be received. If the Government will not receive it, then the Patent is void and so I lose all here. So much for Tyson's valuable assistance in furnishing capital and managing the business in Europe so as to make money. Well, well! "I am young yet". Good night.

Wednesday night, August 5, 1846. - Have done very little except stroll about all day. Dine every day with Brewster of whom I shall have a great deal to say to you. Last night I met at <u>that ball</u> a Swiss gentleman with whom I was acquainted in St. Petersburg. Has a sister at St. Petersburg from whom he learned that all <u>your</u> friends (for mine there are yours) were well. Good night.

Friday morning, August 7, 1846. – I come home from Brewster's very late every night and in consequence do not write every night. Yesterday I visited the Louvre (loo-ver) where I saw the statuary and paintings which have made that exhibition so celebrated. Afternoon visited the almost equally celebrated Pere la Chaise which you have so often read of as being the most remarkable burying place in the world. <u>Mount</u> <u>Auburn</u>, near Boston, possesses ten thousand natural beauties that Pere la Chaise can never have. I saw thee the tomb of Heloise and Abelard which is still visited by unhappy lovers and is strewed constantly with wreaths of "live-for-ever".

(Of what I have seen this morning I shall never attempt a description. I will however say that there is a great hospital for the treatment of "certain diseases" as they are advertised in our newspapers. Dr. Brewster called for me very early this morning and drove me out to the hospital and introduced me to Dr. Ricord, the Surgeon (an American). We went through several very long rooms, filled with double rows beds – each having an occupant suffering from some form of <u>the</u> disease. Dr. Ricord followed by 20 or 30 students gave a sort of running lecture upon each that he visited – exhibiting its type – explaining, prescribing etc. I think every young man or boy should see something of this sort. I saw one bed (and there may have been many) in which the sheet was drawn over the face of the occupant – His sufferings were at an end.)

Tomorrow morning I start for <u>home</u> and hope to reach it before the gales of September. You will perhaps think it strange – but I have been on the lookout all the time since I came here for some little thing, within my means to buy, for you and the children; but have seen nothing – absolutely nothing worth carrying home either for its novelty or beauty – and this is exactly what Parmly wrote me while I was at St. Petersburg. I thought of getting a suit of clothes here for myself but have given it up – thought of buying you a watch and after enquiring the prices of and examining a dozen have given <u>that</u> up also.

The celebrated beauty of French women I have not had the fortune to see; and all their <u>superior grace</u> <u>of</u> <u>action</u> is attributable, I imagine, to their freedom from what we call modest restraint – a thing I should not be willing to exchange for all <u>their</u> merit. Night. Brewster tells me that I can secure a place here as well as at Liverpool for a steamer, and I have concluded to stop another day and try to do so.

Passing a window I saw a peculiar corset and bought it – "You shall see what you shall see" <u>when you see it</u>. This visit to Paris has given me a great insight to the European practice of Dentistry. I do not at all wonder that so much dissatisfaction attends it. The Legation here has given me some despatches for Washington – so that I shall be Bearer of Despatches again. Good night.

Saturday night, August 8, 1846. – I found all as Brewster told me about the steamers – and I consider myself very fortunate in having secured my passage here because I should probably have lost it by waiting until I arrive at England. I am to leave Liverpool in the Great Britain on the 28th of this month and expect to arrive at <u>New York</u> about the 8th of September. Tomorrow morning I leave Paris for <u>home</u> – I must go to bed as it is past midnight. Good night.

Ostend, (Belgium) Monday night, August 10, 1846. – Arrived at Brussels last night and came her on this P.M. Tomorrow morning I take the steamer for Dover and from thence go to London by railway. Nothing that Brewster could offer me foe amusement would induce me to remain another day in Paris. He offered to devote himself for the whole day (Sunday) to visiting the country around Paris if I would stay but I was so impatient to be on my way home that I declined accepting his offer. I am sitting in a little 10 by 12, 7 feet high room at the Hotel de Flandre, my cup of tea before me <u>within</u> me a feeling that if you were here – no –not that; - but if I were with you at Cooperstown taking tea I should feel less lonesome than I do. It will be a touch of relief to me to once get home and get "settled down" to business that I look forward to the time with anticipation of much pleasure.

May your dreams be sweet. Good night.

Golden Cross Hotel, London Tuesday night, August 11, 1846. – Arrived here this P.M. Was a little sea sick while crossing the channel – just enough to remind me of my old sufferings and give me a foretaste of those to come. I expected some delay and trouble at the custom house, but had none of either – my baggage scarcely being looked into when they learned I was a <u>Courier</u>. My despatch bag was in a travelling bag and I was not even required to show it, having already politely handed the Officer my passport with a request that he would be so kind as to look at it. I hear good accounts of the Steamer in which I am to go. She seems to have gained favor. Good night.

Wednesday night, August 12, 1846. – I called this morning to pay my postage bill at the House of Harrison, Winans and Eastwick and found there a letter from Parmly who writes me that he will sail from Rotterdam for London to meet <u>and</u> <u>talk</u> (but not to return to America) on Saturday next. This will make it necessary for me to remain here instead of going into the country, for three or four days. It is so expensive staying here that I wish to get away as soon as I can – and besides I wish to see something of English Country life. As I have written to Parmly tonight I must close by wishing you good night.

Friday night, August 13, 1846. – I find that a letter passed through our Legation here on the 28th (I believe) of last month from America, for me. It was sent to Brussels and must have been received by Mr. Clemson after I left Belgium. I have written to have it sent here and shall expect it on Monday next. I scarcely dare hope it is from you, but I wish it may prove to be. I have not quite finished my business here but hope to do so tomorrow. You will recollect that I told you when I was here before that I saw a great many pretty and good things which I should be glad to get for you – so it is now – but you know why I don't get them. I should also be glad to get something for each of our dear friends who have been so kind to you in my absence but I must forgo the pleasure of doing so. I had no idea there was so much expense necessarily attending a traveler in Europe. I have cramped and pinched myself in living and avoided expenses that I should have incurred if I had money to spare, in order that I might get home <u>whole</u> and perhaps bring a few souvenirs of my travels; but shall only be able to show you a few maps of routes, views of buildings, and such cheap things as would aid me in telling my stories of travel. I feel mortified and grieved at this; and I feel that you will all be disappointed; but I have done all that I could. I should be as much pleased as any one of you to bring you such rich presents; but with the exception of <u>the</u> <u>ring</u> given me by the Grand Duchess Helen, which will be yours, I shall have nothing of value to give. I have a little picture book of soldiers and a little box of bricks for George and John to play with – very cheap things, but the best I can buy. I see occasionally some things that would be very useful to you and the children and such as we cannot get at home, and if I could afford it should feel more disposed to get such things than those of luxury merely.

Mr. Ralston called upon me last night and was greatly disappointed to learn that I had not made a fortune by my invention. He regretted that I had not my pistol with me as he believed he could put me in the way of doing something here etc., etc., etc., etc. So it goes – everybody thinks that everybody must like it and if they have money must be anxious to but the Patent etc., etc. I have heard so much of this thing that I am tired of it. I don't like to think of it – and if I could forget all about the invention I am not sure but it would be the best thing for me.

I have been thinking about going to Cooperstown on my arrival at New York and have come to the conclusion to leave it to you to decide. If you would rather go to Washington as early as the 10th September then take John to take care of you and the children and go to the City Hotel, New York on the 8th September and wait for me. If you would rather I should go to Cooperstown write me so and direct to me at the City Hotel, N.Y. and across the end of the letter writ "Passenger by the Great Britain from Europe" – and write so that your letter will be in New York on the 8th. I confess that I would rather go to Cooperstown for a little while on account of the weather which will be still too warm for you and the children at Washington and to see our friends; so if you are not anxious to get home for a week or so I think it would be better that I go to Cooperstown. But I am disposed to leave the matter entirely to your decision, as there may be things to influence you of which I can know nothing. Or, if you prefer it, leave the children at Cooperstown and go with John to New York and we will go back to Cooperstown together. Perhaps this will suit you better. Should you go to New York it would be well to send your card to my brother's house so that he may show you the attention he would wish to show. John will easily find his house as it is in the first street above Union Place turning to the right; - house on the left hand after he enters the street. If he is in town he will endeavor to make your stay pleasant. I will write him that I am coming by the Great Britain and that perhaps you will be at the city Hotel on the 8th to wait for me. Good night.

Saturday night, August 14, 1846. - I have procured the Patents for England, Ireland and Scotland from the men who had charge of them here, and have sent them to Mr. Clemson; - have paid all my postage bills here and when I get that letter from Mr. Clemson I shall have finished my business here. Had I any feeling for enjoyment here there are a thousand things to gratify it – but I have none – and I should feel blessed if I could sleep until the hour of my departure from London.   I could perhaps obtain entrance into some of the Hospitals here and perhaps other instructive places but cannot consent so by favors from Englishmen yet. As for the letters I brought introducing me etc. – they are not to my taste. I could not use them without an implied obligation to say as much for the writers; and I do not choose to let anything of that sort curtail my freedom of speech or action. I have a letter to Mr. Cartwright (an eminent Dentist here), from Dr. Harris, and as I am rather anxious to know him, I may present the letter.

I expect Parmly tonight and when he comes I shall have some occupation for my time. I shall send a letter to Major Smith for him and Tyson to meet me in New York to make some arrangement about our affairs; and another to brother Mops saying that you will probably be at the City Hotel on the 8th September to wait for me and asking him to show you any attentions that he can conveniently. About your going to New York – if the children are, either of them, at all unwell don't leave them on any account, and I will hurry with all speed to meet you at Cooperstown. I am so anxious to see you and so nervous about the children that I fear you will judge, from my letter, that I have lost my reason. Good night.

Sunday night, August 15, 1846. – Parmly came this morning and seemed to be as glad to see me as if I had been his brother. He has been operating for some member (or one at least) of the Royal Family of Holland and for several of the Nobility. He is to return there and remain some months and then go to Italy and then perhaps to Vienna, Berlin etc. round to Holland again next summer and then return home in the autumn. Perhaps he will visit St. Petersburg also before his return. The Royal Family of Holland is nearly related to the Imperial Family of Russia, and it is not at all improbable that he will have the door opened for him at the latter place by Royalty at the Hague. I wish him success, and I think he would have it certainly if he had a few more years experience of the world. We have had a long walk and talk together – recounting our adventures. He has business for a few days here and then will be glad to join me and go into the country; or if I choose he will come to me if I do not choose to wait. As he may make my time pass more agreeably I think I shall wait as the difference in expense will be small for so short a time and I may see something to tell of. Good night and for a little while good bye for I must close this for tomorrow but I will not tonight – I'll wait to see if I hear from you in the morning – Good night.

Monday night. – August 16, 1846. – Having learned that I could keep my letter another day I have delayed closing it, hoping to receive your letter; but it does not come. This afternoon I saw a party of ladies and gentlemen – eleven together – ascend in a balloon – the particulars concerning which I will relate at home. Our arrangements now are to go into the country (and perhaps visit Birmingham, Sheffield and Manchester on my way to Liverpool) day after tomorrow. I have nothing in particular to say about home matters except that I hope to bring home enough of my earnings to pay any debts that may have been contracted. My earnings have been, as you know, very handsome, or I should have been compelled to borrow money to get home. I have, as you also know, lived some of the time very uncomfortably in order to save money to pay my debts out of my earnings; or at least to diminish the debts and save my credit. I would send you some money by this letter if I were not to follow it in a few days and so be able to save the commission, exchange, brokerage etc.

This is the last letter probably that I shall write to you from Europe, before you get it I shall be half way across the Atlantic and consequently you may expect me in about a week after receiving it. Remember me affectionately to all the family. Kiss our dear little boys for their papa, and try to be as cheerful as you can for your own and for the sake of the children as well as for mine. Good bye – May Heaven protect and preserve you and our children.

To My Dear Ellen – Forever Your Edward

Chapter 24
Dr. Maynard's Life at Home

Above: Dr. Edward Maynard, Courtesy of the Library of Congress.

Edward Maynard returned safely to America in early September 1846. Though he did not realize a fortune with his invention in Europe, his trip could be viewed as having been successful.   He successfully sold the rights to his invention for Denmark and Sweden for $2,500 for each country or a total of $5,000, a fairly substantial amount in 1846.

Above: Dr. Maynard's Prussian Order of the Red Eagle, awarded to him by the King of Prussia. Courtesy: National Museum of American History, Smithsonian Institution.

For his contribution to the science of dentistry and his firearms inventions, he would be made a Chevalier of the Military Order of the Red Eagle by the King of Prussia and likewise he would receive a Gold Medal of Merit from the King of Sweden.

He managed to get his Tape Primer Lock patented in France, Belgium, England, Scotland and Ireland which would lay the foundation for future sales. In 1855 the British Government would contract to buy 6,000 Model 1855 "British Model" Sharps carbines and 2,000 Greene carbines modified with Maynard's tape primer lock for use in the Crimean War in 1856.

Dr. Maynard was given the magnificent ring by Her Imperial Highness the Grand Duchess Helen of Russia as a token of appreciation for his exceptional dental work performed for the Imperial Family while in St. Petersburg. This ring he would give to his wife, Ellen and they would treasure it for the rest of their lives.

Professionally, Dr. Maynard returned with the enhancement of his reputation by having been Dentist to the Imperial Family of Russia. The Emperor Nicholas I offered to create the title of "Actual Dentist to the Imperial Family," with the rank of Major, if he would agree to remain in Russia for ten years and practice and teach his ways of practice; Dr. Maynard to be attached to the court with a salary or practice privately, whichever he might choose. This was an offer that he respectfully declined.

He had the opportunity to see the world and to meet and befriend a number of interesting and notable people. He met the King of Belgium who complimented him in person regarding his tape primer lock as the "author of such a beautiful invention." He earned a handsome amount of money by performing dental surgery and by introducing the use of gold foil to fill teeth of patients in the cities he visited across Europe. From 1857 until his death, Dr. Maynard held the Chair of Theory and Practice at the Baltimore College of Dental Surgery, established in 1840; it was the first dental college in the world. He held the same position from 1887 until his death in 1891 at the National University in Washington, D.C. He was an Honorary Member of the American Academy of Dental Sciences and the European Society of American Dentists, as well as a Member of the International Medical Congress. He received Honorary degrees of A.M., M.D., and D.D.S. His patients included several U.S. Presidents, numerous Cabinet officers, U.S. Senators, Representatives, high ranking officers of the Army and Navy and many Foreign Ministers. He designed the logo for the American Society of Dental Surgeons and in 1878 the Virginia State Dental Association designated him the "Prince of Dentists."

He returned to a family that would never be the same with the loss of his eldest son Edward. Within a year of his return home, his wife Ellen would give birth to the first of four daughters; Marcia Ellen "Nellie" Maynard was born August 6, 1847, followed by Josephine Gardette Maynard in 1849, Marie Maynard in 1852, and Virginia Dumont Maynard in 1854. Dr. Maynard and Ellen bought their summer home, the oldest house in Cooperstown, N.Y., in 1855. Located at the corner of River and Main Street, it was valued at $3,000, which puts the $75,000 that Maynard realized from the sale of his tape primer lock in 1855 to the U.S. Government for the U.S. Model 1855 Percussion Rifle Musket into proper perspective. The large sums of money that Maynard realized from both the sale of his inventions and from his thriving dental practice, through which he was known to charge high fees due to his skills as an exceptionally gifted and gentle dental surgeon, allowed him to acquire sizable wealth and live extremely well. That same year they bought two additional properties just outside of town. By 1860 they had sold the Main Street house but held on to the Mill House and the land bordering Otsego Lake.

Dr. Maynard was invited by and employed by the U.S. Government to make the first experiments with the manufacture of Damascus steel in conjunction with the authorities in Belgium. In June 1863, he was invited by the Secretary of War to attend the examination of the Cadets of the Military Academy at West Point, where he became an early proponent for the creation of a Corps of Dental Surgeons to be attached to the Army and Navy for the care of the teeth of both officers and enlisted men.

Sadly, his wife Ellen died of heart disease at the young age of 46 in October 1863 and she is buried in Lakewood Cemetery in Cooperstown. Within a month of Ellen's death, Dr. Maynard sold his two remaining properties in Cooperstown for $5,000. Distraught by the death of his wife and with the Civil War heating up, it is speculated that Maynard wished to return to Washington to concentrate on procuring contracts for his guns from the Government.

The Gunnell House (right) owned by Maynard in the 1850's.   Dr. Maynard's Mansion in the late 1860's.
Both Pictures Courtesy of The Historical Society of Washington D.C.

Dr. Maynard owned several different homes and offices during his years in Washington and they were all within walking distance of both the White House and the Capital. His patients and friends included the cities social and political elite and he was a friend of Jefferson Davis and both Presidents Franklin Pierce and Abraham Lincoln. In the early 1870's, Dr. Maynard sold his Washington, D.C. Mansion at 2425 L Street (pictured above right) to the Columbia Hospital for Women. Originally built in 1812 and known as the Ringgold House, it had previously been used on two separate occasions as the residence for two British Ministers to the United States. In late 1865, two years after he sold his Cooperstown homes he bought as a second home "The Castle" in Tarrytown, N.Y. The Castle, also known as Ericstan Castle, was a magnificent and imposing home on the East Bank of the Hudson River at Tarrytown. He owned it for several years but with the cessation of the Civil War and the U.S. Government subsequently cancelling many of its contracts, including its contracts with Maynard, he hastily sold it in early 1869 and returned to Washington.

Above Right: Maynard's Castle at Tarrytown, on a hill overlooking the Tappan Zee; view from the west.

Right: South view to include the tree covered Porte Cochere at Maynard's Castle. All Castle photos courtesy of: The Historical Society, Inc., Serving Sleepy Hollow and Tarrytown.

172

THE CASTLE.—EAST VIEW.

Above: Dr. Maynard's Tarrytown Castle East View with the Porte Cochere at left.

The story of Dr. Maynard's selling Ericstan Castle is relayed by Anthony W. Dimock in his book "Wall Street and the Wilds" published in 1915. Anthony Dimock bought it from Dr. Maynard in 1869. Dimock was a successful Wall Street financier and avid sportsman and outdoorsman who vigorously pursued his passions for hunting and fishing. He describes the Castle as the most attractive edifice located on the east bank of the Hudson at Tarrytown. It ruined its builder John J. Herrick who was a successful dry goods merchant who spent a staggering $60,000 to have it built. It was completed in 1859 but due to high maintenance costs Herrick quickly sold it and it came to be known as Herrick's Folly. Dr. Maynard bought it from Herrick in 1865 and according to Anthony Dimock, about the day Maynard had paid for the house, the contract that Maynard had with the Government was abrogated. Dimock was invited to spend the night at Maynard's Castle through a mutual friend in January 1869. According to Dimock and recounted in his book;

"As we drove up the porte cochere in the early evening I saw through the window sitting by an open fire with a book in his hand a man of patriarchal appearance. He wore some manner of flowing garment and beneath his long, iron gray beard a crimson scarf was loosely knotted. There was a suggestion of the Orient in the surroundings and in the stateliness of his reception of me. He was a wonderful conversationalist and he had me hypnotized from the start. After a long evening that passed like a dream I was conducted to the guest chamber, overlooking the Tappan Zee then flooded with the light of the full moon. I sat by the window almost the night through. I was a silent guest at the breakfast table until the Doctor asked me how I liked the place, when I replied:

173

"I only wish it were for sale"

"It is" was the reply.

"How much?' I asked and I have forgotten the price he named, remembering only that it was much more than a hundred thousand dollars and that I accepted at once. With equal promptness I paid seven thousand dollars for the carved oak furniture in the mansion. After the sale of his Castle, which has since been torn down, Dr. Maynard returned to Washington where he would reside for the rest of his life.

Maynard's eldest son George Willoughby Maynard would grow up to become a noted artist specializing in figure, marine and mural painting. He would study art at the National Academy of Design in New York and have apprenticeships in Florence and Antwerp. He would marry Louise Brownell of Brooklyn, NY in 1907.

Below: Eldest son and artist George Willoughby Maynard.

Many of his painting reside in well known museums today but perhaps his most notable works are paintings that make up various murals, panels and ceilings on the second floor of the Library of Congress. Some of these include the four panels that he painted depicting the virtues; Wisdom, Understanding, Knowledge, and Philosophy in the North Corridor. A series of eight panels representing The Virtues in the four corners of the Great Hall; Industry and Concord, Fortitude and Justice, Temperance and Prudence, and Patriotism and Courage. In addition he painted the domed Pavilion of Discoveries at the far end of the Treasures Gallery which include Adventure, Discovery, Conquest and Civilization as well as the four qualities he deemed most appropriate to these four stages of a nation's development: Courage, Valor, Fortitude and Achievement. He was a member of the Society of American Artists, the American Water Color Society, the Tile Club, the Players Club and the Century Club. He was President of the Salmagundi Club and a National Academician.

John Doty Maynard his second eldest son would follow in his father's footsteps and become a dentist. He married and had three daughters. He lived in both New York City and Rochester, N.Y.

Nellie Maynard, his eldest daughter would marry James L. Hatch, son of Jesse Hatch, an early pioneer settler of Rochester New York and a Rochester Shoe manufacturer. James and Nellie married at Dr. Maynard's Tarrytown, New York home, Ericstan Castle, in October of 1868. James was in the shoe business for the better part of his adult life and he owned several shoe patents. He and Nellie would have three children, George Edward, Marie Virginia and Marion Lindsay. Marie Virginia would die in infancy.

Below: Nellie Maynard Hatch.

Josephine Gardette Maynard would marry Andrew Jackson Hatch, the older brother of James Hatch. They lived in Rochester, New York. He and Josephine would have five children, three daughters and two sons, Josephine, Andrew Jackson, Marcia Geraldine, Marguerite and Andrew Maynard; all would die at a young age.

His two remaining daughters Marie and Virginia Dumont would lead long lives though neither would marry or have children. Marie was an artist and lived until 1927. Virginia was a music teacher and lived until 1926. Both Marie and Virginia lived in Rochester, New York in their later years and they are both buried in Congressional Cemetery in Washington, D.C.

In 1869, Dr. Maynard married his second wife Nellie Long of Savannah, Georgia and they had one daughter, Edna Long Maynard. Edna would marry Edwin Laselle and live in Troy, New York with her husband. After Dr. Maynard's death in 1891, his widow Nellie would end up living with her daughter and son in law in Troy.

While Dr. Maynard is mostly known for his successes in the fields of dentistry and firearms development and manufacture, it should be noted that he was an accomplished artist, architect, wood engraver and surveyor. He was for many years a member of the Sketch Club in Washington, D.C. He was also an active member of the Freemasons. Those who knew him described him as being very aristocratic and dignified in appearance, yet modest and retiring in his nature. He was reserved and refined, always gentlemanly. He had a poetic and genial nature which gave charm and grace to his presence. Known for being a consummate conversationalist on all topics, he had warm personal friendships with a large and varied circle of acquaintances among leading men of society.

Below: Joint Resolution of Congress dated March 1, 1853 authorizing the Secretary of War to procure the right of Edward Maynard to improve the firearms of the United States.

31st CONGRESS,
2d Session.

S. 60.

IN THE SENATE OF THE UNITED STATES,

MARCH 1, 1851.

By unanimous consent, Mr. DICKINSON obtained leave to bring in the following joint resolution; which was read and passed to a second reading, and ordered to be printed.

JOINT RESOLUTION

Authorizing the Secretary of War to procure the right of Edward Maynard to improve the fire arms of the United States.

1   *Resolved by the Senate and House of Representa-*

2   *tives of the United States of America in Congress*

3   *assembled,* That the Secretary of War be, and he is

4   hereby, authorized to contract with Edward Maynard for

5   the right to use his patent altering muzzle loading rifles,

6   so as to make them breech loading arms, at a price in his

7   discretion not exceeding ten cents for each arm.

Chapter 25

Dr. Maynard's Contributions to the Civil War

Dr. Edward Maynard circa 1864, photograph by Alexander Gardner (1821-1882).
Courtesy: National Portrait Gallery, Smithsonian Institution.

Dr. Maynard would go on to have many more gun inventions and file more than twenty patents. His most notable inventions after the tape primer lock were for the invention of the first metallic cartridge and the first breech loading rifle famed for its use in the Civil War. Five years after his return to America in 1851, Dr. Maynard had his tape-primer-lock exhibited at the

Crystal Palace Exposition in London, England. The Crystal Palace Exhibition also known as the Great Exhibition of the Works of Industry of all Nations was an international exhibition that took place in Hyde Park, London from May 1st to October 15th 1851. It was the first in a series of World's Fair exhibitions of culture and industry that were to become popular in the 19th century. Apparently the interest in Maynard's invention was second only to that of the Colt revolving pistol. The patents Maynard acquired for his invention while in Europe in 1846 would have been useful for him to do business at this later date. Several European countries expressed interest in Maynard's tape primer system, but it wasn't until the mid 1850's that this interest escalated. In the mid 1850's Dr. Maynard was awarded a silver medal by the Metropolitan Mechanics Institute for his tape primer invention. The Massachusetts Arms Company acquired the right to install the tape primer lock on guns that it manufactured, thus it started appearing on more and more U.S. Government guns and on guns privately made. On September 9, 1854, the U.S. Government awarded a contract to E. Remington & Son for 20,000 of Maynard's tape primer locks and a contract to convert 20,000 flint-lock muskets to Dr. Maynard's patented system. The bulk of guns that were thus altered were the Model 1816 flint-lock muskets. In 1855 the British Government contracted to buy 6,000 Model 1855 "British Model" Sharps carbines and 2,000 Greene carbines modified for use with the tape primer lock for use in the Crimean War. In 1855 the United States Army ordered 400 "US Model" 1855 Sharps carbines and that same year the United States Navy ordered some 200 with 28 ¼ inch barrels with bayonet studs.

In July 1855, Secretary of War Jefferson Davis endorsed the recommendations of the U.S. Ordnance Board that a new musket be built in .58 caliber with a forty inch barrel and the incorporation of the Maynard tape primer lock. There were additional recommendations incorporating these features for both a rifle-musket and a rifle, each capable of accommodating the Maynard lock with a roll of fifty Maynard primers, while a pistol- carbine would be built with 25 Maynard primers. These guns were mass produced at the two national armories, at Harpers Ferry and at Springfield. These guns were to be known as the U.S. Model 1855 Rifle Musket, Rifle and Pistol-Carbine. Dr. Maynard was to receive a total of $75,000 from the U.S. Government for his tape-primer-lock inclusive of monies paid to him for his contract of 1845. There were over 59,273 U.S. Model 1855 Percussion Rifle-Muskets produced from 1857 to 1861 and it was a primary arm of the Union Army at the onset of the Civil War. It was the first U.S martial arm that used the .58 caliber Minie bullet. A small number of these Model 1855 Rifle-Muskets were also made by the gun manufacturers A.M. Burt, J.F. Hodge, A. Jenks & Sons, J.D. Mowry, J. Mulholland and E. Whitney and the locks made by these firms are so marked. From 1857 to 1861 there were 7,317 U.S. Model 1855 Percussion Rifles made with the Maynard system at Harpers Ferry. These Rifles had 33" barrels and two barrel bands versus three bands on the Rifle-Muskets. Additionally there were 4,021 Model 1855 Percussion Pistol Carbines made at Springfield Armory. Maynard's lock system can also be found on arms manufactured by Merrill, Symmes, Soule, and Burnside. It was also used on pistols such as the U.S. Model 1836 flintlock, and pistols made by the Massachusetts Arms Company, Derringer and Stevens to name a few.

By the early 1860's, it was found that in use, the Maynard tape primer system did not always perform as well as hoped. In inclement weather the tape would sometime fail to fire or the cut off mechanism would fail to cleanly cut off an individual cap. Also the caps would sometimes fail to "fall off" the nipple, blocking the way for the next cap. By 1862, it appears that the manufacture of the Maynard tape primer lock system had been all but discontinued.

Below: Harpers Ferry Model 1855 U.S. Percussion Rifle with Maynard Tape Primer Lock dated 1857.

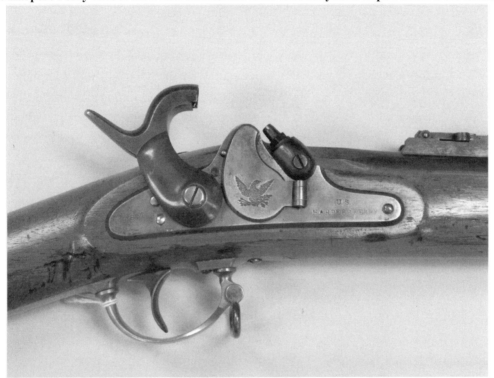

Dr. Maynard would revolutionize cartridges which had been made of paper by designing a metallic cartridge which was the result of two patents; the first patent number 15,411 was issued June 17, 1856 and was for a metallic cartridge with its rear aperture closed by waxed paper.

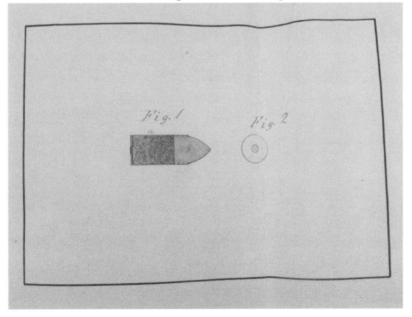

It was further modified and refined by patent number 22,565 issued on January 11, 1859.

Below: Maynard's patent No 22,565 for the metallic cartridge.

E. MAYNARD.

Cartridge.

No. 22,565.   Patented Jan. 11, 1859.

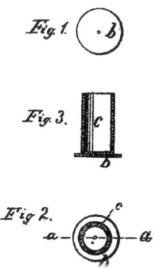

The Maynard cartridge was basically a large rim with a centrally located hole, soldered to the base of a cylindrical brass shell.

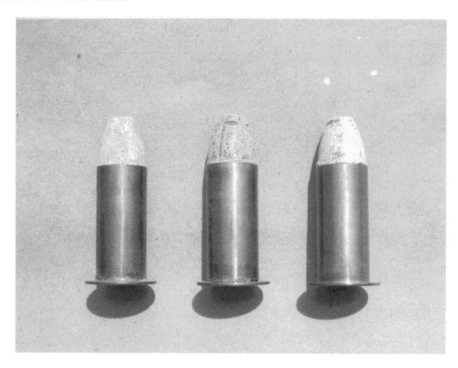

This cartridge was designed to be used in the Maynard designed lever action rifle with a tip up breech known as the Maynard Carbine which was the result of two patents. The first patent numbered 8,126 was issued May 27, 1851 and the second patent numbered 26,264 was issued December 6, 1859. The development and use of the metallic cartridge designed for this rifle not only increased accuracy but also proved to be able to withstand rough handling in the field. The metallic cartridge was eventually adopted by the United States Government, by all manufactures of breach loading arms and eventually became the standard cartridge for all rifles worldwide. Dr. Maynard would patent several improvements in cartridge design over the course of his life.

Below: Maynard's Patent number 8,126 dated 1851 for tip up breech action.

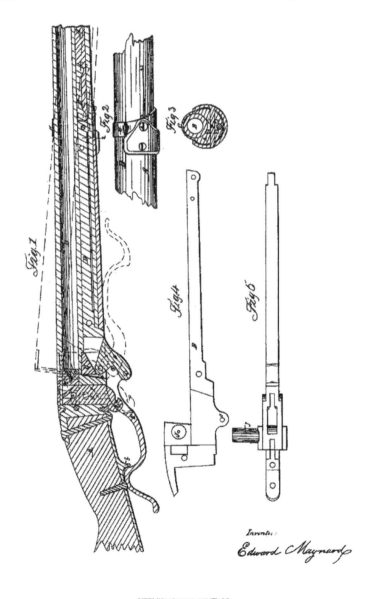

E. MAYNARD.

Breech-Loading Fire-Arm.

No. 8,126.

Patented May 27, 1851.

Below: Maynard's Patent Number 26,364 dated 1859 for Breech Loading Rifle.

E. MAYNARD.

Breech-Loading Fire-Arm.

No 26.364.

Patented Dec. 6. 1859

Witnesses.

Inventor.

The first model Maynard carbine incorporated the Maynard tape priming system and was available in both 35 and 50 caliber. As early as 1853, Dr. Maynard had a prototype of this rifle made by Springfield Armory at a cost of $116.37. This carbine was tested under the supervision of Major William Bell on May 16, 1856 at the Washington Armory with the actual test firings performed by Lieutenant Benton. At the end of his report, Major Bell pronounced Maynard's rifle "the best breechloader for military or civil purposes" he had seen.

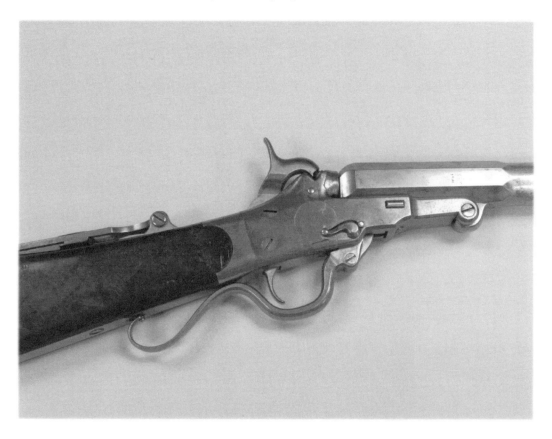

Above: Maynard's Prototype of the Maynard Carbine manufactured in 1853 by Springfield Armory. This Maynard Prototype carbine remains in excellent condition and is in its original finish.

As a result of the success of these 1856 trails, Dr. Maynard and several enthusiastic investors formed the Maynard Arms Company of Washington, D.C. on April 28, 1857. Maynard retained a twenty five percent share of the company and William Corcoran was elected President with William Freeman serving as Secretary of the company. The Maynard Arms Company contracted all of its manufacturing with the Massachusetts Arms Company of Chicopee Falls, Mass. and in August 1857 the Maynard Arms Company entered into an agreement with The Massachusetts Arms Company to have five thousand Maynard Carbines produced at a cost of $17.50 per gun. Of these five thousand, four thousand were made in the larger .50 caliber and one thousand were made in .35 caliber. In addition, the Maynard Arms Company signed an agreement with the American Flask and Cap Company of Waterbury, Connecticut for the production of the metallic cartridges used in the guns and it signed an agreement with T.C. LeRoy and Company of New York for the manufacture of the bullets.

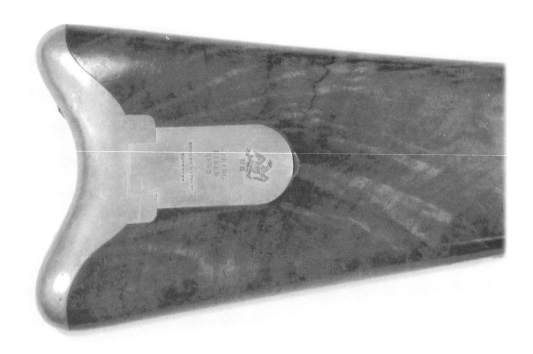

Above: Maynard Rifle / Carbine Prototype stock manufactured by Springfield Armory in 1853, stamped with Federal Eagle over U.S., Springfield 1853 and Edward Maynard Patentee.

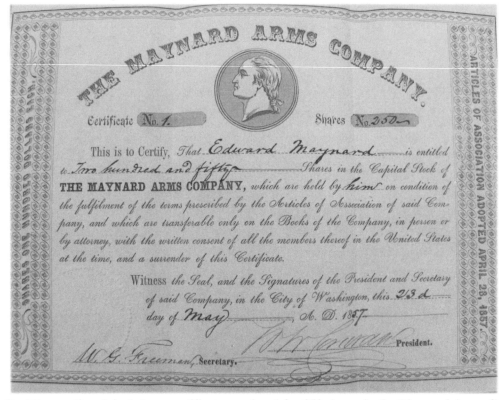

Above: Dr. Maynard's original share certificate number 1 for 250 shares in the Maynard Arms Company.

Some of these early Maynard produced rifles were purchased by affluent sportsmen who were also part of the business and political elite. Some of them included Congressman John H. Potter of Michigan, Senator Robert Toombs of Georgia, Wade Hampton of South Carolina and Vice President J. C. Breckenridge. It is interesting to note that several of these gentlemen sided with the Confederacy during the Civil War and also became Generals for the Confederacy. Senator Toombs was a personal friend of Maynard's and it is likely Maynard was friendly with the others.

In 1857 the U.S. Ordnance Department purchased four hundred first model Maynard rifles and in 1859 the U.S. Treasury Department purchased two hundred for the Revenue Cutter Service. In the spring of 1859, Lieutenant Colonel B.S. Roberts who was a mounted rifleman with the U.S. Army and one of the Army's best shots declared the Maynard "the best gun in the world". In Early 1860 the U.S. Navy bought sixty carbines. By October 1860 the Maynard Arms Company had sold about fourteen hundred of its previously produced five thousand carbines. W. J. Syms & Bros. of 300 Broadway in New York City had signed an agreement on January 11, 1859 to be sole agent for Maynard Arms and all of these sales would have emanated through them. With the election of Abraham Lincoln to President in November 1860, the remaining inventory of Maynard carbines was quickly bought up by numerous southern militia companies and the states of Florida, Georgia and Mississippi contracted to buy another approximately 2,450 carbines for their own state militias.

An untimely fire on the night of January 28, 1861 would see the destruction of the Massachusetts Arms Company factory and the cessation of gun production by this firm until 1863. With the successful manufacture and delivery of the previously manufactured Maynard guns through mid 1861, Dr. Maynard decided to shutter the Maynard Arms Company and buy out his smaller stockholders.

By 1863, Dr. Maynard, through the Massachusetts Arms Company which had rebuilt its production facilities, signed an agreement to sell to the U.S. Ordnance Department 20,000 of his second model Maynard carbines for $24.20 each. The second model Maynard Carbine was a simplified version of his first model carbine without the tape primer. These guns were delivered between June 22, 1864 and May 19, 1865 and totaled 20,002 carbines. With the cessation of the Civil War, the Massachusetts Arms Company continued to sell the Maynard carbine in different center fire calibers and in a shotgun configuration for civilian use until 1890.

During the period that this simplified second model carbine was being produced for the U.S. Government, Dr. Maynard also offered sporting models of this rifle in .35, .40 and .50 calibers which had interchangeable barrels. It was also offered as a shotgun in a .64 caliber shot which was somewhere between a 16 and 20 gauge shotgun. The shotgun barrel could be easily switched with the rifle barrels, thus offering maximum flexibility for the owner to switch from a shotgun to a rifle configuration.

Below: Right side of Maynard First Model Carbine, note lever for opening tape primer compartment, stamped Maynard Arms Co. Washington on right side of action.

Below: Second Model Maynard Carbine with tape primer storage container, unopened tape primer roll and two fired metal cartridge casings. (Authors Collection)

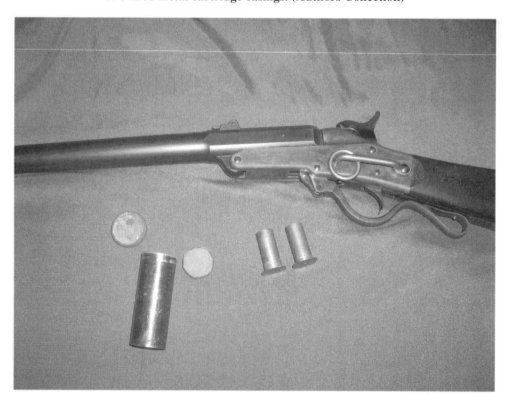

Chapter 26

Dr. Maynard and the Post Civil War Years

Dr. Maynard 1870's, Courtesy of the Dr. Samuel D. Harris National Museum of Dentistry Baltimore, Maryland.

After the Civil War Dr. Maynard continued developing improvements to both firearms and to priming metallic cartridges. These modifications however were not all commercially successful.

On June 27, 1865, Dr. Maynard filed Patent Number 48,423 for a new and useful improvement in the solid hinged breech block of a breech loading musket as seen in his patent filing diagram below.

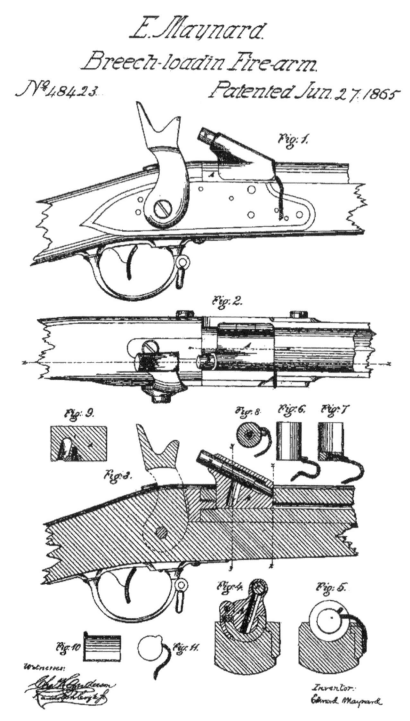

Dr. Maynard had at least three prototype muskets built with this breech block improvement as seen in the following pictures. One applied to a Springfield musket dated 1840, one to a Norwich musket dated 1863 and one to an unmarked and undated musket.

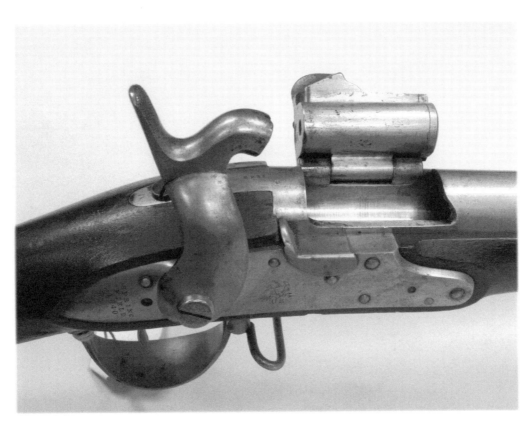

Above: Maynard prototype with 1865 patent improvement for a breech loading conversion on a Springfield musket dated 1840. (1st of 3 known prototypes) Below: Prototype with similar conversion (2nd of 3 known)

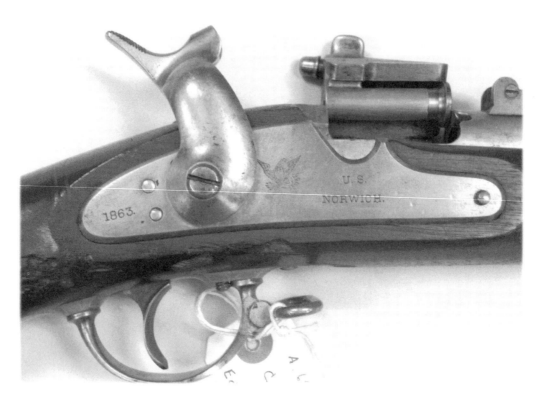

Above and below: Another Maynard Prototype model based on the inventors 1865 patent for a breech loading conversion system on a 1863 U.S. Norwich marked musket. (3rd of 3 known prototypes)

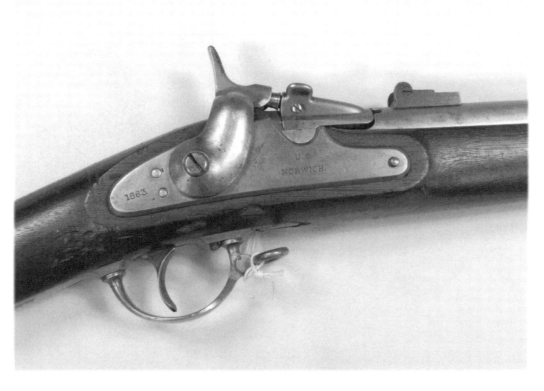

190

On October 20, 1868, Dr. Maynard filed Patent Number 83,194 for an improvement in the method that the forward end of barrels in double barreled shotguns are united so as to allow expansion and contraction of each barrel independently from each other while maintaining their relative position and lateral adjustment.

Below: Maynard's Patent Number 83,194 dated 1868 for Double Barreled Fire Arm.

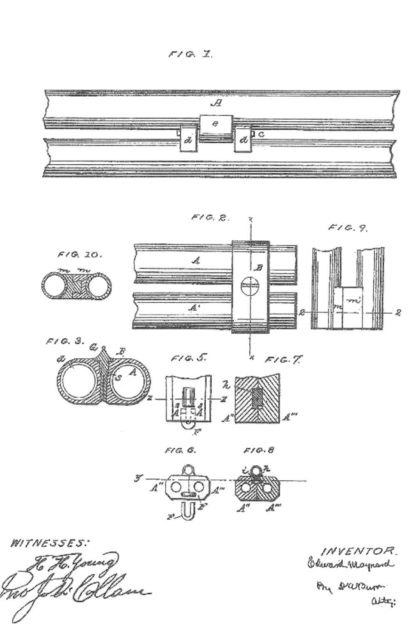

On February 2, 1869, Dr. Maynard filed a patent # 86,556 for the improvement in breech loading firearms which are closed by a sliding bolt, with his improvements being of such nature as to admit of being readily combined with the ordinary muzzle loading Springfield rifles, so as to convert them into breech loaders adopted to the use of the regulation cartridges of the United States service. As seen in his patent papers below, this improvement attempted to adopt a bolt action onto a pre-existing musket while using the pre-existing hammer.

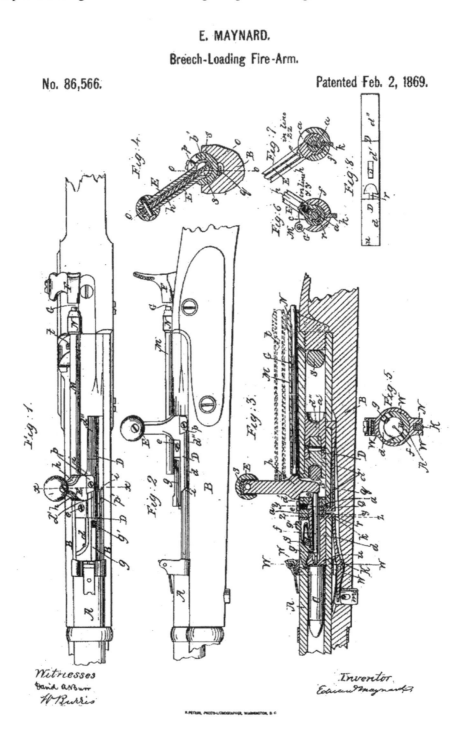

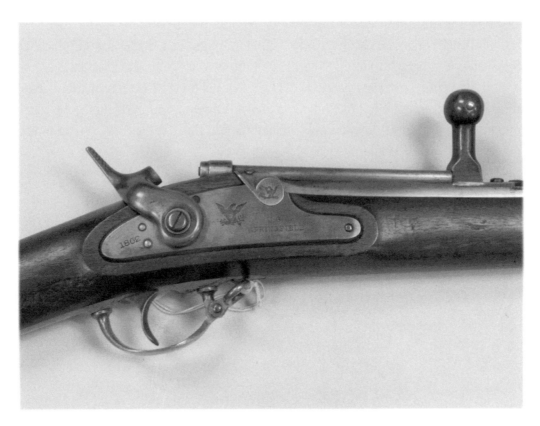

Above and below: Prototype model of Dr. Maynard's 1869 patented bolt action conversion to an 1862 dated Springfield musket. (One of two known Maynard bolt conversion prototypes based on his 1869 patent)

Always the consummate entrepreneur and always striving to keep abreast of the ever evolving gun and ammunition market, Dr. Maynard filed a patent Number 135,928 on February 18, 1873 for the improvement in breech loading firearms that allowed for his breechloader designed rifle to use individually primed metallic cartridges. This gave his breechloader a distinguishable new look from his wartime percussion breechloaders and this new design allowed the Massachusetts Arms Company the opportunity to manufacture and market this new gun to civilian hunters and target shooters in post Civil War America.

Below: Dr. Maynard's Patent Number 135,928 for the Maynard Model 1873 Breech-Loader.

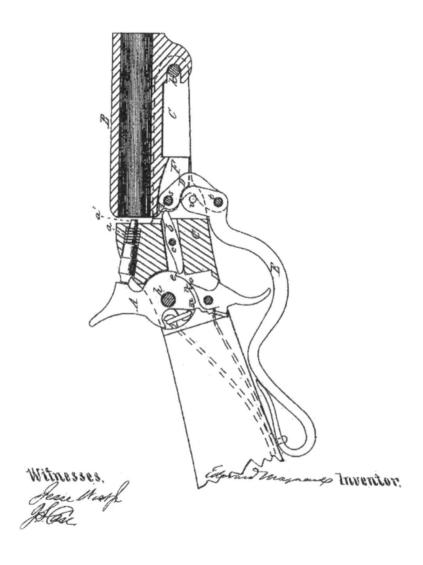

E. MAYNARD.

Breech-Loading Fire-Arms.

No. 135,928.   Patented Feb. 18, 1873.

This new gun was called the Model 1873 Maynard and in conjunction with its production was the introduction of fourteen new center fire cartridges to be offered for use with it. Additionally, the Massachusetts Arms Company offered the 1873 Maynard in several different styles and

Below: Dr. Maynard's personal Maynard hunting outfit; four barrel set to include two shotgun barrels and two rifle barrels of differing lengths with silver engraved stock oval "Edward Maynard" and all accessories in its original case. Of particular note is the unusual bayonet attachment that could be used as a machete.

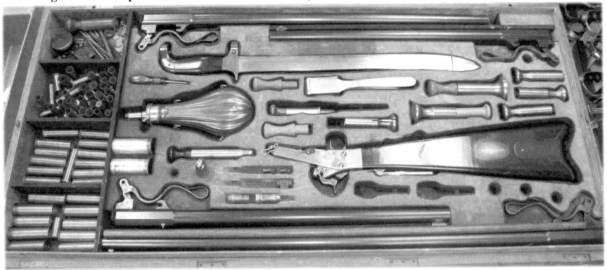

grades, so as to appeal to a wider segment of the shooting public. This gun was also made available in a shotgun configuration and the easy interchangeability of barrels allowed the purchaser ease in switching from having a rifle to having a shotgun. This new design insured continued production of a Maynard breechloader well into the latter half of the nineteenth century. The one drawback of the Model 1873 Maynard Rifles is that they only accepted Maynard proprietary ammunition that was not usable in any non Maynard guns and they could not use any other manufactured ammunition. This ultimately limited their appeal and would lead to further improvements by Dr. Maynard.

Above: Numerous accessories were available for the post war Maynard rifles and shotguns. Above left: Brass canister for Maynard tape primers. Above right: Brass canister for Maynard gun lubricant / oil.

In 1882 an improved model of the Model 1873 Maynard was made available. This gun accepted more widely used center fire cartridges and it was named the Model 1882 Maynard. Both the Model 1873 Maynard and Model 1882 Maynard, in rifle and shotgun configurations, remained popular with the hunting and target shooting public through the late 1800's. After Dr. Maynard's death in 1891, production of his Maynard designed rifles and shotguns gradually declined and production ceased in the mid 1890's. This was due partially to the death of Dr. Maynard, no doubt a driving force behind the production of his guns, and equally to the high cost of producing his high quality arms, which required a fair amount of hand fitting and individual attention to maintain quality control. In an age of ever increasing mass produced machine made guns, the Massachusetts Arms Company was unable to compete with its cheaper mass produced competition. The Massachusetts Arms Company was bought by J. Stevens Arms & Tool Company in 1895. The Stevens Arms Company continued to sell single shot rifles based on the Maynard action until 1930. They produced a Stevens Maynard Jr. rifle Number 15 in .22 rim fire from 1902 to 1912. They produced the Stevens Featherweight Number 101 shotgun on a Maynard type action from 1914 to 1916 and they produced the Stevens Marksman Number 12 based on the Maynard action from 1911 until 1930.

Dr. Maynard's last firearms invention of note, which he received Patent Number 343,471 for on June 8 1886, was an invention for indicating the number of cartridges in the magazine of a repeating firearm at any time. This was considered of particular value to both military men and to hunters.

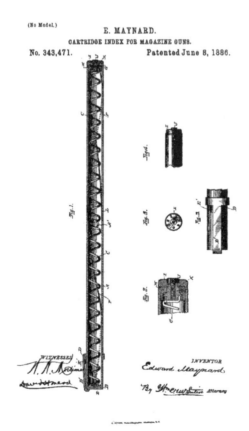

In addition to Dr. Maynard's lifelong interests in improving firearms designs and cartridge development and his practicing and teaching Dentistry and Dental surgery, he also filed patents for numerous non gun related items over his career. Some of these patents were for improvements in buttons, photographic albums, and various tools.

Below is a list of Dr. Maynard's Patents:

Patent Number	Patent Date	Patent Purpose
4,208	September 22, 1845 Antedated March 22, 1845	Percussion primer and gun-lock
8,126	May 27, 1851	Breech Loading Firearm Improvement
15,141	June 17, 1856	Cartridge Improvement
22,565	January 11, 1859	Metallic Cartridge Improvement
25,663	October 4, 1859	Back Sight for Firearm Improvement
25,664	October 4, 1859	Nipple for Firearm Improvement
26,364	December 6, 1859	Breech loading Firearm Improvement
39,823	September 8, 1863	Metallic Cartridge Improvement
40,111	September 29, 1863	Cartridge Improvement
40,112	September 29, 1863	Cartridge Improvement
42,388	April 19, 1864	Improvement in Metallic Wad for Cartridges
43,696	August 2, 1864	Photographic Album
45,420	December 13, 1864	Improvement in Priming Metallic Cartridges
47,843	May 23, 1865	Improvement in Buttons
48,423	June 27, 1865	Breech loading Firearm Improvement
49,130	August 1, 1865	Breech loading Firearm Improvement
59,044	October 23, 1866	Improvement in Priming Metallic Cartridges
61,225	January 15, 1867	Improvement in Priming Metallic Cartridges
83,194	October 20, 1868	Double Barrel Firearm Improvement
86,566	February 2, 1869	Breech loading Firearm Improvement
135,928	February 18, 1873	Breech loading Firearm Improvement
343,471	June 8, 1886	Cartridge Index for Magazine Guns

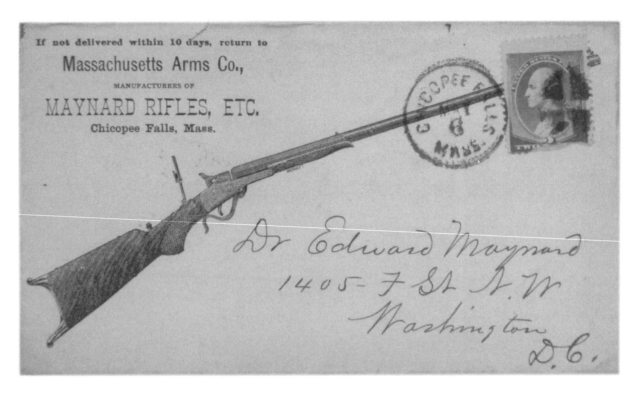

Above: Envelope from the Massachusetts Arms Co. which was the manufacturer of Dr. Maynard's Rifles; This particular letter was addressed to Dr. Edward Maynard in Washington, D.C.

In the late 1800's and early 1900's, all of Dr. Maynard's gun models, his prototype guns, his medals and decorations were on display at the National Museum at Washington in cases especially set apart for them, for the purpose of showing everything in the line of firearms of his inventions from the earliest to the latest. The National Museum was the forerunner to the Smithsonian Institution and the Dr. Edward Maynard Family gun collection remains at the Smithsonian to this day.

Despite his having made several fortunes from his gun inventions and the profits from his successful Washington dental practice, it appears Dr. Maynard was not a proficient money manager as he spent his money as quickly as he made it. When he passed away his fortune was all but spent.

After a long and successful career as both dental surgeon and firearms inventor and manufacturer, Dr. Maynard retired in 1890 and passed away at the age of 78 on May 4, 1891 after a long painful illness. He is buried in the Maynard Family plot at Congressional Cemetery in Washington, D.C. in a grave marked by a granite obelisk that reads Dr. Edward Maynard - Surgeon - Dentist and Inventor 1813-1891.

Bibliography

"A Collection of Annual Reports and Other Important Papers Relating to the Ordnance Department" Volume II 1880, The Bobst Library New York University

Dimock, Anthony Weston, *Wall Street and the Wilds* New York Outing Publishing Company 1915

Flayderman, Norm, *Flayderman's Guide to Antique Firearms, 7th Edition*, Krause Publiactions 1998

Koch, Charles R.E. DDS *History of Dental Surgery* Volume III pp 217-223 National Art Publishing Company, Fort Wayne, Indiana 1910

Layman, George. *A Guide to the Maynard Breech-Loader* 1993 Nashoba Publications Incorporated

Lustyik, Andrew F. *Dr. Maynard's Tape Primer* (Gun Report Sept, Oct, Nov, Dec, 1965)

Maynard Arms Company Letters, Smithsonian Institution

The Maynard Papers, 1836-1867 Library of Congress,

Michaels, Howard. *Cooperstown and Edward Maynard, Surgeon, Dentist and Inventor* June 1980

McAuley, John D., *Carbines of the Civil War 1861-1865* Pioneer Press Union City Tennessee 1981

McAuley, John D., *Civil War Carbines Volume II The Early Years* Andrew Mowbray Inc Publishers PO Box 460 Lincoln, RI 1991

Nonte, George, *Firearms Encyclopedia* Harper and Row 1973

Southern Dental Journal 1891

Southern Dental Journal 1894

Taylor, J.A., *History of Dentistry* Lea & Febiger Philadelphia 1922

"Dr. Edward Maynard Obituary" Dental Cosmos 33 (June 1891) p. 493

"Dr. Edward Maynard Obituary" Archives of Dentistry 8 (July 1891) pp 299-303

"Dr. Edward Maynard Obituary" International Dental Journal 12 (June 1891) pp 413-416.

"Dr. Edward Maynard Obituary" The New York Times May 5, 1891

"Dr. Maynard's Drill Stock" American Journal of Dental Science 3 (March 1843) p 228

Acknowledgement

Smithsonian Institution National Museum of American History, Division of Military History and Diplomacy, Division of Medicine and science, Division of information Technology and Communications

Cooperstown, NY Historical Society

The Historical Society, Inc. Serving Sleepy Hollow and Tarrytown

The National Portrait Gallery, Washington, D.C.

The Dr. Samuel D. Harris National Museum of Dentistry, Baltimore, MD

United States Patent Office, Washington, D.C.

Index

202

About the Author

Rodney Hatch is Dr. Edward Maynard's great-great-great grandson. He was born and raised in Rochester, New York, where seven Hatch generations have lived since 1822. He received his B.A. in Political Science from Williams College and he received his M.B.A. from Fordham University, Graduate School of Business Administration in New York City. In addition to his interests in genealogy, American History and military history, he is an avid saltwater fisherman and golfer. He is a life member of both the General Society of Mayflower Descendents and the National Society Sons of the American Revolution. He resides in Westchester County, New York with his wife Lydia and their two yellow Labs, Westley and Oakley.

Westley and Oakley

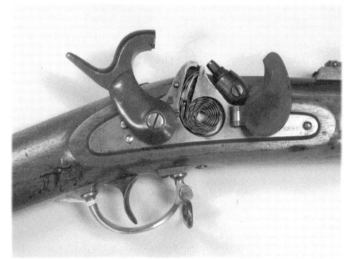